BREAKING THROUGH THE

WORLD OF STATISTICS

First Edition

By Kristofor Paulson
University of North Dakota

cognella® | ACADEMIC PUBLISHING

Bassim Hamadeh, CEO and Publisher
Kassie Graves, Director of Acquisitions and Sales
Jamie Giganti, Senior Managing Editor
Miguel Macias, Senior Graphic Designer
Angela Schultz, Senior Field Acquisitions Editor
Michelle Piehl, Project Editor
Alexa Lucido, Licensing Coordinator
Christian Berk, Associate Production Editor
Chris Snipes, Interior Designer

Printed in the United States of America

ISBN: 978-1-5165-0876-1 (pb) / 978-1-5165-0877-8 (br)

cognella® ACADEMIC PUBLISHING

Table of Contents

1 Statistics and Their Measurement

INTRODUCTION

"Statistics may prove something and nothing at the same time." Every day when we wake up and visit our favorite news sources, whether it be the computer, radio, television, or, more importantly, our smart phones, we are blasted with numbers, facts, and figures. Depending on the source, we might question exactly how this information was collected or if there was any bias in reporting the numbers. Examples of statements you might see (some are more clearly stated):

- "The report found that tuition in Arizona has risen by 83.6% since 2008, or $4,734 per student, after adjusting for inflation." (Emily Jane Fox, "Where Public University Tuition Has Skyrocketed," *CNN Money*, May 13, 2015, http://money.cnn.com/2015/05/13/pf/college/public-university-tuition-increase/.)
- "The 2013 six-year graduation rate for first-time, full-time undergraduate students who began their pursuit of a bachelor's degree at a four-year degree-granting institution in fall 2007 was 59%. That is, 59% of first-time, full-time students who began seeking a bachelor's degree at a four-year institution in fall 2007 completed the degree at that institution by 2013." ("Fast Facts," from the website for the National Center for Education Statistics, accessed 5/19/2016, http://nces.ed.gov/fastfacts/display.asp?id=40.)

The goal of this textbook is to provide the student/learner of statistics with the necessary tools to collect, organize, analyze, and present data. It will guide you in the selection and collection of relevant data as well as providing the correct procedure for analysis. The book will use a three-stage approach. The first stage is the introduction; the second step is application; and the third, which connects the first two stages, is the practice or evaluation stage.

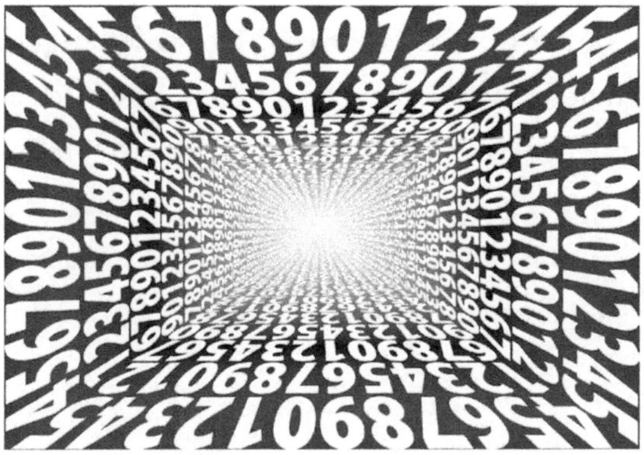

Figure: 1.1 Numbers

STATISTICS, DATA, ELEMENTS, AND VARIABLES

Statistics refers to the process of collecting, organizing, analyzing, and presenting data. **Data** are the facts and figures that are collected and used for interpretation or analysis. An **element**, or observation, is a single unit of data that represents a person, place, or thing. A **variable** is a characteristic or feature used to describe an element or observation. A data set consists of all observations and variables. The size of the data set is simply the multiplication of the number of observations times the number of variables (Observations*Variables).

Data can represent actual quantities such as age, the number of miles a student lives from campus, or a characteristic about something, like a favorite color or type of vehicle. Data can be divided into two categories: quantitative and qualitative. Quantitative data, which is always numeric, answers the questions "how much?" or "how many?" Qualitative data may be numeric or nonnumeric and represent a trait or characteristic of an observation.

Quantitative data can be divided into two categories: (1) continuous and (2) discrete. Quantitative data, which answers the question "how much?" is referred to as continuous data. Time, weight, and distance are some of the most common examples of continuous data. Marathon times are a good example. Marathon times are measured in hours, minutes, seconds, and tenths—even hundredths—of a second. The distance you live from campus is another example. It is possible to measure continuous variables more precisely.

Quantitative data that answers the question "how many?" is classified as discrete data. A good example of discrete data is the number of classes you are enrolled in each semester (zero, one, two, three, four, and so on) or your current checking/savings account balance. Other examples include the number of bedrooms in a house, the number of students who would prefer to attend class four days instead of five, and the number of tails viewed in five tosses of a coin.

Qualitative data are used to describe traits or characteristics that are not easily quantifiable by numbers. Take, for example, the calculation of the grade point average. Universities use a four-point scale and assign each letter grade a certain number (A = 4, B = 3, C = 2, and D = 1). If you received straight As and you were enrolled in five three-credit classes, you cannot very easily multiply the total number of credits (fifteen) by the letter grade (A) and interpret the result. In designating each letter grade a value (in this case, A = 4), the calculation is straightforward (GPA for a student who is enrolled in five classes and earned all As: (15*4)/15). The GPA calculation is a weighted average calculation (GPA = Σ [# of Credits of Each letter grade]*[Value of Letter]). (Remember the value of each letter: A = 4, B = 3, C = 2, D = 1). Other examples include credit card numbers, barcodes, and Likert scales (student evaluation and customer satisfaction surveys).

STATISTICS CAN BE MADE TO PROVE ANYTHING—EVEN THE TRUTH

Carol C. Riddick and Ruth V. Russell

Excerpt from: Carol C. Riddick and Ruth V. Russell, "Step 14A: Analyze Quantitative Data'," *Research in Recreation, Parks, Sport, and Tourism*, pp. 290-293. Copyright © 2008 by Sagamore Publishing LLC. Reprinted with permission.

SCALE OF MEASUREMENT

Analysis of information does not happen in a vacuum between collecting data and interpreting it. In fact, thinking about how the data analysis might be carried out should be an integral part of the initial study design process. Otherwise you could end up with a mish-mash of information, which no analysis procedure can redeem (Robson, 2002).

Information that is initially gathered from interviews, questionnaires, case study notes, field observation journals, rating forms, and the like is not typically organized. Ordering and then analyzing such information is necessary because, generally speaking, data in their "raw" form do not speak for themselves.

When it gets down to it, the information that is gathered or measured in research is in one of two forms. First, there is ***numerical data,*** meaning information presented as numbers. Examples of numerical data include:

- Number of participants in an adult fitness program.
- Percentage of the black diamond ski trail users who prefer longer operating hours.
- Participants' accuracy of shot scores following a basketball clinic.

Information can also be presented in ***non-numerical*** or text form. Illustrations of non-numerical data are:

- Descriptive adjectives used by aquatics supervisors to describe lifeguards' performances.
- Ideas for new services voiced by infrequent health club users.
- Hand written notes of an observation of outdoor adventure leaders during a mountain climbing expedition.

This chapter focuses on making sense of numerical information, or ***quantitative analysis.*** The next chapter will examine how to handle non-numerical information collected in the research process, or ***qualitative analysis.***

A vast extended family of quantitative data-analysis tools exists. This chapter will focus primarily on the more popular univariate statistics that are used to handle quantitative data. ***Univariate statistics*** focus on one variable at a time and are descriptive statistics that include such things as frequency distributions, proportions, ratios, rates, measures of central tendency, and measures of variability. Additionally, towards the end of the chapter, you will also be introduced to some ***bivariate statistics,*** meaning some of the statistical tools used to examine relationships and differences between two variables. Finally, we will round the chapter out by presenting some thoughts about computer statistical software.

A forewarning is in order before we proceed. Please recognize that in this as well as the following chapter, we are only able to introduce you to a small selection of all the statistical tools available. Thus, we recommend that your professional preparation include a course in statistics, and/or that you ask for help from a consultant when analyzing data from your studies.

LEVELS OF NUMERICAL MEASUREMENT

In order to select the appropriate statistical tool, you first must know the level of numerical measurement that was used. Whenever a variable is measured four ***levels of measurement*** are used: nominal, ordinal, interval, and ratio.

As shown in Figure 1.1, the measurement levels can be ordered in a hierarchy according to the amount of specificity. This is because nominal and ordinal levels are categorical levels, which are more primitive measurements than interval and ratio levels, which are numerically continuous. If you read from top to bottom in Figure 1.1, you should see the precision increases when moving from nominal to ordinal levels and again transitioning between interval to ratio levels.

Level of Measurement	Defined	Example	Amount of Precision
Nominal	Categorical	Males, females	Least meticulous; no math can be used
Ordinal	Nominal with rank order	1st, 2nd, 3rd place finishers in a track meet	More meticulous than nominal yet no math can be used
Interval	Ordinal with equal distances between units of measurement	Water temperature	More meticulous than ordinal; math can be applied—yet because of a meaningless zero, ratios cannot be calculated
Ratio	Interval with meaningful zero	Minutes to swim first lap in race	Most meticulous; all math operations can be applied

Figure: 1.1 Levels of Measurement of Variables.

NOMINAL DATA

The ***nominal*** level consists of measurement using labels or categorizes. The word nominal means "having to do with names" (Figure 1.2). Many demographic variables are measured nominally.

Variable	Nominal Measurement
Gender	Male or female
Ethnicity	African American, Asian, Hispanic, Caucasian, etc.
Residence	Rural, suburban, urban
Job titles	Department head, division head, supervisor, leader, assistant, volunteer.
Football player positions	Quarterback, lineman, linebacker, etc.

Figure: 1.2 Nominal Data Examples.

Since nominal data consist of discrete categorical distinctions rather than numerical distinctions, no arithmetic-based functions (such as addition and subtraction) can be applied. For instance, it would be inappropriate to "value" females with a score of "2" and males with a score of "1."

ORDINAL DATA

The ***ordinal*** measurement level ranks categorical information in terms of size or magnitude. As the word ordinal implies, data are arranged in rank order.

Examples of ordinal data are:

- A supervisor is asked to rank his playground leaders in terms of creativity. The resulting data indicate which leader the supervisor considers most creative, second most creative, and so on.
- The number of first-place, second-place, and third-place finishes for the swim club in the city meet.
- College class standing (first-year, sophomores, juniors, and seniors).

Like nominal data, ordinal data, while using numbers (1st, 2nd, 3rd, etc.), cannot be worked mathematically. The numbers just measure relative magnitude, meaning something is more or less.

This mathematical limitation for both nominal and ordinal data is overcome with interval and ratio levels of measurement. Interval and ratio data can be treated mathematically.

INTERVAL DATA

Interval data have the rank-order characteristic of ordinal data yet go one step beyond ordinal data. That is, for interval data, the distance between the numbers are equal units of measurement. What does this mean? Look at a ruler. A one-inch interval is the same size at every location on the ruler, so that the distance between two inches and four inches is equal to the distance between seven inches and nine inches. Examples of interval data are water temperature and air temperature.

Interval data provide a more highly refined level of measurement than nominal and ordinal, yet interval data also have a limitation. That is, a ratio cannot be determined with interval data because the zero point is arbitrary. While equal intervals between numbers reflect equal differences in magnitude, the interval level of measurement does not have an absolute zero point, or an absence of the quality being measured. For instance, zero degrees Fahrenheit for water temperature certainly doesn't mean you will feel an absence of temperature when you jump in! Guess you'd be ice skating!

It needs to be pointed out that when applying statistical procedures, some people wind up treating ordinal data as interval data. Admittedly, this practice has both proponents and critics (Case 1).

CASE 1. NEARLY INTERVAL?

Researchers disagree about whether certain widely used measures, such as an attitude questionnaire, meet interval or ordinal data requirements. For example, suppose you ask respondents how much they favor an admission fee increase for the public pool. The following answer categories are used: "Strongly Agree," "Agree," "Neither Agree nor Disagree," "Disagree," "Strongly Disagree." Are these possible answers an example of ordinal or interval data? To be honest, in similar situations, some researchers treat the provided answers as an interval measurement level and then go on to use statistical tools that require interval data. Contrastingly, others consider these answers as exemplifying ordinal data and consequently turn to statistical tools that require an ordinal level of measurement. What do you think? Is this type of scale ordinal, interval, or "nearly interval?"

RATIO DATA

The ***ratio*** level is the highest measurement level. This is because ratio data are defined as having a rank order, with equal units of measurement, and an absolute zero. You can think of ratio data as interval data but with the added characteristic of an absolute zero point.

An example of ratio data is annual salary. The difference between a yearly salary of $25,000 and $35,000 is the same as the difference between $90,000 and $100,000. Further, an annual salary of $0 is truly an absence of salary. This means that for information collected as ratio data we can apply mathematical operations, such as the salary of $100,000 is twice that of a salary of $50,000.

CROSS-SECTIONAL AND TIME SERIES DATA

Data may or may not have a time frame associated with it. For example, data that is collected during roughly the same time period is referred to as cross-sectional data. One example is the percentage of graduates who finished their undergraduate degree in four years or six years in all North Dakota four-year universities in 2013. This information is presented in Table 1.1 below. As you can see, the four-year degree is more of a myth than a reality.

TABLE 1.1 GRADUATION RATES AND OTHER DATA FOR NORTH DAKOTA 4-YEAR INSTITUTIONS

Graduation and Other Data (4-year Institutions), North Dakota Universities 2013					
4-Year Institution	Grad. Rate (4 yr)	Grad. Rate (6 yr)	Completion per 100	Total Spending Completion	Students with Pell
University of North Dakota	24.10%	53.30%	16.7	$108,164	20.90%
North Dakota State	25.60%	53.10%	18	$60,098	22.50%
Valley City State	22.80%	46.20%	21.6	$63,240	26.40%
Dickinson State	15.30%	37.90%	22.9	$49,919	23.40%
Minot State	14.40%	37.30%	21.1	$49,842	23.20%
Mayville State	20.90%	36.00%	17.1	$71,599	29.70%

Data collected over a period of time is referred to as time series data. Most macroeconomic variables fall under this type of data. Examples include the Gross Domestic Product (GDP), the Consumer Price Index (CPI), and the unemployment rate. With time series data, statisticians usually focus on how a particular variable changes over time. Table 1.2 below illustrates the unemployment rate in the United States for the years 2014 and 2015. The unemployment rate has decreased from January 2014 to Dec 2015.

TABLE 1.2 UNITED STATES UNEMPLOYMENT RATE 2014–15

Year	Jan	Feb	Mar	Apr	May	Jun	Jul	Aug	Sep	Oct	Nov	Dec
2014	6.6	6.7	6.7	6.2	6.2	6.1	6.2	6.2	6	5.7	5.8	5.6
2015	5.7	5.5	5.5	5.4	5.5	5.3	5.3	5.1	5.1	5	5	5

PAYING FOR DATA? CONSTRAINTS OF DATA COLLECTION, SAMPLES, THE POPULATION, AND THE PROCESS OF STATISTICAL INFERENCE

More data is preferred to less. Why? Having more data gives statisticians and other interpreters of data a clearer picture. In describing how well a student preformed in a class, you would not just use a single exam but a collection of all exams, assignments, and quizzes. Sure, the student may have done better on one exam, but the overall grade is a collection of the exams and other work.

Data collection suffers from two big constraints: time and money. The more time available, the more complete and accurate your project or experiment will be. This does not mean you have to collect every single data point in the study. A collection of all possible observations or elements of a study is referred to as the population. The correct notation (symbol) for the population is N. Usually a subset of the population will suffice. A data set that consists of only a proportion or subset of the population is referred to as a sample. The symbol that represents a sample is n.

Should you pay for data? If so, how much should you pay for data? It depends. It is a marginal-cost-versus-marginal-benefit scenario in which the decision maker weighs the cost of obtaining the data versus the time savings or increased decision-making ability. The cost of obtaining the data should not outweigh the benefits received from it. A consumer would never pay more for a product or service than the value it offers to them.

When the entire set of observations cannot be collected for a particular study because it is too large or the population size is unknown (e.g., manufacturing process), statisticians/researchers make conclusions or judgements about the population by using sample data. This is called the inference process. This is different from descriptive statistics, in which data is summarized by percentages, graphs, or tables and no references or conclusions are made about the population. More explanation of descriptive statistics will follow in Chapter 2. Notice the difference between the two statements below. The first one illustrates descriptive statistics, and the second one illustrates statistical inference (the production of 60-watt LED light bulbs is a continuous process).

Statement 1: A sample of one hundred 60-watt LED lightbulbs was taken to test their lifespan. The average (mean) turned out to be 42,500 hours.

Statement 2: Given that the average life span of one hundred 60-watt LED lightbulbs was 42,500 hours, all 60-watt LED bulbs have a life span of 42,500 hours (using sample data to make inferences about the population).

ETHICAL GUIDELINES AND DATA SOURCES

As Samuel Langhorne Clemens (better known as Mark Twain) stated, "There are lies, damn lies, and statistics." ("Lies, Damned Lies, and Statistics," *Wikipedia*, last modified February 22, 2017, https://en.wikipedia.org/wiki/Lies,_damned_lies,_and_statistics). It is very easy to manipulate or disregard data points that are not in alignment with our expectations. When conducting statistical analysis, be open to new ideas and surprising outcomes.

The American Statistical Association has published a set of ethical guidelines to assist researchers/statisticians in the learning process. There are eight guidelines that should be followed when conducting statistical analysis. These eight guidelines are presented on their website ("Ethical Guidelines for Statistical Practice," http://www.amstat.org/about/ethicalguidelines.cfm#responsibilities). These will help your analysis. There are many good websites for collecting data. The idea, when researching or testing a claim, is to be as fair and ethical as possible. Listed below are a few reliable websites that can be used to collect data.

1. Business Websites
    A. Economics and Finance/Accounting:
        i. Bureau of Labor Statistics (www.bls.gov)—macroeconomic data; unemployment, inflation, productivity, pay, and benefit data
        ii. Fred2 (https://research.stlouisfed.org/fred2/)—macroeconomic data, expenditures, money supply, interest rates, and exchange rates
        iii. Bureau of Economic Analysis (http://www.bea.gov/index.htm)—international, national, and state-level economic data
        iv. Bloomberg (http://www.bloomberg.com/)—financial and world news
        v. CNBC—(http://www.cnbc.com/world/?region=world)—investment and world news
        vi. Securities and Exchange Commission (www.sec.gov)—information on publicly traded companies (earnings, strengths, weaknesses, competitors, and accounting statements [10K and 10Q])
        vii. Internal Revenue Service (www.irs.gov)—tax information and questions
        viii. World Bank (https://www.wto.org/)—international trade and fairness
        ix. Marketing Websites (http://60secondmarketer.com/blog/2010/06/08/18 great-websites-for-marketers/)
    B. Health Websites
        i. World Health Organization (WTO) (http://www.who.int/en/)—data on life expectancy, diseases, and other health-related topics
        ii. Centers for Disease Control and Prevention (CDC) (http://www.cdc.gov/)—data on viruses, fitness, traveling, and overall health of countries
        iii. WebMD (http://www.webmd.com/)—health topics and news
    C. Sports Websites
        i. NHL.com, NBA.com, NFL.com, MLB.com, and MLSsoccer.com—professional sports statistics and news
        ii. American Statistical Association's "Sports Data Resources" page (http://community.amstat.org/sis/sportsdataresources)—statistics about sports
        iii. Sportsreference.com—all professional sports as well as the Olympics
        iv. NCAA.com (www.ncaa.com)—college sports, with schedules and statistics
        v. USCHO.com—college hockey statistics, power rankings, and schedules

CONCLUSION

Statistics is a process, not necessarily a concept. There are three general steps for statistical analysis. The process starts with data collection, followed by description and organization, and then finally the analysis and conclusion.

Collecting and organizing data from trustworthy websites, using the correct statistical procedures, and presenting the results in a clear and concise manner will help readers and stakeholders make better-informed decisions. Following the ethical guidelines will help make sure your project is fair and unbiased. The next chapter continues with data organization.

IMAGE CREDITS

- Fig. 1.1: Gerd Altmann / Pixabay, “Numbers,” https://pixabay.com/en/pay-digit-number-fill-count-mass-1036477/. Copyright in the Public Domain.

Data Organization

2

Figure: 2.1 Golfer Silhouette

Figure: 2.2 Golf Course

INTRODUCTION

Chapter 1 described the types of data and the scale of measurement. Data collection is the first step of the process. Chapter 2 will explore the organization and summarization of data. The type of data collected (categorical or quantitative) will determine the appropriate method of organization and pieces of information one can learn. The goal is to organize and present the data in a clear and concise manner. The presentation methods include tables and graphs.

Some methods of organization work with both quantitative and qualitative data. The methods used to describe data are descriptive statistics. These methods include frequencies, percent frequencies, and relative frequencies, while others—such as the cumulative frequencies, cumulative percent frequencies, and cumulative relative frequencies—are unique to quantitative data.

DESCRIBING NUMERICAL DATA

FREQUENCY, RELATIVE FREQUENCY, AND PERCENT FREQUENCY DISTRIBUTIONS: QUALITATIVE AND QUANTITATIVE DATA

Qualitative data describes a trait or characteristic (like the variables gender and interest level in the table above). When working with qualitative data, the goal is to determine how many observations are associated with each class. Each data point belongs to one and only one class.

The **frequency** of a class is the number of data points in that class. A frequency distribution indicates the number of observations in each class. The relative frequency is the fraction of data points that belong to a class (frequency of class/total number of observations). The percent frequency is the percentage of data points that belong to a certain class or simply the relative frequency multiplied by 100 (Relative Frequency*100). The following example uses qualitative data to explain the favorite golf courses played near the city of Hackersville.

TABLE 2.1 FAVORITE GOLF COURSE TO PLAY

Favorite Golf Course to Play			
Slicer's Dream	Tall Oaks	Rolling Hills	Rolling Hills
Rolling Hills	Rolling Hills	Tall Oaks	Lost Balls
Five Ponds	Five Ponds	Five Ponds	Lost Balls
Tall Oaks	Slicer's Dream	Slicer's Dream	Slicer's Dream
Lost Balls	Hacker's Villa	Lost Balls	Lost Balls
Hacker's Villa	Tall Oaks	Hacker's Villa	Tall Oaks
Lost Balls	Rolling Hills	Lost Balls	Tall Oaks
Lost Balls	Five Ponds	Lost Balls	Five Ponds
Slicer's Dream	Hackers Villa	Slicer's Dream	Slicer's Dream
Lost Balls	Slicer's Dream	Lost Balls	Hacker's Villa

There are six main golf courses located around Hackersville. The courses are Slicer's Dream, Rolling Hills, Five Ponds, Tall Oaks, Hacker's Villa, and Lost Balls. This alone does not give any insight into which course golfers prefer. The frequency, relative frequency, and percent frequency table gives us insight into which courses are most preferred and least preferred. Looking at Table 2.2 below, the

TABLE 2.2 DESCRIPTIVE STATISTICS OF GOLF COURSES

Course	Frequency	Relative Frequency	Percent Frequency
Tall Oaks	8	0.16	16%
Rolling Hills	7	0.14	14%
Lost Balls	13	0.26	26%
Five Ponds	7	0.14	14%
Hacker's Villa	6	0.12	12%
Slicer's Dream	9	0.18	18%

golfers' favorite course is Lost Balls, and the least preferred golf course is Hacker's Villa (maybe because of the name).

Qualitative data uses pie or bar charts. Figure 2.3 illustrates a percent frequency pie chart.

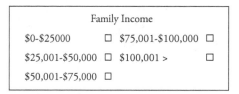

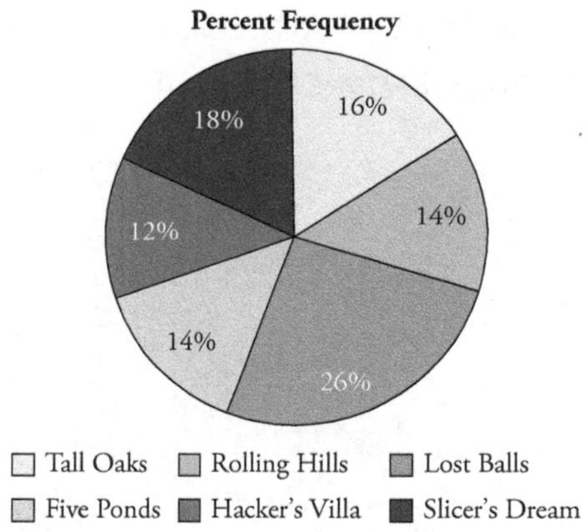

Figure: 2.3 Percent Frequency Pie Chart

Quantitative data is always numeric. When organizing quantitative data, the purpose is to determine how many observations (responses) will belong in each category. For example, when purchasing a product, you may have received a product survey. One of the questions most likely asked is the income of the purchaser. Income is a quantitative variable.

Family Income			
\$0-\$25000	☐	\$75,001-\$100,000	☐
\$25,001-\$50,000	☐	\$100,001 >	☐
\$50,001-\$75,000	☐		

Figure: 2.4 Income of Customers

Quantitative data is used to calculate frequencies, relative frequencies, and percent frequencies. However, labels or names are not used as the classes; numerical ranges (classes) are calculated.

There are three steps in organizing quantitative data. The steps are choosing the desired number of classes, determining the width or bin range for each class (each class should be the same width), and, finally, assigning each data point into one of the nonoverlapping classes. Quantitative data is illustrated using pie charts, histograms, and other graphical representations.

THREE STEP PROCEDURE FOR GROUPING QUANTITATIVE DATA

The goal in organizing quantitative data into groups is to show the variability in the data. In other words, we do not want every data point to have its own class (too many classes), and we do not want all data points in a single class. One method (not an exact science) is to use the 2^k rule. The 2^k rule indicates you should choose a value of k (the number of classes) in which the value of the expression is $2^k \geq n$ (where n is the sample size or number of observations). The larger the sample size (n), the more classes should be used. Using the formula below, if a data set consisted of five hundred observations (n = 500), the value of k would be nine. There should be nine different groups or classes (2^9 = 512). An example follows below.

2^k Rule			
2^1	2	2^6	64
2^2	4	2^7	128
2^3	8	2^8	256
2^4	16	2^9	512
2^5	32	2^10	1024

Figure: 2.5 Powers of 2

Number of Classes (k): $2^k \geq n$

THREE-STEP PROCEDURE FOR ORGANIZING QUANTITATIVE DATA EXAMPLE: APARTMENT RENTS IN A SMALL COLLEGE TOWN

Figure: 2.6 Apartment

A local university is thinking about implementing a housing program for students, whereby students may qualify for housing assistance based on income and rental price of the apartment. To understand the rental market and fully develop a comprehensive housing assistance program, the university collected a sample of apartment rental costs. A sample of sixty one-bedroom apartment rents is shown below in Table 2.3.

TABLE 2.3 1-BEDROOM APARTMENT RENTS

Rent for 1 bedroom apartments					
\$425.00	\$525.00	\$450.00	\$475.00	\$525.00	\$500.00
\$475.00	\$460.00	\$580.00	\$425.00	\$500.00	\$525.00
\$450.00	\$525.00	\$525.00	\$500.00	\$475.00	\$560.00
\$490.00	\$450.00	\$485.00	\$525.00	\$425.00	\$525.00
\$425.00	\$575.00	\$465.00	\$460.00	\$500.00	\$500.00
\$500.00	\$525.00	\$450.00	\$500.00	\$485.00	\$580.00
\$425.00	\$540.00	\$490.00	\$525.00	\$500.00	\$525.00
\$500.00	\$545.00	\$425.00	\$575.00	\$525.00	\$450.00
\$525.00	\$500.00	\$450.00	\$475.00	\$550.00	\$525.00
\$560.00	\$510.00	\$425.00	\$450.00	\$475.00	\$500.00

Decide the number of classes (k) with sixty observations:

k = 6: 2^6 = 64 ≥ n (60)

Determine the class width:

Class Width (Bin Range) = (Maximum Value – Minimum Value)/(# of classes)
Maximum Value = \$560; Minimum Value = \$425; k = 6

($560 – $425)/6 = 22.5; class width of 30 (25 could be used, but will result in seven classes, not six); use a number that ends in a 0 or 5, and each class will have an identical width.

$425–$454	14
$455–484	8
$485–$514	16
$515–$544	14
$545–$574	4
$575–$604	4

Figure: 2.7 Classes and Frequencies (1 Bedroom Apartment Rents)

Decide where to start and end each of the six classes, making sure all of the data points are placed into one and only one class.

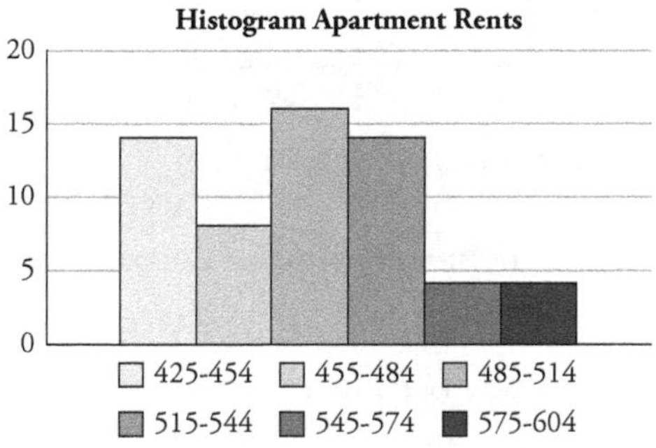

Figure: 2.8 Histogram 1 Bedroom Apartments

Looking at Figure 2.7, fifty percent (thirty out of sixty) apartments have a rental price between $485 and $544. In addition, there are more apartments in the $425–$454 range, compared to the $545–$604 ranges combined. Figure 2.8, below, shows this data as a histogram (bar chart with no spaces).

CUMULATIVE DISTRIBUTIONS FOR QUANTITATIVE DATA

One type of analysis unique to quantitative data is the cumulative distribution. The word cumulative simply means less than or equal to. Cumulative distributions determine the number of observations, the fraction of observations, or the percentages of observations that are equal to or below a certain value. Use Figure 2.8 to calculate the cumulative frequency, cumulative relative frequency, and cumulative percent frequency for the $485–$514 class. Identify the upper limit of the class. In this case, the upper limit of the $485–$514 class is $514.

Cumulative Frequency: All data points that are ≤ $514: 38 observations
Cumulative Relative Frequency (Cumulative Frequency/Total Observations): 38/60
Cumulative Percent Frequency (Cumulative Relative Frequency*100): 63.33%

DESCRIBING DATA USING TWO VARIABLES: CROSS TABULATIONS AND SCATTER PLOTS

In some cases, it is more beneficial to describe data using more than one variable. A cross tabulation is a table that explains two characteristics of an observation. Scatter plots are graphical representations of two quantitative variables.

Figure 2.9 (page 20) is a cross tabulation that describes one-bedroom apartments based on their rent and how far they are from campus. In a cross tabulation, the variables may be both quantitative, both qualitative, or one of each. In most cases, with other things equal, locations closer to the university had more expensive rent.

Distance from University in miles						
Rent	0.25	0.5	0.75	1	1.25	1.5
$425–$454	2	4	3	0	4	1
$455–$484	4	1	2	1	0	0
$485–$514	5	5	4	2	0	0
$515–$544	8	6	0	0	0	0
$545–$574	2	1	1	0	0	0
$575–$604	1	2	1	0	0	0

Figure: 2.9 Crosstabulation: Price and Distance from University

Using Figure 2.9 above, we can determine how many apartments are in a given price range as well as the distance each is away from the university. All of the apartments (14) in $515–$544 class are within one half mile of the university. Only 13.33% (8/60*100) of the apartments in the sample are a mile or more from the university.

A scatter plot or scatter diagram is a graphical representation of two quantitative variables. A scatter plot will help identify if a relationship exists between the two variables. For example, most students would agree there is a positive (direct) relationship between the number of hours studied for an exam and the resulting grade. Simply stated, the more you study, the higher grade you should achieve. Listed below in Table 2.4 is a sample of ten students' results on an exam and the corresponding hours they studied. Figure 2.10 is a scatter plot illustrating the data presented in Table 2.4 (With Added Trend line). The trend line is upward sloping, indicating a positive relationship between study time and the grade earned on the exam.

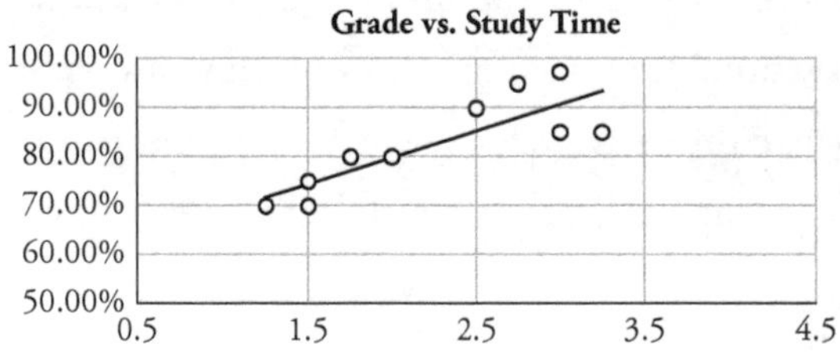

Figure: 2.10 Scatter Plot Study Time versus Score

TABLE 2.4 STUDY TIME VERSUS SCORE

Test	Study Time	Test Score
1	3.25	85.00%
2	3	97.50%
3	1.5	70.00%
4	2	80.00%
5	2.5	90.00%
6	1.25	70.00%
7	1.5	75.00%
8	1.75	80.00%
9	3	85.00%
10	2.75	95.00%

SUMMARY

Grouping data allows for more interpretation, but it still does not give us the entire picture. We can search for the largest (maximum) value ($580) and lowest (minimum) value ($425) or maybe even calculate the average. It does not indicate whether the data is closely grouped or scattered (it only provides ranges), and it does not measure the location, dispersion, or relative position. Chapter 3 will provide these answers.

IMAGE CREDITS

- Fig. 2.1: 27707 / Pixabay, "Golfer Silhouette," https://pixabay.com/en/golf-sport-silhouette-cloud-words-1140860/. Copyright in the Public Domain.
- Fig. 2.2: Unsplash / Pixabay, "Golf Course," https://pixabay.com/en/golf-course-sports-pond-green-828978/. Copyright in the Public Domain.
- Fig. 2.6: Robyn Stewart / Pixabay, "Apartment," https://pixabay.com/en/open-plan-apartment-holiday-home-1336101/. Copyright in the Public Domain.

3 Descriptive Statistics: Location, Variability, and Relationship between Two Variables

This chapter investigates the description and summarization of quantitative data. Quantitative data is characterized in three main areas: the first two look at a single variable, and the third looks at the relationship between two variables. The first step is describing the data by its location; the second is by variability; and, finally, by the interaction between variables. This chapter will have three main sections, covering the group of statistics under each step.

SUMMARIZING LOCATION, SCATTER, AND RELATIVE POSITION

By Priscilla Chaffe-Stengel and Donald N. Stengel

Working with Sample Data: Exploration and Inference, pp. 13-15, 16-18. Copyright © 2011 by Business Expert Press. Reprinted with permission.

MEASURES OF LOCATION

There are three measures of central tendency: the average value or mean, the middle value or median, and the most frequent value or mode. While the mode, by definition, is a member of the original set of data, the mean and the median do not necessarily belong to the original data set.

THE MEAN

The arithmetic average of a set of data is the mean. It is the sum of the individual data values divided by the number of observations. In the study and use of statistics, it is important to know whether the mean is formed using all elements in the population or whether the mean is based on a random sample of elements taken from the population. The population mean is denoted by the symbol μ, pxronounced "*mew*," and the sample mean by the symbol $\overline{x}$. Their computations are the same, boxed for easy reference.

Population and Sample Means

Population Mean: $\mu = \dfrac{\sum x_i}{N}$

where x_i are all the data values in the population and N is the size of the population.

$$\textbf{Sample Mean: } \bar{x} = \frac{\sum x_i}{n}$$

where x_i are the data values randomly sampled and n is the sample size.

The mean is the most frequently used measure for the center of a set of data. The mean is sensitive to the presence of extreme values in a data set, however, and may not be a reliable measurement of the center of a distribution when outliers are present. Microsoft Excel can easily compute the mean for a set of sample data by typing into a spreadsheet cell the function *=average(range for data).*

THE MEDIAN

The middle value of an ordered set of data is the median.

- For an *odd* number of observations, the median is the middle number when the data are put in an ordered array.
- For an *even* number of observations, the median is the average of the middle two values when the data are put in an ordered array.

Unlike the mean, the value of the median is not influenced by the presence of outliers and may provide a more reliable estimate of a distribution's central value when outliers are present. In discussions of residential housing values, for example, we frequently see references to median home values in lieu of average home values because of the potential bias introduced by a few high-value homes into the calculation of the mean home value in a given market. Excel can easily compute the median for a set of sample data by typing into a spreadsheet cell the function *=median(range for data).*

THE MODE

The single most frequently occurring value in a data set is the mode. If there are two values that both occur with highest frequency observed in the data set, the data are said to be bimodal. It is possible that a mode does not exist in a data set. In general, the mode is not as reliable an estimate of the data set's central value, and so the mode is not used as often as the mean or the median to characterize the center of a distribution. Excel can easily compute the mode for a set of sample data by typing into a spreadsheet cell the function *=mode(range for data).*

COMPARING THE MEAN, THE MEDIAN, AND THE MODE

A preliminary estimate of the shape of a distribution can be readily obtained using a comparison of the mean, the median, and the mode. If the value of the mean, the median, and the mode are all roughly equal, the shape of the distribution is said to be symmetric. If the mean is larger than the median and the mode, there are more values in the upper end of the distribution inflating the value of the mean. In that case, the distribution is skewed to the right, or positively skewed, with a longer tail into the right end of the distribution. If, on the other hand, the mean is smaller than the median or the mode, then there are more values in the lower end of the distribution pulling the value of the mean down. In that case, the distribution is skewed to the left, or negatively skewed, with a longer tail into the left end of the distribution. This is a valuable preliminary analysis to conduct, particularly on large data sets where it may be time consuming to build a frequency distribution to examine the shape graphically. With the use of Excel's built-in toolkit, descriptive summary statistics can be prepared easily, giving the analyst a sense of the shape of the distribution relatively quickly.

EXAMPLE: USING THE MEAN, MEDIAN, AND MODE

Listed in Table 3.1 are the average temperatures in February for the state of North Dakota. The temperatures are for a ten-year span ranging from 2006 until 2015. The temperatures are in degrees Fahrenheit.

TABLE 3.1 AVERAGE TEMPERATURES IN NORTH DAKOTA (FEBRUARY 2006–15)

Year	Ave Temp in Feb in ND (*F)
2006	15
2007	7.7
2008	10.3
2009	11.4
2010	9.3
2011	10
2012	21
2013	16.8
2014	5.7
2015	8.4

Sample Mean ($\bar{X}$) = $\sum (X_i)$/n; where X_i is observation i; n = sample size

(15+7.7+10.3+11.4+9.3+10+21+16.8+5.7+8.4)/10
Mean = 115.6 /10 = **<u>15.6*F</u>**

Population Mean $\mu = \sum(Xi/N)$
Median (50th Percentile or 2nd Quartile)—organize the data in ascending order and, because there is an even number of observations, divide the middle two values.
Median = (10 + 10.3)/2 = 10.15*F
Mode: the data value that appears with the highest frequency: not available—each temperature appears only a single time.

TABLE 3.2 TEMPERATURE DATA IN ASCENDING ORDER

5.7
7.7
8.4
9.3
10
10.3
11.4
15
16.8
21

PERCENTILES, QUARTILES, AND OTHER DIVIDERS OF NUMERIC DATA

Two other measures of location that are commonly used are percentiles and quartiles. A percentile is simply a cumulative measure that identifies the number of data points that occur below a certain data value.

Quartiles are certain percentiles and separate the data values into four groups. The first quartile is equal to the 25th percentile, the second quartile is the median, or 50th percentile, and the third quartile is commonly referred to as the 75th percentile.

QUANTILES: MEASURES OF RELATIVE POSITION

A special class of measures is useful in dividing a data set into proportionate segments. They are quantiles, and we have already worked with one of them, the median.

- The *median* is a quantile that divides a data set into two equally populated halves, with 50% of the data set falling above the median and 50% of the data set falling below the median.
- A *quartile* divides a data set further by splitting the lower half and the upper half in two, so that there are four equally populated quarters of the data set, each containing 25% of the data values.
- A *decile* divides a data set into 10 equally populated segments, each containing 10% of the data values.
- A *percentile* divides a data set into 100 equally populated segments, each containing 1% of the data values.

If you have ever taken a national examination, you probably received a scaled score for the exam that was equated to a percentile. A reported score equated to the 87th percentile, for example, means that 87% of the people taking the same test earned scores at or below that reported score and 13% of the people taking the test earned scores at or above the reported score, which establishes a measure of the relative position of the reported score within the entire data set.

To identify a quantile, the data set must first be put in an ordered array, from smallest to largest value. While everyone agrees on the calculation procedure to find the median, differences in procedures can lead to small differences in the values given for other quantiles. One of the simplest procedures to find the first and third quartiles is to apply the procedure for finding the location of the median to the lower and upper halves of the data set. Applying it to the lower half yields the first quartile and applying it to the upper half yields the third quartile. To find the location of a particular percentile, *A*, for example, use the following procedure:

A PROCEDURE TO FIND THE VALUE OF THE A^{TH} PERCENTILE IN A DATA SET

1. Put the data set into an ordered array.
2. To find the location, *L*, at with *A*% of the data fall below that location, use the equation

$$L = \frac{A}{100} \cdot n$$

where L is the location in the data list at which $A\%$ of the data fall below it, and n is the number of data values in the list.

3. If L is not a whole number, the Ath percentile is the value in the data list located at the next largest whole number above L. If L is a whole number, the Ath percentile is the average of the two values in the data list located at the Lth position and at the $(L+1)$st position in the data list.

Excel can easily compute the kth quartile for a set of sample data by typing into a spreadsheet cell the function *=quart(range for data,k)* and can also easily compute the kth percentile for a set of sample data by typing into a spreadsheet cell the function *=percentile(range for data,k)*.

EXAMPLE OF CALCULATING PERCENTILES AND QUARTILES

Listed below in Table 3.3 are Exam 1 results from a random statistics class. The class consisted of twenty-five students (n = 25). Calculate the 25th and the 60th percentiles.

TABLE 3.3 EXAM 1 STATISTICS

70.00%	74.00%	75.00%	76.00%	78.00%	80.00%	80.00%	80.00%	82.00%	82.00%	82.00%	85.00%	85.00%
85.00%	85.00%	85.00%	86.00%	88.00%	90.00%	90.00%	92.00%	94.00%	94.00%	95.00%	98.00%	

Order data in ascending order (Table 3.3 above).

Use the formula L = (A/100)*n, where L is the location of the data point; n is the number of observations.

If L is a mixed number, round up to the nearest integer; if L is an integer, take the average of L and L+1 positions.

25th percentile: A = 25; n = 25 and data in ascending order; (25/100)*25 = 6.25; round up to 7; the 25th percentile is the data value that operates the 7th position; 80%; 25% of the exam scores were equal to or less than 80%.

60th percentile: A = 60: n = 25 and data in ascending order; L = (60/100)*25 = 15; take the average of the 15th and 16th data positions; 15th data position = 85% and 16th position = 85%; (85%+85%)/2 = 85%.

ESTIMATING THE MEAN FROM GROUPED DATA

Sometimes managers may receive reports of data that have already been summarized into a frequency distribution. If the calculated mean is not included in the report, being able to back out an estimated mean is quite useful.

For estimating either the population or the sample mean from grouped data, we use the concept of a weighted average.

ESTIMATED MEAN FROM GROUPED DATA

$$\mu \text{ or } \bar{x} = \frac{\Sigma(\text{each class freeqeuncy} \cdot \text{its class midpoint})}{\text{the sum of the class freeqeuncies}} = \frac{\Sigma f_i \cdot m_i}{n}$$

where f_i is the frequency for class i, m_i the midpoint for class i, and n the number of elements included.

ESTIMATING THE MEAN WITH GROUPED DATA EXAMPLE

Recall from chapter 2 the 1-Bedroom Apartment Rents Frequency Distribution. To calculate the average using the grouped data below, use the following procedure.

TABLE 3.4 FREQUENCY DISTRIBUTION OF RENTS

$425 - $454	14
$455 - $484	8
$485 -$514	16
$515 - $544	14
$545 - $574	4
$575 -$604	4
Total Observations	60

Locate the midpoint of each class:

Class 1 Midpoint: 439.5
Class 2 Midpoint: 469.5
Class 3 Midpoint: 499.5
Class 4 Midpoint: 529.5
Class 5 Midpoint: 559.5
Class 6 Midpoint: 589.5

Multiply each midpoint by its class frequency and add the results:

$439.50*14 + $469.50*8 + $499.50*16 + $529.50*14 + $559.50*4 + $589.50*4 = $29,910

Divide the answer in step 2 by the total number of observations:

$29,910/60 = $498.50.

MEASURES OF SPREAD

In addition to determining the center of a distribution, describing the concentration of data around its center is important. We will cover three measures of spread or dispersion: the range, the variance, and the standard deviation.

THE RANGE

A preliminary sense of the spread among data is given by the range over which the data vary, from the smallest value to the largest value in the data set. The range is technically defined as the difference between the maximum and the minimum values, although we often say that the data range from one value to the other, describing the range by stating the location of the two end points of the distribution. Because the range is established by the two extremes of the distribution, it is both the most sensitive of the measures of spread to the presence of outliers and the least representative of the dispersion among the complete set of data. Excel can easily compute the range for a set of sample data by typing into spreadsheet cells each of two functions

=max(range for data)
=min(range for data)

and then subtracting the minimum value from the maximum value.

THE VARIANCE

The variance is a frequently used measure of spread whose numerator is the sum of the squared differences of each value from its mean. When the population mean, μ, is known, the numerator is divided by the population size, N. The resulting measure is the population variance, σ^2, pronounced "*sigma-squared*." When the population mean is not known but is estimated by $\bar{x}$, the numerator is divided by the sample size minus one, $(n - 1)$. By dividing by one less than the sample size, we allow for more fluctuation in small samples. When samples are comparatively large, subtracting one from n does not make a significant impact on the overall value. The resulting measure is the sample variance, s^2.

POPULATION AND SAMPLE VARIANCE

$$\textbf{Population Variance: } \sigma^2 = \frac{\Sigma(x_i - \mu)^2}{N}$$

where x_i are all the data values in the population, μ is the population mean, and N is the size of the population.

$$\textbf{Sample Variance: } s^2 = \frac{\sum(x_i - \overline{x})^2}{n-1}$$

where x_i are the data values randomly sampled, $\overline{x}$ is the sample mean, and n is the sample size.

Excel can easily compute the variance for the set of population data by typing into a spreadsheet cell the function *=varp(range for data)* and can also compute the variance for the set of sample data by typing into a spreadsheet cell the function *=var(range for data)*.

THE STANDARD DEVIATION

The standard deviation is the positive square root of variance. For a population, the standard deviation is σ, or *sigma*, and for the sample, the standard deviation is s. Where the variance is given in squared units, the standard deviation is given in the same units the mean is reported in. So, if we are discussing the average value of a mutual fund in dollars, its variance is in squared dollars, but its standard deviation is in dollars, as the mean is reported. And that is a good part of its virtue.

A particularly useful expression of dispersion is given by the coefficient of variation, which is the standard deviation divided by the mean of the data set, written as a percent.

COEFFICIENT OF VARIATION

$$\textbf{For a population: } CV = \frac{\sigma}{\mu}\cdot 100$$

$$\textbf{For a sample: } CV = \frac{s}{\overline{x}}\cdot 100$$

In computing the coefficient of variation, we can compare the relative amount of dispersion across a number of sets of data, where the means and their standard deviations may be otherwise quite disparate. For example, coefficients of variation can be compared for "penny" stocks and for blue chip stocks, despite the fact that the mean value of "penny" stocks will be quite different from the mean value of the blue chip stocks. Making such comparisons yields measures of comparative risk or stability as a percent of the mean value of the stock. Excel can easily compute the standard deviation for a set of sample data by typing into a spreadsheet cell the function *=stdev(range for data)*. Alternatively, if we have already computed the sample variance, we can simply take the square root of the sample variance by entering into a cell the equation *=sqrt(variance)*. When calculating the standard deviation for a set of population data, the Excel formula is *=stdevp(range for data)*.

PRACTICING THE MEASURES OF SPREAD

Table 3.5 is a summary of three random student's results from a psychology course. As you can see, each student averaged a 90% in the class, but the test scores of the students were different.

TABLE 3.5 TEST SCORES AND AVERAGES OF THREE STUDENTS

Test	A	B	C
1	90.00%	88.00%	85.00%
2	90.00%	90.00%	95.00%
3	90.00%	92.00%	80.00%
4	90.00%	90.00%	100.00%
Average	90.00%	90.00%	90.00%

Range = (Maximum – Minimum Value); for Student B, Max is 92%, and the Min is 88%.

Range = 0.92 – 0.88 = .04, or 4%.

Sample Variance $s^2 = \dfrac{\sum(\text{Xi} - \bar{\text{X}})^2}{n-1}$

Calculate the average: (∑Xi)/n = 90%.

Calculate the distance (deviation) each data point is away from the mean, square the result, and add the numbers together.

For Student B: (0.88 – .90)^2 + (0.90 – 0.90)^2 + (0.92 – 0.90)^2 + (0.90 – 0.90)^2 =

(0.0004 + 0 + 0.0004 + 0) = 0.0008.

Divide the result in step 2 by (n – 1):

s^2 = 0.008/3 = 0.000266.

Population Variance $\sigma^2 = \dfrac{\sum(X_i - \mu)^2}{N}$

Sample Standard Deviation—square root of sample variance $\sqrt{s\wedge 2}$ (0.0002667)^.5 = s = 0.01633.

Population Standard Deviation – $\sqrt{\sigma^2}$

Interquartile Range (IQR)—middle 50% of your data; (Quartile 3 – Quartile 1) or 75th percentile – 25th percentile.

For Student C:

25th percentile: L = (A/100)/n; A = 25 and n = 4; 25/100*4 = 1 = L; average the data values in the 1st and 2nd positions after data is in ascending order; 1st position value is 80%, and the 2nd position value is 85%; (.80+.85)/2 = Q1 = 0.825.

75th percentile: A = 75 and n = 4 Q3 = (75/100)*4 = 3; take the average of the data values that operate in the 3rd and 4th positions; (0.95+1.00)/2 = Q3 = 0.975.

IQR = (Q3–Q1) = 0.975 – 0.825 = 0.15.

TABLE 3.6 THREE STUDENTS TEST STATISTICS

Test	A	B	C
1	90.00%	88.00%	85.00%
2	90.00%	90.00%	95.00%
3	90.00%	92.00%	80.00%
4	90.00%	90.00%	100.00%
Average	90.00%	90.00%	90.00%
Median	90.00%	90.00%	90.00%
Range	0.00%	4.00%	20.00%
Sample Variance	0.00%	0.03%	0.83%
Sample St. Dev	0.00%	1.63%	9.13%
Interquartile Rate	0.00%	1.00%	15.00%

TESTING FOR OUTLIERS

An outlier is a relatively high or low value, compared to the other data values. The value may be due to a large variability in the data or statistical anomaly. A high (or low) outlier is any data value that is unusually high (or low) compared to the other data values. The test for outliers uses the interquartile range:

Testing for High Outliers: High Outlier > Q3 + 1.5*(IQR), where Q3 is Quartile 3 and IQR (Q3 – Q1).

Testing for Low Outliers: Low Outlier < Q1 – 1.5*(IQR), where Q1 is Quartile 1 and IQR is (Q3 – Q1).

EXAMPLE: TESTING FOR OUTLIERS: PET EXPENDITURES

Table 3.7 (page 35) is a list of the last five trips to the pet store Treat Play Love. Treat Play Love is a pet store dedicated to the well-being of cats and dogs. The store sells a variety of high-quality cat and dog foods and treats, leashes, beds, and other pet supplies. Test to see if $62.49 is an outlier, with the data already organized in ascending order.

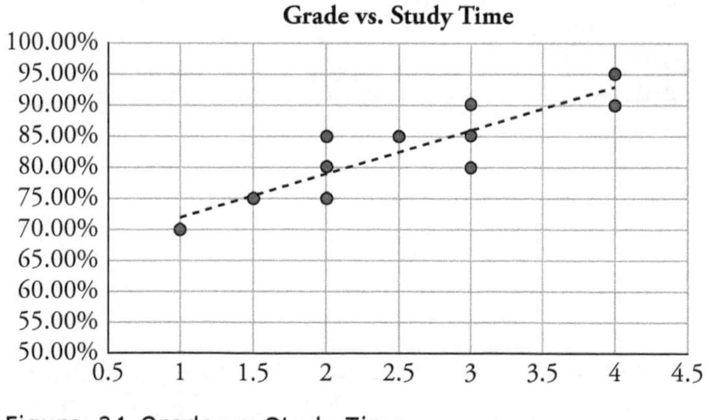

Figure: 3.1 Grade vs. Study Time

Equation: High Outlier if Data Value (\$62.49) > Q3 +1.5*(IQR)

Q3 = \$18.75, Q1 = 14.86, IQR = 3.89; \$62.49 > \$18.75 + 1.5*(\$3.89).

\$62.49 > \$24.59; any data value (in this case, \$62.49) that is above \$24.59 is an outlier.

TABLE 3.7 EXPENDITURES AT TREAT PLAY LOVE

Last 5 trips to Treat, Play, Love	
Trip #	Spending
1	\$12.46
4	\$14.86
2	\$15.25
5	\$18.75
3	\$62.49

ASSOCIATION OF TWO VARIABLES

All the statistical analysis up to now has focused on a single variable. In statistics, however, it may be beneficial to look at the interaction or relationship between two or more variables. We are referring to the correlation between two variables, not causation. The two main statistics measuring the linear association of two variables are the covariance and correlation coefficient. Be careful: just because two variables move in the same or opposite directions does not indicate one caused the other one to move. Association does not mean causation.

Figure: 3.2 Grade Versus Study Time

The covariance investigates the possible linear relationship between two variables, X and Y. Table 3.8 illustrates the positive relationship between study time and exam grade. The interpretation is the more time you study, the higher the grade. The sign, either positive or negative, indicates the relationship between the two variables X and Y. If the result is positive, there is a direct or positive relationship. Variables X and Y move in the same direction. Looking at Figure 3.1 (page 34), there seems to be a positive relationship between study time and the grade received on a test.

The formula for the covariance is below. Using the formula and the data presented in Table 3.8, the sample covariance is 0.065, which confirms our suspicion of a positive relationship.

$$\text{Sample Covariance} = s_{xy} = \frac{\sum (xi - \bar{x})(yi - \bar{y})}{n-1}$$

TABLE 3.8 EXAM SCORES AND STUDY TIME

Grade on Exam	Study Time
95.00%	4
85.00%	3
90.00%	4
75.00%	2
80.00%	3
90.00%	3
85.00%	2.5
85.00%	2
75.00%	1.5
70.00%	1
75.00%	1.5
80.00%	2

The second statistic, the correlation coefficient (or more formally, the Pearson's correlation coefficient), is a preferred measure of the association between two variables. It is preferred because it not only indicates the relationship, direct or indirect, but it also gives an idea of how strong the relationship is between the two variables. The correlation coefficient's range is between –1 and +1. A correlation of –1, referred to as perfectly negative correlation, indicates that X and Y move in opposite directions by the same amount. In a perfectly positive correlation ($r_{xy} = -1$), the variables X and Y move in the same direction. The closer the correlation coefficient is to –1 or 1, the stronger the relationship is between the two variables. The formula for the correlation coefficient is below.

$r_{xy} = sxy / (sx * sy)$, where r_{xy} is the correlation coefficient; s_x is the sample standard deviation of x; s_y is the standard deviation of y. Both the covariance and correlation coefficient lead to the same conclusion.

The sample correlation coefficient, using the data in Table 3.8, is 0.89. There is a strong positive relationship between study time and your exam grade. The more you study, the higher grade you can expect.

SUMMARY

The previous chapter focused on the visual representation of data with tables, graphs, charts, and other summaries, whereas in the current chapter, we used numerical descriptive statistics and a number line to illustrate data position, variation of a single variable, and the linear association of two variables. Descriptive statistics provides a simple summary of the data.

Extension of Chapter 3: Practicing Measures of Location and Variability

This section allows for the practicing and a further explanation of the measures of location and variability presented earlier in the chapter. The following example uses the average February temperature in the state of North Dakota for the years 2006 to 2015.

PRACTICING THE MEASURES OF LOCATION (MEAN, MEDIAN, AND MODE)

TABLE 3.1 AVERAGE TEMPERATURES IN NORTH DAKOTA (FEBRUARY 2006–15)

Year	Ave Temp in Feb in ND (*F)
2006	15
2007	7.7
2008	10.3
2009	11.4
2010	9.3
2011	10
2012	21
2013	16.8
2014	5.7
2015	8.4

Listed in Table 3.1 are the average temperatures in February for the state of North Dakota. The temperatures are for a ten-year span ranging from 2006 until 2015. The temperatures are in degrees Fahrenheit.

Sample Mean ($\overline{X}$) = $\Sigma(X\text{i})/\text{n}$, where Xi is observation i; n = sample size

(15+7.7+10.3+11.4+9.3+10+21+16.8+5.7+8.4)/10

Mean = 115.6 /10 = **15.6*F**

The mean is one of the most commonly calculated measures of location, but it is influenced by very large or very small data values. The mean can be positive, negative, or equal to zero.

Median (50th Percentile or 2nd Quartile)—the median tries to remedy the main problem with the mean, taking out the influence of very large or small data values. The median is the middle data point. It divides the data into halves. Fifty percent of the data is above the median and fifty percent of the data values are below.

To calculate the median:

1. Organize the data in ascending order.
2. If there is an odd number of values, the median is the middle value; if there is an even number of observations, take the average of the middle two data values.

Median = (10+10.3)/2 = 10.15*F.

Mode: the data value that appears with the highest frequency: not available—each temperature appears only a single time.

TABLE 3.2 TEMPERATURE DATA IN ASCENDING ORDER

5.7
7.7
8.4
9.3
10
10.3
11.4
15
16.8
21

PRACTICING PERCENTILES AND QUARTILES

Two other measures of location that are commonly used are percentiles and quartiles. A percentile is simply a cumulative measure that identifies the number of data points that occur at or below a certain data value.

Quartiles are certain percentiles and separate the data values into four groups. The first quartile is equal to the 25th percentile, the second quartile is the median, or 50th percentile, and the third quartile is commonly referred to as the 75th percentile.

Example of Calculating Percentiles and Quartiles

Listed in Table 3.2 are exam 1 results from a random statistics class. The class consisted of twenty-five students (n = 25). Calculate the 25th and the 60th percentiles.

TABLE 3.3 EXAM 1 STATISTICS

70.00%	74.00%	75.00%	76.00%	78.00%	80.00%	80.00%	80.00%	82.00%	82.00%	82.00%	85.00%	85.00%
85.00%	85.00%	85.00%	86.00%	88.00%	90.00%	90.00%	92.00%	94.00%	94.00%	95.00%	98.00%	

Order data in ascending order (Table 3.3 above).

Use the formula L = (A/100)*n, where L is the location of the data point; n is the number of observations.

If L is a mixed number, round up to the nearest integer; if L is an integer, take the average of L and L+1 positions.

(1st Quartile) 25th Percentile: A = 25; n = 25 and data in ascending order; (25/100)*25 = 6.25; round up to 7; the 25th percentile is the data value that operates the 7th position; 80%; 25% of the exam scores were equal to or less than 80%.

60th Percentile: A = 60: n = 25 and data in ascending order; L = (60/100)*25 = 15; take the average of the 15th and 16th data positions; 15th data position = 85% and 16th position = 85%; (85%+85%)/2 = 85%.

ESTIMATING THE MEAN WITH GROUPED DATA EXAMPLE

Recall from Chapter 2 the One-Bedroom Apartment Rents Frequency Distribution. To calculate the average using the grouped data below, use the following procedure.

Locate the midpoint of each class:

Class 1 Midpoint: 439.5
Class 2 Midpoint: 469.5
Class 3 Midpoint: 499.5
Class 4 Midpoint: 529.5
Class 5 Midpoint: 559.5
Class 6 Midpoint: 589.5

TABLE 3.4 FREQUENCY DISTRIBUTION OF RENTS

$425 – $454	14
$455 – $484	8
$485 – $514	16
$515 – $544	14
$545 – $574	4
$575 – $604	4
Total Observations	60

Multiply each midpoint by its class frequency and add the results:

$439.50*14 + $469.50*8 + $499.50*16 + $529.50*14 + $559.50*4 + $589.50*4 = $29,910.

Divide the answer in step 2 by the total number of observations:

$29,910/60 = $498.50.

TABLE 3.5 TEST SCORES AND AVERAGES OF THREE STUDENTS

Test	A	B	C
1	90.00%	88.00%	85.00%
2	90.00%	90.00%	95.00%
3	90.00%	92.00%	80.00%
4	90.00%	90.00%	100.00%
Average	90.00%	90.00%	90.00%

PRACTICING THE MEASURES OF VARIABILITY (SPREAD)

Table 3.5 above is a summary of three random student's results from a psychology course. As you can see, each student averaged a 90% in the class, but the test scores of the students were different.

The simplest measure of variability is the range. The range is the difference between the maximum value and the minimum value (Max – Min). The range is never negative, and the smallest value it can assume is 0. The problem with the range is that it only uses two data values.

Range—(for Student B): Max is 92%, and the Min is 88%.

Range = 0.92 – 0.88 = .04 or 4%.

Another simple measure of variability is the interquartile range. Instead of using only two data points, like the range, the interquartile uses 50% percent of the observations. It is an incomplete measure.

Interquartile Range (IQR)—middle 50% of your data; (Quartile 3 – Quartile 1) or 75th percentile – 25th Percentile.

For Student C:

25th percentile: L = (A/100)/n; A = 25 and n = 4; 25/100*4 = 1 = L; average the data values in the 1st and 2nd position after data is in ascending order; 1st position value is 80%, and the 2nd position value is 85%; (.80+.85)/2 = Q1 = 0.825.

75th percentile: A = 75 and n = 4 Q3 = (75/100)*4 = 3; take the average of the data values that operate in the 3rd and 4th positions; (0.95+1.00)/2 = Q3 = 0.975.

IQR = (Q3–Q1) = 0.975 – 0.825 = 0.15.

The two preferred measures of variability are the variance and standard deviation. Both measures use all the data observations. The variance is the average squared deviations a data value is from the mean and the standard deviation measures the average distance a data value is from the mean. The standard deviation is the preferred measure because it is measured in the same units as your data (variance is measured in units squared).

Calculating the Sample Variance $s^2 = \dfrac{\sum\left(Xi - \bar{X}\right)^2}{n-1}$

Calculate the average: (ΣXi)/n = 90%.

Calculate the distance (deviation) each data point is away from the mean, square the result, and add the numbers together.

For Student B: (0.88 – .90)^2 + (0.90 – 0.90)^2 + (0.92 – 0.90)^2 + (0.90 – 0.90)^2 = (0.0004 + 0 + 0.0004 + 0) = 0.0008.

Divide the result in step 2 by (n – 1):

s^2 = 0.008/3 = 0.000266.

Population Variance $\sigma^2 = \dfrac{\sum\left(Xi - \mu\right)^2}{N}$

Sample Standard Deviation—square root of sample variance $\sqrt{s^{\wedge}2}$ (0.0002667)^.5 =

s = 0.01633.

Population Standard Deviation = $\sqrt{\sigma^2}$

Table 3.6 (page 41) presents various descriptive statistics of three students. Measures of location and variability should be used together to draw conclusions. One statistic does not tell the whole story.

TESTING FOR OUTLIERS

An outlier is a relatively high or low value compared to the other data values. The value may be due to a large variability in the data or a statistical anomaly. A high (or low) outlier is any data value that is an unusually high (or low) compared to the other data values. The test for outliers uses the interquartile range:

Testing for High Outliers: **High Outlier > Q3 + 1.5*(IQR)**, where Q3 is Quartile 3 and IQR (Q3 – Q1).

Testing for Low Outliers: **Low Outlier < Q1 – 1.5*(IQR)**, where Q1 is Quartile 1 and IQR is (Q3 – Q1).

TABLE 3.6 THREE STUDENTS TEST STATISTICS

Test	A	B	C
1	90.00%	88.00%	85.00%
2	90.00%	90.00%	95.00%
3	90.00%	92.00%	80.00%
4	90.00%	90.00%	100.00%
Average	90.00%	90.00%	90.00%
Median	90.00%	90.00%	90.00%
Range	0.00%	4.00%	20.00%
Sample Variance	0.00%	0.03%	0.83%
Sample St. Dev	0.00%	1.63%	9.13%
Interquartile Rate	0.00%	1.00%	15.00%

EXAMPLE: TESTING FOR OUTLIERS: PET EXPENDITURES

An outlier is a relatively high or low data value, compared to the other data observations. Outliers can inflate or deflate the mean. If a data point is large or small, compared to the others, it should not be disregarded. Table 3.7 is a list of the last five trips to the pet store Treat Play Love. Treat Play Love is a pet store dedicated to the well-being of cats and dogs. The store sells a variety of high-quality cat and dog foods and treats, leashes, beds, and other pet supplies. Test to see if $62.49 is an outlier, with the data already organized in ascending order.

Figure: 3.2 Grade Versus Study Time

TABLE 3.7 EXPENDITURES AT TREAT PLAY LOVE

Last 5 trips to Treat, Play, Love	
Trip #	Spending
1	$12.46
4	$14.86
2	$15.25
5	$18.75
3	$62.49

Equation: High Outlier if Data Value ($62.49) > Q3 +1.5*(IQR)

Q3 = $18.75, Q1 = 14.86, IQR = 3.89; $62.49 > $18.75 + 1.5*($3.89).

$62.49 > $24.59; any data value (in this case, $62.49) that is above $24.59 is an outlier.

SUMMARY

The Extension of Chapter 3 reinforces the calculation of the main descriptive statistics: measures of location and variability. Testing for outliers was also examined. No single measure of location or variability should be used by itself. It is the use of both location and variability together that make statistical analysis more complete.

IMAGE CREDITS

- Tab. 3.1: NOAA, "Average Temperatures in North Dakota (February 2006-15)," http://www.ncdc.noaa.gov/cag/time-series/us/110/0/tavg/1/2/2005-2015?base_prd=true&firstbaseyear=1901&lastbaseyear=2000. Copyright in the Public Domain.
- Tab. 3.2: NOAA, "Temperature Data in Ascending Order," http://www.ncdc.noaa.gov/cag/time-series/us/110/0/tavg/1/2/2005-2015?base_prd=true&firstbaseyear=1901&lastbaseyear=2000. Copyright in the Public Domain.
- Fig. 3.1: Copyright © by Treat Play Love. Reprinted with permission.

Probability

4

"So you are telling me there's a chance." Probability is simply that. It is the likelihood or belief an event may or may not occur. Probability ranges from (inclusive of) zero, indicating the event will not happen, to one, indicating the event will certainly happen. Whether it be sports, the weather, or the state of the economy, it is all a guessing game. As Benjamin Franklin said, "there are only two certainties in life: death and taxes."

An experiment is any procedure or process that produces well-defined outcomes. The goals of this chapter are to determine the number of outcomes, assign probabilities to each outcome, and investigate the relationship between two events.

COUNTING RULES, COMBINATIONS, AND PERMUTATIONS

DETERMINING THE NUMBER OF OUTCOMES

THE MULTISTAGE EXPERIMENT

The total number of outcomes of a multistage experiment can be determined by multiplying the number of outcomes at each stage by each other. Take, for example, tossing a coin three times. Each toss is a stage. For each toss of the coin, there are two possible outcomes. There are eight total outcomes, listed in Table 4.1.

# of Outcomes = (n1)*(n2)*(n3) = 2*2*2 = 8.

TABLE 4.1 POSSIBLE OUTCOMES TOSSING A COIN THREE TIMES

8 Outcomes	
T, T, T	H, T, T
T, T, H	H, T, H
T, H, T	H, H, T
T, T, H	H, H, H

PERMUTATIONS AND COMBINATIONS

There are two methods for determining the number of outcomes when organizing items into groups. They are permutations and combinations. The difference between the two is deciding if the order of selection matters. If the order of selection is important, then it is a permutation. This result would also yield the number of outcomes. If the order does not matter, it is a combination. (The key is whether the order of selection matters.)

$$P_n^N = n!\binom{N}{n} = \frac{N!}{(N-n)!} \qquad C_n^N = \binom{N}{n} = \frac{N!}{n(N-n)!}$$

Where n = the number of items per group and N is the total number of items.

Example: Scheduling Employees at Food Mart

There are fourteen work shifts in a week (two shifts a day, Monday through Sunday) that have to be filled by seven employees (Employees A, B, C, D, E, F, and G) at Food Mart. How many groups of two can be formed? How many different combinations can be formed?

Constraints:

*Employees cannot work two shifts in a given day.

*Only one employee is needed for each shift.

TABLE 4.2 NUMBER OF OUTCOMES

Number of Possible Outcomes = 42						
A, B	B, A	C, A	D, A	E, A	F, A	G, A
A, C	B, C	C, B	D, B	E, B	F, B	G, B
A, D	B, D	C, D	D, C	E, C	F, C	G, C
A, E	B, E	C, E	D, E	E, D	F, D	G, D
A, F	B, F	C, F	D, F	E, F	F, E	G, E
A, G	B, G	C, G	D, G	E, G	F, G	G, F

The total number of outcomes, the number of permutations, is equal to forty-two (N = 7 (workers to choose from, n = 2 (two workers per day)). The number of combinations, remembering order does not matter, is twenty-one. There are doubles of each group (A, B and B, A count as one group under combinations and two separate groups for permutations).

Permutations = N!/(N – n)! = 7!/(7 – 2)! = (7*6*5*4*3*2*1)/(5*4*3*2*1) = 42.

Combinations = N!/(n!(N – n)!) = 7!/(2!*(7 – 2)!) = (7*6*5*4*3*2*1)/(2*1*5*4*3*2*1) = 21.

Probability Applied to Sports

PROBABILITY

By Andrew Wiesner

The discussion of probability in elementary statistics can often present much confusion for students. The topic tends to contain some of the more difficult concepts for students to grasp. They either understand the concept but not the formula, or vice versa. Fortunately, there exists in sports many examples that can readily explain these concepts and provide a foundation for their understanding. For instance, consider the following two conversations between two friends:

Conversation One

Friend One: What chance do you give New England in beating the Giants in the Super Bowl?

Friend Two: I'd say it's about 50/50.

Friend One: What if Brady can't play?

Friend Two: Then New England has no chance.

Conversation Two

Friend One: What chance do you give New England in beating the Giants in the Super Bowl?

Friend Two: I'd say it's about 50/50.

Friend One: What if their second string quarterback, Brian Hoyer, gets hurt and can't play?

Friend Two: So what, that won't matter. I still give them a 50/50 shot.

If you can appreciate both conversations, then you already have a basic grasp of probability concepts such as **subjective probability**, **conditional probability**, and **independent events**.

4.1 DEFINING PROBABILITIES

The idea of **probability** is simply the chance that some event occurs (or doesn't occur). From a numeric standpoint, this implies that an event either has no chance of happening (probability of 0), will absolutely occur (probability of 1), or somewhere in between. Thus, the probability of any event taking place ranges from 0 to 1. This is easy enough, and to most of us it is common sense, but *how* the probability of an event is found is another issue.

In general, there are three common types of probabilities: **Classical**, **relative frequency**, and **subjective**. *Classical probability* relates to the number of times an outcome can occur out of the total number of possible outcomes, assuming all outcomes are equally likely. For those who enjoy a bit of gambling, think of flipping a coin, rolling a die, or choosing a card from a standard deck of cards. Relatively, the probability of a head is 1/2, the probability of getting a "1" is 1/6, and the probability of getting the ace of spades is 1/52. Or, if you believe in the parity of the NFL, each team has a 1/32 chance of winning the Super Bowl before the season starts! *Relative frequency probability* is defined as what occurs in the long run or over a long number of trials. Consider two evenly matched teams playing a game; you would give each team a 1/2, or 0.5, probability of winning the game. If these teams played twice with Team A, winning both times, does this necessarily change the probability? No. This is the idea of "over a long-run number of trials." The idea is that if the two teams played over and over and over again, the numbers would eventually even out to where both teams won an equal number of times. Applying this to the classical probability examples, think of rolling the die. You may roll the die 10 times and never get a 1. Assuming the die is fair, if you rolled the die many, many times you would expect about 1/6 of these many roles to produce a 1. This raises another concept called the **law of large numbers**. *Subjective* probability is when one sets the probability of some outcome on personal views. This is sometimes referred to as *personal probability*—the belief a person gives to an outcome happening. This is illustrated in the above conversations. Friend Two is giving the Patriots a 50/50 chance of winning. There is no long-run series of trials on which to base this probability—they have only played once before in the Super Bowl (2008)—and the teams playing in 2012 are not exactly the same.

4.2 TERMINOLOGY, NOTATION, AND MATH RULES

TERMINOLOGY

Sample Space: The set of all possible outcomes.

Event: A subset of the sample space.

Disjoint Events or Mutually Exclusive Events: These are events that do not have any outcomes in common. That is, they do not share any outcomes: If an outcome occurs in one event. This outcome cannot occur in another event. By rule, if events are disjoint they cannot also be independent. That is, if events are disjoint, they are also dependent.

Independent Events: Events are independent when one event does not "influence" the chance another event occurs. (See Conversation Two at the beginning of the chapter.)

Complement Events: These are all events not in the event of interest. By rule, complementary events are also disjoint events.

Intersection of Events: This consists of all outcomes shared by events. Unlike disjoint events, intersection represents the outcomes that events have in common.

Union of Events: The combined outcome of two or more events.

Conditional Probability: When the occurrence of one event influences the probability that another event occurs. (See Conversation One at the beginning of the chapter.)

Simple Events: These are events that have only one outcome.

NOTATION

With probability, events are often defined by a long phrase. For instance, we might be interested in the event "Giants win Super Bowl" or "Giants win Super Bowl and Manning throws for over 300 yards." To simplify things, single letters are given to represent these wordy events. The usual choice of lettering is "A" and "B" when discussing two events, and then "C" if three events, etc. What is important, however, is to not let this labeling confuse you: just think of it as shorthand. For instance, one might say, "Let A be the event the Giants win the Super Bowl." However, one could just as easily say, "Let G be the event the Giants win the Super Bowl." Other than using A or G, the meaning is the same: We are interested in the outcome, Giants win the Super Bowl. The important idea is that you identify what the lettering represents, as once you identify the events with simple labels, you use the labels!

P(A): The probability that event A occurs. Remember, by earlier definition of probability, the probability of any event ranges from 0 to 1, or $0 \le P(A) \le 1$.

P(A and B) or P(A $\cap$ B): The probability that events A and B occur. This is the notation form for the intersection of two events. Think of the symbol $\cap$ as an "A" without the connecting line. This is also referred to as the **joint probability**.

P(A or B) or P(A $\cup$ B): The probability that events A or B occur. This is the notation form for the union of two events. Think of the symbol $\cup$ as representing union.

P(A') or P(A^c): The probability of the complement to event A.

P(A|B): The probability event A occurs *given* event B has occurred. The symbol "|" should not be confused with "divide by." That is, do not think of this as "A divided by B." This notation represents the conditional probability of "event A occurs given event B occurred."

P(B|A): The probability event B occurs *given* event A has occurred. As with the prior notation, the symbol "|" should not be confused with "divide by." That is, do not think of this as "B divided by A." This notation represents the conditional probability of "event B occurs given event A occurred."

PROBABILITY RULES

Complement Rule: $P(A) + P(A^c) = 1$ or equivalently, $P(A) = 1 - P(A^c)$. In words, the probability of an event plus the probability of the complement to that event equals one.

Independence Rule: If two events, say event A and event B, (remember, don't get hung up on notation, as this could be any lettering used!) are independent events, then the P(A and B) = P(A)*P(B). In words, if two events are independent, then the probability of their intersection is equal to the product of the individual event probabilities.

Addition Rule for Union: P(A or B) = P(A) + P(B) – P(A and B). In other words, the probability of the union of two events is found by adding the individual event probabilities, then subtracting the joint probability (i.e., the probability of the intersection of the two events).

Conditional Probability: $P(A\,|\,B) = \dfrac{P(A \text{ and } B)}{P(B)}$ and conversely, $P(B\,|\,A) = \dfrac{P(A \text{ and } B)}{P(A)}$.

Notice that in both equations, the numerator is the probability of the intersection of the two events. The denominator is the probability of the given event.

TWO SPECIAL RULES:

1. If two events, A and B, are disjoint, or mutually exclusive, then the P(A and B) is zero. This makes sense by the definition of disjoint, which says two events are disjoint if they do not share any outcomes in common. Thus, if two events are disjoint, the intersection of the events must be zero, as they would not have any outcomes in common. So if two events are disjoint, P(A or B) = P(A) + P(B). Note this only applies when we know the events are disjoint; otherwise use the addition rule for unions. Remember, disjoint and mutually exclusive mean the same thing.
2. If two events, A and B, are independent then P(A|B) = P(A) and P(B|A) = P(B). This, too, should make sense when you consider the meaning of independence. Recall that two events are independent when the occurrence of one event does not affect the chance another event occurs. Therefore, if A and B are independent events, then knowing event B occurred would not change the probability event A occurs, i.e., P(A|B) = P(A). This same logic applies to P(B|A). For those who prefer to see this mathematically, consider the following, keeping in mind the **independence rule** that says P(A and B) = P(A)*P(B). Applying this rule to two independent events:

$$P(A \mid B) = \frac{P(A \text{ and } B)}{P(B)} = \frac{P(A) * P(B)}{P(B)} = \frac{P(A) * P(B)}{P(B)} = P(A)$$

[Same math logic for P(B|A)]

The key to Special Rule 2 is to remember that this ONLY applies when the events are independent. If independence is not known or is not true, then you need to use the conditional probability rules.

RULES FOR INDEPENDENT EVENTS

If asked to show if two events are independent, one only needs to verify if any *ONE* of the following is true. If one of the following is true, then so are the other two, and the events would be labeled as independent.

1. P(A and B) = P(A)*P(B)
2. P(A|B) = P(A)
3. P(B|A) = P(B)

4.3 APPLYING PROBABILITY RULES: SOME EXAMPLES

Probabilities are generally provided in one of two ways: You are either given the probability (e.g., the probability Team A beats Team B is 0.25) or you can calculate the probability from a series of outcomes displayed in a table. We will look at both. NOTE: These examples use probability based on relative frequency, since it is based on what has transpired over time.

EXAMPLE 1: WORLD SERIES GAME 7

Since the World Series went to a best-of-7 format in 1905 through 2011, there have been 36 fall classics that extended the full seven games. Below is a breakdown of home team (AL or NL) and whether that home team won game 7. This particular type of table is called a **two-by-two table**, as the table is composed of two rows of data and two columns of data *excluding the rows and columns for totals*!

TABLE 4.1.1 TWO-BY-TWO TABLE OF GAME 7.

Home	Lost	Won	Total
AL	10	10	20
NL	7	9	16
Total	17	19	36

Question 1: What is the probability that the home team was from the American League (AL)?
Question 2: What is the probability that the home team won game 7?
Question 3: What is the probability the home team won *given* the home team was from the American League?
Question 4: Are the events "Home team AL" and "Home Team Won" independent events?

Answer 1: The probability the home team was from the AL can be found by the number of total times the AL was home team (20) divided by the total number of games (36). The answer is therefore 20/36 = 0.555.

Answer 2: The probability the home team won can be found by the number of total times the home team won (19) divided by the total number of games (36). The answer is therefore 19/36 = 0.528.

Answer 3: This is a *conditional probability* and we start with the *given* event, which is the home team was from the AL. From the table, there were 20 instances where the home team was from the AL. Then, of these 20, the home team won 10 times. The probability could be written as follows: P(Home Wins | Home AL) = 10/20 = 0.50.

Answer 4: Recall that to state independence, we need to show that *one* of the following is true:

P(A)*P(B) = P(A and B) or P(A|B) = P(A) or P(B|A) = P(B)

From the table, we can calculate the probability that "Home Team AL" and "Home Team Wins" from taking the number of times these two events occur together (10) divided by the total number of games (36). So the P(Home Team AL and Home Team Wins) = 10/36 = 0.28.

Starting with using some notation, let's define A as "Home Team AL" and B as "Home Team Wins." Applying this to the above formulas:

P(A and B) = 0.28 and from answers to Questions 1 and 2, P(A)*P(B)
= 0.555*0.528 = 0.29.

Pretty close! And this presents one possible problem: rounding! If we had rounded to more (or fewer) decimal places, the answer may have been more clear. In this case, one could reasonably conclude that these are "close enough" to assume independent. However, technically speaking, since they are not *exactly* the same, one might say they are not independent. Fortunately, statistics can help provide us with an answer to this question of, "Are they close enough?" which is a topic we will discuss starting in Chapter 6.

From Answer 3, we have P(B|A) = 0.50 and from Answer 2, we have P(B) = 0.528. Again, pretty close—which it should be, as the decision on independence should be the same regardless of which equation you use. Note that the final probability may not be the same—that is, above we are comparing 0.28 to 0.29 and here we are comparing 0.50 to 0.528—but the decision you make will be the same. So once more, like before, possibly too close to call!

What one can conclude from this information is that, in general, there is no advantage to playing game 7 at home. However, a possible lurking variable (remember these from Chapter 2!) could be the weather or starting pitcher. For example, maybe northern teams are more likely to win game 7 at home compared to if the game were played in the South, as the October/November weather in the North could be a factor. Perhaps a team's best pitcher had to be used in game 6, leaving that team to play against the other team's ace.

EXAMPLE 2: PREDICTING SUPER BOWL WINNERS

Some say, "Offense is what makes the game exciting," but does this translate to winning the Super Bowl? From reviewing the regular season points per game (ppg) averages for teams playing in the Super Bowl (see www.nfl.com), the probability is 0.57 that the team with the higher ppg average during the regular season wins the Super Bowl. The probability is 0.52 that the team with the higher ppg is from the American Football Conference (AFC). Finally, the probability is 0.27 that the team with the higher ppg is from the AFC and wins the Super Bowl.

Question 1: What is the probability that the team with the higher ppg *loses* the Super Bowl?
Question 2: Are the events "Higher ppg wins Super Bowl" and "Team with higher ppg is from AFC" independent?

Answer 1: This question requires that we look at the *complement* of an event. Since the team can either win or lose the Super Bowl (disjoint events since a team cannot both win *and* lose the same game!), the probability the team with the higher ppg loses the Super Bowl can be found by:

---

1 – P(Team with higher ppg wins Super Bowl) = 1 – 0.57 = 0.43

Answer 2: Again, for independence, think of using any one of the above mentioned formulas in Example 1. Since we are given a "joint probability" (remember these are "and" probabilities), we can use the P(A and B) = P(A)*P(B) to check for independence.

If we define A as "Team with higher ppg wins" and B as "Team with higher ppg is from AFC," then from the example we have:

P(A) = 0.57, P(B) = 0.52 and P(A and B) = 0.27

Plugging these probabilities into our equation P(A)*P(B) we have:

(0.57)*(0.52) = 0.29, which is again close to our P(A and B) of 0.27! You can see how frustrating probability can be, as the results are not always so clear!

From this information, it would appear that having the higher scoring offense in the regular season does not translate into an advantage in the Super Bowl. We leave it to you to research www.nfl.com or some other resource to see if defense would play a role; that is, is the team with the lower ppg allowed during the regular season more likely to win the Super Bowl?

EXAMPLE 3: IS THERE A HOME FIELD ADVANTAGE IN NFL CHAMPIONSHIP GAMES?

There have been 46 Super Bowls through 2012, meaning there have been 92 conference championships: 46 in each league. For each of those championship games, the game is played on one team's home field. If there was no home field advantage, then what would be the probability that either team would win? If you said 50/50, that would be correct: Any team—road or home—would have an equal chance of winning. Applying this to the 92 games, this would mean that 46 times the road team won and 46 times the home team won, or at least very close to this outcome. If we let "W" represent the event "Win Championship Game," then 0.50 would represent P(W), or the probability of winning the championship game. If we let "H" represent "Playing Championship at Home," then if winning is independent of playing the game at home—that is, no home field advantage—the conditional probability of P(W|H) would also be 0.50, or just the probability of winning. Playing at home would offer no advantage. However, in reviewing these 92 championship games, 61 times the home team has won. This translates into roughly 2/3 of the time the home team has won. In other words, the conditional probability of winning the game given playing at home is 0.66, which is not equal to the 0.50 probability of winning if no home field advantage. From this, one could conclude that playing at home does offer a better chance of winning; a home field advantage exists in NFL championship games.

EXPRESSIONS AND FORMULAS

1. P(A) stands for the "probability that some event called A occurs."
2. P(A and B) or P(A $\cap$ B) is the probability of the " intersection of event A and event B.". This is where the two events overlap or the outcomes that occur in both event A and event B.
3. P(A or B) or P(A $\cup$ B) is the probability of the " union of event A and event B."
4. P(A') or P(A^c) represents the probability of the "complement" of event A. This would be all outcomes that do NOT occur in event A.
5. P(A|B) represents a "conditional" probability. The probability event A occurs *given* event B has already occurred. Similarly, P(B|A) would be the conditional probability that event B occurs *given* event A has already occurred.
6. P(A) = 1 – P(A^c), known as the complement rule.
7. P(A)*P(B) is the independence rule and can *only* be used if known that event A and event B are independent.

8. $P(A \text{ or } B) = P(A) + P(B) - P(A \text{ and } B)$ is the addition rule for the union of event A and event B.

9. $P(A \mid B) = \frac{P(A \text{ and } B)}{P(B)}$ and $P(B \mid A) = \frac{P(A \text{ and } B)}{P(A)}$ are the formulas for conditional probabilities for event A and event B.

10. To show if two events are independent, we need to verify that any *one* of the following is true:
    1. $P(A \text{ and } B) = P(A)*P(B)$
    2. $P(A|B) = P(A)$
    3. $P(B|A) = P(B)$.

SUMMARY

This chapter introduced probability as the likelihood that some event would occur. There is a three-step process used in determining the probability. The first is determining the number of outcomes; the second is assigning the probabilities to the outcomes, using one of the three methods; and, finally, investigating the relationship between probability and another event. Probabilities can range from zero to one. Some probabilities are easy to determine: for example, there is a 50/50 chance when you toss a coin that the result will be heads, or when you roll a die, the probability of a certain number showing (1–6) is 16.67% (1/6). Other events, such as the chance it will rain or the likelihood you will earn an A in this class, are a little more challenging. These events require analyzing other key variables, past performance, and making a judgement call. If two variables move in the same direction or opposite direction, that does not mean one caused the other one to move.

5 Discrete Probability Distributions

A discrete random variable is a quantitative variable that answers the question “how many?” Discrete random variables describe persons, places, or things. Discrete random variables use integers counting numbers (no mixed numbers), and the lowest value a discrete random variable can assume is zero. A discrete probability distribution is the set of possible outcomes of an experiment and their associated probabilities. There will be three main discrete probability distributions discussed in this chapter: the Relative Frequency, the Binomial, and the Poisson distribution.

DISCRETE PROBABILITY DISTRIBUTIONS

By Jin W. Choi

A discrete probability distribution describes the probability of a discrete random variable occurring. A discrete variable is an observation (or a data) that is measured in a discrete unit such as categorical data of yes-or-no and discrete numerical data obtained from a counting process such as a number of customers in line, phone calls received, customer orders taken, etc. A **random variable** is a data set whose values are observed randomly without any managed plans of selecting them.

Among discrete probability distributions, however, the binomial distribution and the Poisson distribution are the most prominent. The binomial distribution allows a probability assessment of an event that has only two outcomes of either yes-or-no, failure-or-success, or one-or-the-other-group. The Poisson distribution, on the other hand, allows the probability assessment of an outcome based on an average number of occurrences observed.

Before discussing these distributions, alternative but very powerful concepts of calculating the mean and the variance of a discrete random variable by the use of the expectations operator are first in order.

A. Definitions

1. The Mean = The Expected Value of a Discrete Random Variable = E(X) = The First Moment about the Origin = μ

$$\mu = E(X) = \sum_{i=1}^{m} X_i \cdot P(X_i)$$

where X_i = the i-th observation of X = the i-th X value and $P(X_i)$ = the probability of X_i occurring

Example 1

Given 10, 9, 10, 11, and 10 as a population, the arithmetic average (=the population mean) is calculated as:

$$\mu = \frac{\sum_{i=1}^{N} X_i}{N} = \frac{9+10+10+10+11}{5} = 10$$

Note that there are one 9, three 10s, and one 11, out of 5 observations.
Alternatively, therefore, the mean (=the expected value) of X can be calculated as:

$$\mu = \frac{1}{5}\cdot 9 + \frac{3}{5}\cdot 10 + \frac{1}{5}\cdot 11 = 10 \rightarrow \mu = \sum_{i=1}^{m} P(X_i)\cdot X_i = E(X)$$

where $P(X_i)$ is the probability of X_i occurring. This calculation emphasizes the relative frequency (=probability) of 9, 10 and 11 occurring in the population. → This method is useful if only the probabilities of certain outcomes to occur are known. That is, you need not know all the observation values as is the case of calculating the arithmetic average.
Note: The expected value of X, E(X), is the mean of X, μ.

Example 2

Howie Mandel's "Deal or No Deal" TV Game Show[1]:

Given the following suit cases of \$5; \$300; \$50,000; and \$1 million are to be opened, the Banker offers \$165,000. Will you take it? Deal? Or No Deal? If you base your decision purely on the expected value concept, will you make a deal or not?

1 This game starts with 26 brief cases with values, ranging between \$0.01 and \$1 million, that are written inside each brief case. To start the game, the contestant initially picks 6 brief cases to be opened, except the one he/she keeps to his/her side and the number of brief cases to be opened decreases as the game progresses.

Answer:

The answer to this question will critically depend on your risk preference. However, if you are to make a decision solely based on the mathematical expectation, you should reject the deal because the offer is far lower than the expected value of the game as shown below:

$$E(X) = \frac{5+300+50000+1000000}{4} = \frac{1050305}{4} = 262576.25$$

In reality, the contestant took the deal and stopped the game. Was he irrational?

Example 3

A survey showed that Americans exercise an average of 20 minutes daily. However, only 20% of Americans exercise daily. How long do you think these exercising Americans exercise every day?

Answer:

$$\text{Because } E(X) = 0.2 \times X + 0.8 \times 0 = 20, \text{ X} = 100 \text{ minutes.}$$

Example 4

How would you determine the annual premium of a $500,000 life insurance policy for a 29-year-old male? Suppose that 5 out of 10,000 29-year old male die each year.

Answer:

Identify the probability of a 29-year-old male dying in one year → That is, the mortality rate for a 29-year-old male is 0.0005 (=5/10,000). Then, calculate the break-even point for the premium paid by the insured and the death benefit to be received by the beneficiary as follows:

Noting that a payment is a negative number to the insured individual whereas a receipt is a positive number, we can identify:

Break-even = E(Cash Flow) = 0 = (–X)*(1 – 0.0005) + $500,000 (0.0005)

Solving for X, the insurance premium, we find: X = $250.13 per year.

2. The Variance, σ^2 = The 2nd Moment about the Mean

$$\sigma^2 = E(X^2) = \sum_{i=1}^{m} P(X_i) \cdot [X_i - E(X)]^2 = \sum_{i=1}^{m} P(X_i) \cdot [X_i - \mu]^2$$

e.g., Given a population of 10, 9, 10, 11, and 10 and thus, the population size (N) = 5, the population variance, σ^2, is calculated as:

$$\sigma^2 = \frac{\sum_{i=1}^{N} (X_i - \mu)^2}{N} = \frac{(9-10)^2 + 0^2 + 0^2 + 0^2 + (11-10)^2}{5} = \frac{2}{5} = 0.4$$

Alternatively, the population variance of X can be calculated as:

$$\sigma^2 = \frac{1}{5} \cdot (9-10)^2 + \frac{3}{5} \cdot (10-10)^2 + \frac{1}{5} \cdot (11-10)^2 = \frac{2}{5} = 0.4$$

$$\text{because } \sigma^2 = E(X^2) = \sum_{i=1}^{m} P(X_i) \cdot [X_i - \mu]^2$$

3. The Standard Deviation, σ

$$\sigma = \sqrt{\sigma^2} \quad \rightarrow \sigma = \sqrt{04} = 0.6324$$

Note 1: The standard deviation is a square root of the variance. Thus, without the variance, the standard deviation can not be calculated.

Note 2: Traditionally, a standard deviation is written as a positive number even though $(\pm\sigma)^2 = \sigma^2$ clearly shows the existence of a negative standard deviation.

B. The Binomial Distribution

The binomial (probability) distribution measure the probability of success (=yes) and failure (=no) in a sample of n observations → Only 2 outcomes are possible[2].

1. Assumptions
   a. Each trial can have only two mutually exclusive outcomes or can be grouped into two mutually exclusive outcomes. Thus, each outcome can be classified as either a success or a failure.
   b. The number of trials, n, is known.
   c. The outcomes of each trial are independent of each other.
   d. The probability of a success (or a failure) remains the same for each trial.

Examples:

a. Does a 3 coin toss follow a binomial distribution?

Yes. In a 3 coin toss (either tossing 3 coins at the same time or tossing 1 coin three times), (a) outcomes are classified as either a head (=success) or a tail (=failure); (b) there is a fixed number of trials – 1 trial of 3 coins or 3 trials of 1 coin; (c) each coin toss is independent of one another; and (4) the probability of a head remains the same at 0.5. Thus, all conditions (=assumptions) of a binomial distribution is fulfilled in this case.

b. Can rolling a die be considered as following a binomial probability distribution?

Yes, if 2 (for example) is a success and the rest of the numbers such as 1, 3, 4, 5, and 6 are grouped as a failure. The success probability is, then, 1/6 whereas the failure probability is 5/6 (= 1 – 1/6).

2 If three outcomes are possible, then the probability distribution is called the trinomial probability distribution.

2. The Binomial Probability Function

$$P(X) = {}_nC_X \cdot p^X \cdot (1-p)^{n-X} = \frac{n!}{X!(n-X)!} \cdot p^X (1-p)^{n-X}$$

a. The Mean of the Binomial Distribution

$$\mu = E(X) = np$$

b. The Variance of the Binomial Distribution

$$\sigma^2 = np(1 - \text{p})$$

c. The Standard Deviation of the Binomial Distribution

$$\sigma = \sqrt{np(1-p)}$$

3. The Methodology of Applying the Binomial Distribution

Step 1: Assess if the binomial distribution is appropriate by examining the number of outcomes possible. If appropriate, identify the probability of success, p, and the probability of failure, (1 − p). If we let q = (1 − p), then the above equations can be simplified somewhat. For example, $\sigma^2 = npq$ and $\sigma = \sqrt{npq}$.

Step 2: Identify the number of trials, n, and the number of successes, X.

Step 3: Apply these values to the binomial probability function to obtain the binomial probability, P(X).

C. Examples

1. What is the probability of having 2 heads in 3 coin tosses?

Note: p = probability of a head in a single coin toss = 0.5
Number of Heads = successes = X = 2
Number of trials = number of observations = n = 3

a. Numerical Solution:

$$P(X=2) = {}_3C_2 \cdot (0.5)^2 \cdot (1-0.5)^{3-2} = \frac{3!}{2!(3-2)!} \cdot 0.5^2 (1-0.5)^{3-2}$$

$$= 3 \times 0.125 = 3 \times \frac{1}{8}$$

b. Enumerative Solution:

i. What is the number of possible outcomes from 3 coin tosses?

$$2 \times 2 \times 2 = 2^3 = 8 \text{ ways}$$

Alternatively, we find the 8 ways to be:

HHH	(HHT)	(HTH)	HTT
(THH)	THT	TTH	TTT

ii. What is the probability of 2 heads in 3 coin tosses?

As shown above, 3 cases of 2 heads out of 8 possible outcomes are found by enumeration.

Alternatively, we can use the rule of combination to count the number of outcomes because the order of a head appearing does not matter → unordered → use the rule of combination as follows:

$$n^C X = \frac{n!}{X!(n-X)!} = \frac{3!}{2!(3-2)!} = 3$$

Therefore,

$$P(\text{2 heads})=3 \text{ cases} \times \text{probability of } 1/8 = 3\times\frac{1}{8} = 3\times 0.125 = 0.375$$

2. On average, how many times will you see a head in these 3 trials of coin tosses? What is the corresponding standard deviation?

$$\mu = np = 3\cdot 0.5 = 1.5$$

$$\sigma = \sqrt{np(1-p)} = \sqrt{3\cdot 0.5\cdot(1-0.5)} = 0.866$$

3. What is the probability of having 1 or 2 heads in 4 coin tosses?

Note: p = probability of a head in a single coin toss = 0.5
Number of Heads = number of successes = X = 1 **or** 2
Number of trials = number of observations = n = 4

Solution:

$$P(X=1) = P(1) = \frac{4!}{1!(4-1)!}\cdot 0.5^1(1-0.5)^{4-1} = 0.25$$

$$P(X=2) = P(2) = \frac{4!}{2!(4-2)!}\cdot 0.5^2(1-0.5)^{4-2} = 0.375$$

Therefore,

$$P(1 \text{ or } 2) = P(0<X<3) = P(1) + P(2) = 0.25 + 0.375 = 0.625$$

Note 1: You can use the Excel Spreadsheet command of

"**=BINOMDIST(X,n,p,true)**" for cumulative probability and
"**=BINOMDIST(X,n,p,false)**" for relative probability.

Note 2: You can look up the binomial probability value from the following partial Binomial Probability Table → the probability, p, can be found in the first row, and n and X are found under their respective columns. For example, given p=0.5, n=4, and X=l, you should find P(X=1) = 0.25.

		P								
n	X	0.1	0.2	0.3	0.4	0.5	0.6	0.7	0.8	0.9
2	0	0.8100	0.6400	0.4900	0.3600	0.2500	0.1600	0.0900	0.0400	0.0100
	1	0.1800	0.3200	0.4200	0.4800	0.5000	0.4800	0.4200	0.3200	0.1800
	2	0.0100	0.0400	0.0900	0.1600	0.2500	0.3600	0.4900	0.6400	0.8100
3	0	0.7290	0.5120	0.3430	0.2160	0.1250	0.0640	0.0270	0.0080	0.0010
	1	0.2430	0.3840	0.4410	0.4320	0.3750	0.2880	0.1890	0.0960	0.0270
	2	0.0270	0.0960	0.1890	0.2880	0.3750	0.4320	0.4410	0.3840	0.2430
	3	0.0010	0.0080	0.0270	0.0640	0.1250	0.2160	0.3430	0.5120	0.7290
4	0	0.6561	0.4096	0.2401	0.1296	0.0625	0.0256	0.0081	0.0016	0.0001
	1	0.2916	0.4096	0.4116	0.3456	0.2500	0.1536	0.0756	0.0256	0.0036
	2	0.0486	0.1536	0.2646	0.3456	0.3750	0.3456	0.2646	0.1536	0.0486
	3	0.0036	0.0256	0.0756	0.1536	0.2500	0.3456	0.4116	0.4096	0.2916
	4	0.0001	0.0016	0.0081	0.0256	0.0625	0.1296	0.2401	0.4096	0.6561
5	0	0.5905	0.3277	0.1681	0.0778	0.0313	0.0102	0.0024	0.0003	0.0000
	1	0.3281	0.4096	0.3602	0.2592	0.1563	0.0768	0.0284	0.0064	0.0005
	2	0.0729	0.2048	0.3087	0.3456	0.3125	0.2304	0.1323	0.0512	0.0081
	3	0.0081	0.0512	0.1323	0.2304	0.3125	0.3456	0.3087	0.2048	0.0729
	4	0.0005	0.0064	0.0284	0.0768	0.1563	0.2592	0.3602	0.4096	0.3281
	5	0.0000	0.0003	0.0024	0.0102	0.0313	0.0778	0.1681	0.3277	0.5905
6	0	0.5314	0.2621	0.1176	0.0467	0.0156	0.0041	0.0007	0.0001	0.0000
	1	0.3543	0.3932	0.3025	0.1866	0.0938	0.0369	0.0102	0.0015	0.0001
	2	0.0984	0.2458	0.3241	0.3110	0.2344	0.1382	0.0595	0.0154	0.0012
	3	0.0146	0.0819	0.1852	0.2765	0.3125	0.2765	0.1852	0.0819	0.0146
	4	0.0012	0.0154	0.0595	0.1382	0.2344	0.3110	0.3241	0.2458	0.0984
	5	0.0001	0.0015	0.0102	0.0369	0.0938	0.1866	0.3025	0.3932	0.3543
	6	0.0000	0.0001	0.0007	0.0041	0.0156	0.0467	0.1176	0.2621	0.5314

4. On average, how many times will you see a head in these 4 trials of coin tosses? What is the corresponding standard deviation?

$$\mu = np = 4 \cdot 0.5 = 2$$

$$\sigma = \sqrt{np(1-p)} = \sqrt{4 \cdot 0.5 \cdot (1-0.5)} = 1$$

---

5. Applications
   a. Assume that Julie can hit the bull's eye 60% of the time. If she shoots 3 bullets, what is the probability that she will hit the bull's eye 2 times?

Answer: Given n = 3, X = 2, and p = 0.6,

$$P(X=2) = P(2) = \frac{3!}{2!(3-2)!} \cdot 0.6^2 (1-0.6)^{3-2} = 0.432$$

   b. When taking a 10-question true-false quiz, a student guesses the answers by flipping a coin. What is the probability that she will get 6 out of 10 answers correctly?

Answer: Given n = 10, X = 6, and p = 0.5,

$$P(X=6) = P(6) = \frac{10!}{6!(10-6)!} \cdot 0.5^6 (1-0.5)^{10-6} = 0.205 \approx 20.5\%$$

$\rightarrow$ one chance out of 5 trials

   c. A basketball player can make free throws 80% of time. What is the probability that he will make next 3 free throws in a row?

Answer: Given n = 3, X = 3, and p = 0.8,

$$P(X=3) = \frac{3!}{3!(3-3)!} \cdot 0.8^3 (1-0.8)^{3-3} = 0.512 \approx 51.2\%$$

$\rightarrow$ one chance out of 2 situations to make 3 consecutive free throws.

Note: The same result can be found as:

$$0.8 \times 0.8 \times 0.8 = 0.8^3 = 0.512 \rightarrow 51.2\%$$

The reason for this identical outcome is based on the assumption that all three free throws are independent from one another.

d. Assume that a sharp shooter can hit the bull's eye 90% of the time. If she shoots 100 bullets, what are the mean (=average) and the standard deviation of the number of her hitting the bull's eye?

Answer: Given n = 100 and p = 0.9, $\mu = np = 100 \cdot 0.9 = 90$ and

$$\sigma = \sqrt{np(1-p)} = \sqrt{100 \cdot 0.9 \cdot (1-0.9)} = 3$$

e. If 5% of the people who take aspirin get a headache, what is the probability that one out of 6 people who take the aspirin will get a headache?

Answer: Given n = 6, X = 1, and p = 0.05,

$$P(X=1) = \frac{6!}{1!(6-1)!} \cdot 0.05^1 (1-0.05)^{6-1} = 0.2321 \approx 23.21\%$$

D. The Poisson Distribution

The Poisson distribution measures the probability of an event occurring within a time block or a specified space → note that the event is comprised of discrete units such as a number of people, a number of phone calls, a number of books ordered, etc.

The Poisson Distribution is named after its originator, Simeon D. Poisson (1781–1840), and used to calculate a probability associated with situations where an event of one's interest occurs over a specific time period, geographical space, or volume, etc.

1. The Poisson Probability Function

$$P(X) = \frac{e^{-\lambda} \cdot \lambda^X}{X!} \qquad where \quad e = 2.718281828 \approx 2.7183$$

a. The Mean of the Poisson Distribution: $\mu = E(X) = \lambda$

b. The Variance of the Poisson Distribution: $\sigma^2 = \lambda$

c. The Standard Deviation of the Poisson Distribution: $\sigma = \sqrt{\lambda}$

2. The Methodology of Applying the Poisson Distribution

Step 1 : Assess if the Poisson distribution is appropriate by examining the number of outcomes possible. If appropriate, identify the average number of occurrences, λ. $\rightarrow$ no probability of successes or failures is needed.

Step 2: Identify the number of successes, X. $\rightarrow$ the number of trial, n, is not needed.

Step 3: Apply these values to the Poisson probability function to obtain the probability, P(X).

Always you are assumed to know the value of lambda, λ, which is what is expected or observed based on one's experience or data analysis[3]. That is, lambda, λ, is the mean or the average value of the variable of one's interest. **Given that you know the value of lambda, λ, you now want to know the probability of an event, X, occurring.**

Note: The binomial and the Poisson distributions are like close cousins because both deal with discrete probability. Therefore, the Poisson distribution can yield a probability value that is quite close to the binomial distribution when $n \geq 20$ and the success rate, $p \leq 0.05$. **However, unlike the binomial distribution, the Poisson distribution deals with the number of occurrences, not yes-or-no issues.**

3. Examples

a. Suppose that you know that there are on average 10 people standing in line for a coffee at Starbuck's during the rush hour. What is the probability that there will be no one in line this morning?

3 In some business situations, one can hypothesize its value based on prior experiences.

Answer:

Hint 1: There is no probability of successes or failures given and the number of trials, n, is not given → the Binomial Distribution is **not** appropriate → However, because the number of people is measured in a discrete unit, the Poisson Distribution is appropriate.

Hint 2: Therefore, we identify $\lambda = 10$ and $X = 0$.

Therefore, $P(0) = \dfrac{e^{-10} \cdot 10^0}{0!} = 0.0000454$

b. What is the probability of less than 3 people in line?

Answer:

Hint: P(X<3) = P(0) + P(l) + P(2)

Therefore, We first calculate: $P(0) = \dfrac{e^{-10} \cdot 10^0}{0!} = 0.0000454$

$P(1) = \dfrac{e^{-10} \cdot 10^1}{1!} = 0.000454$ and $P(2) = \dfrac{e^{-10} \cdot 10^2}{2!} = 0.00227$

Therefore, P(X<3) = 0.0000454+0.000454+0.00227=0.00277

Note 1: You can use the Excel Spreadsheet command of **"=POISSON(X,lambda,true)"** for cumulative probability and **"=POISSON(X,lambda,false)"** for relative probability

Note 2: You can look up thc Poisson probability value from the following partial Poisson Probability Table → Some selected Lambda values are listed in the first row and X values under the X column. For example, given $\lambda = 10$, and X = 2, you may find P(2) = 0.0023, which is a rounded number of 0.00227. → Lambda and X values not listed in this table must be calculated by using the above Excel command for a relative Poisson probability.

The following Poisson probability distribution table is produced by the Excel command of "**=POISSON(X,lambda,false)**" for relative probability

X	Lambda									
	1	2	3	4	5	6	7	8	9	10
0	0.3679	0.1353	0.0498	0.0183	0.0067	0.0025	0.0009	0.0003	0.0001	0.0000
1	0.3679	0.2707	0.1494	0.0733	0.0337	0.0149	0.0064	0.0027	0.0011	0.0005
2	0.1839	0.2707	0.2240	0.1465	0.0842	0.0446	0.0223	0.0107	0.0050	0.0023
3	0.0613	0.1804	0.2240	0.1954	0.1404	0.0892	0.0521	0.0286	0.0150	0.0076
4	0.0153	0.0902	0.1680	0.1954	0.1755	0.1339	0.0912	0.0573	0.0337	0.0189
5	0.0031	0.0361	0.1008	0.1563	0.1755	0.1606	0.1277	0.0916	0.0607	0.0378
6	0.0005	0.0120	0.0504	0.1042	0.1462	0.1606	0.1490	0.1221	0.0911	0.0631
7	0.0001	0.0034	0.0216	0.0595	0.1044	0.1377	0.1490	0.1396	0.1171	0.0901
8	0.0000	0.0009	0.0081	0.0298	0.0653	0.1033	0.1304	0.1396	0.1318	0.1126
9	0.0000	0.0002	0.0027	0.0132	0.0363	0.0688	0.1014	0.1241	0.1318	0.1251
10	0.0000	0.0000	0.0008	0.0053	0.0181	0.0413	0.0710	0.0993	0.1186	0.1251
11	0.0000	0.0000	0.0002	0.0019	0.0082	0.0225	0.0452	0.0722	0.0970	0.1137
12	0.0000	0.0000	0.0001	0.0006	0.0034	0.0113	0.0263	0.0481	0.0728	0.0948
13	0.0000	0.0000	0.0000	0.0002	0.0013	0.0052	0.0142	0.0296	0.0504	0.0729
14	0.0000	0.0000	0.0000	0.0001	0.0005	0.0022	0.0071	0.0169	0.0324	0.0521
15	0.0000	0.0000	0.0000	0.0000	0.0002	0.0009	0.0033	0.0090	0.0194	0.0347
16	0.0000	0.0000	0.0000	0.0000	0.0000	0.0003	0.0014	0.0045	0.0109	0.0217
17	0.0000	0.0000	0.0000	0.0000	0.0000	0.0001	0.0006	0.0021	0.0058	0.0128
18	0.0000	0.0000	0.0000	0.0000	0.0000	0.0000	0.0002	0.0009	0.0029	0.0071
19	0.0000	0.0000	0.0000	0.0000	0.0000	0.0000	0.0001	0.0004	0.0014	0.0037
20	0.0000	0.0000	0.0000	0.0000	0.0000	0.0000	0.0000	0.0002	0.0006	0.0019

c. What is the probability of more than 9 people in line?

Answer:

$P(X>9) = P(10) + P(11) + \dots\dots + \infty$

$= 1 - P(X\leq 9) = 1 - [P(0)+P(1)+ \dots +P(9)] = 1 - 0.458 = 0.542$

Note 1: $P(0) + P(1) + \dots + P(9) = 0.458$
is obtained from the Poisson probability table shown in the above Poisson Probability Table.

Note 2: Does this P(X>9) = 0.542 make an intuitive sense?

Yes, given that the mean is 10 which may be the median, the probability of greater than 9 should be larger than 0.5 such as 0.542.

d. What is the probability of between 3 and 9 people in line?

Answer: Because "between 3 and 9" technically excludes 3 and 9,

$$P(3 < X < 9) = P(4) + P(5) + P(6) + P(7) + P(8) = 0.3301$$

Alternatively, $P(3 < X < 9) = 1 - [P(X<3) + P(X>9)]$

$= 1 - [0.0104 + 0.6595]$

$= 1 - [0.6699] = 0.3301$

4. Advanced Applications of the Poisson Distribution

Example 1 Assume that a telemarketing company gets on average 5 orders per 1000 calls it makes. If an employee of the company makes 400 calls today, what is the probability that the employee will get 4 orders or more?

Answer:

Given that there is on average 5 orders per 1000 calls, the probability of getting an order is 0.005 (=5/1000). Thus, if 400 calls are made, then one can expect on average of 2 orders (=400 calls × 0.005). Thus, the value of Lambda, λ, is 2 and the probability can be calculated as follows:

$$P(X \geq 4) = P(X > 3) = 1 - P(X \leq 3) = 1 - [P(0) + P(1) + P(2) + P(3)]$$

where $P(0) = \dfrac{e^{-2} \cdot 2^0}{0!} = 0.1353$ $P(1) = \dfrac{e^{-2} \cdot 2^1}{1!} = 0.27067$

$P(2) = \dfrac{e^{-2} \cdot 2^2}{2!} = 0.27067$ and $P(3) = \dfrac{e^{-2} \cdot 2^3}{3!} = 0.1804$

Therefore, $P(X \geq 4) = P(X>3) = 1 - P(X \leq 3)$

$= 1 - [0.1353+0.2706+0.2706+0.1804] = 1 - 0.8569 = 0.1431$

Note: The key to solving this problem lies with the identification of the Lambda value (=the average).

Example 2 Assume that the average number of inquiries to a toll-free telephone number for a computer company is 10 per business hour. Each inquiry takes about 6 minutes on average to be resolved. What is the probability of getting exactly 15 calls per business hour today?

Answer:

$$P(15) = \frac{e^{-10} \cdot 10^{15}}{15!} = 0.0347$$

Note: The information of 6 minutes has no role to play in probability calculation.

Example 3 An order taker at an online shopping company normally has 5 errors per day when filling the orders. What is the probability that a newly hired order taker will have 6 errors or less today (assuming that the new hire has the same skill as an average order taker)?

Answer:

$P(X \leq 6) = P(0) + P(1) + P(2) + P(3) + P(4) + P(5) + P(6)$

$= 0.0067 + 0.0337 + 0.0842 + 0.1404 + 0.1755 + 0.1755 + 0.1462$

$= 0.7622 \rightarrow 76.22\%$

Or alternatively, by using the Excel command of "**=POISSON(6,5,1)**" we find:

0.762183

Note that in Excel command, the last number, 1, indicates a cumulative probability. If we were to calculate a relative probability, it should have been "0".

EXERCISE PROBLEMS ON DISCRETE PROBABILITY DISTRIBUTIONS

This set of exercise problems has 16 problems, worth a total of 20 points.

1. The expected value of a discrete random variable X is the same as the ______.
   a. mean of X
   b. arithmetic average of X
   c. geometric average of X
   d. only (a) and (b) of the above
   e. only (a) and (c) of the above

2. As the Chief Financial Officer (CFO) of your firm, you are discussing the future sales prospect of your firm's products in a board of directors meeting. If you tabulated the following sales data for the last 10 years and used them to forecast sales, what would be your expected sales?

   $1 million sales occurred 3 times.
   $2 million sales occurred 5 times.
   $3 million sales occurred 2 times.

   a. $1.5 million
   b. $1.9 million
   c. $2 million
   d. $2.1 million
   e. $2.5 million

3. What is the standard deviation of your sales estimate (or forecast), using the above information?
   a. $0.4 million
   b. $0.49 million
   c. $0.5 million
   d. $0.6 million
   e. $0.7 million

4. Suppose that one of the board members suggests the following:
   She expects that a 30% chance of booming economy with a possible sales of $4 million, a 50% chance of so-so economy with a possible sales of $3 million, and a 20% chance of bad economy with a possible sales of $0.5 million. Under this scenario, what would be the expected sales?
   a. $4 million
   b. $3 million
   c. $2.8 million
   d. $2.5 million
   e. not calculable

5. Which of the following is the underlying assumption(s) of the binomial probability distribution?
   a. each trial can have only two outcomes.
   b. the number of trials is known.
   c. the outcomes of each trial are independent of each other.
   d. all of the above
   e. only (a) and (c) of the above

6. What is the probability of having 5 heads in 8 coin tosses?

a. 0.0179
b. 0.0039
c. 0.2188
d. 0.6250
e. none of the above

7. The mean and the standard deviation of a binomial distribution with p=0.4 and n=20 is _____ and ______, respectively.

a. 10; 4.8
b. 8; 4.8
c. 10; 2.1909
d. 8; 2.1909
e. 12; 2.1909

8. Given that there is a 30% chance of a head appearing in a coin toss (and thus, there is a 70% chance of a tail appearing), what will be the expected number of heads that will appear if the coin is tossed 30 times?

a. 9
b. 15
c. 21
d. 30
e. unknown

9. A fair coin is a coin whose head and tail appears in an equal probability of 50% each. What is the probability of obtaining either 5 heads or 6 heads in 10 tosses of a fair coin? Pick a number as close as it comes by carrying 6 decimal points in calculating this probability.

a. 0.5
b. 0.45
c. 0.3
d. 0.55
e. 0.6

10. If President George Bush has a 30% approval rating from the U.S. citizens, what will be the probability that you will find 5 Bush supporters in a crowd of 10 people? Pick a number as close as it comes by carrying 6 decimal points in calculating this probability.

a. 0.3
b. 0.2
c. 0.1
d. 0.05
e. 0

11. The Poisson distribution is used to calculate the probability associated with an event occurring _____.

a. in a specific time block
b. in a geographical space
c. in a specific volume
d. all of the above
e. none of the above

12. The Poisson distribution uses the exponential value of *e* which has a numerical value of _____.

a. 0
b. 1
c. 2.5
d. 2.71828
e. 3.14159

The following questions are worth 2 points each.

13. Assume that as a quality control manager of a firm that produces chocolate-chip cookies, you believe that the number of chocolate chips on a cookie is distributed as a Poisson distribution. Assume further that your machine is designed to put 10 chocolate chips per cookie. The industry standard accepts 8 or more chocolate chips per cookie. What is the probability that you will find a cookie with exactly 8 chocolate chips?

    a. 0.8
    b. 0.8944
    c. 0.1126
    d. 0.2203
    e. 0.5

14. Assume the same situation as above. That is, your machine is designed to put 10 chocolate chips per cookie. The industry standard accepts 8 or more chocolate chips per cookie. What is the probability that you will find a cookie with less than 8 chocolate chips which is below the industry standard?

    a. 0.4765
    b. 0.8944
    c. 0.1126
    d. 0.2203
    e. 0.5324

15. Assume the same situation as above. That is, assume that your machine is designed to put 10 chocolate chips per cookie. What is the probability that you will find cookies with between 7 and 12 chocolate chips (i.e., more than 7 chocolate chips and less than 12 chocolate chips) per cookie?

    a. 0.5324
    b. 0.3639
    c. 0.4765
    d. 0.8001
    e. 0.9

16. Assume the same situation as above. That is, assume that your machine is designed to put 10 chocolate chips per cookie. What is the probability that you will find a cookie with more than 11 chocolate chips per cookie?

    a. 0.2203
    b. 0.3032
    c. 0.4765
    d. 0.6968
    e. 0.8

SUMMARY

A discrete random variable is one that answers the question "how many?" A discrete random variable uses the counting numbers (0, 1, 2, 3 and so on) and can either be finite or infinite in nature. Examples include viewing a certain number of heads in three tosses of a coin, the number of students enrolled in a statistics class, or the number of customers a grocery clerk helps in a given period of time. In the first two examples, there is an upper limit of values x (the discrete random variable) can assume. The third example represents an infinite stream of customers. A discrete probability distribution is a table that illustrates the values the discrete random variable can assume and their corresponding probabilities. The sum of the probabilities of all outcomes will be equal to one. In the next chapter, we explore continuous random variables.

6 Continuous Probability Distributions

In the previous chapter, we explored discrete random variables, their probabilities, and their probability distributions. Remember that a discrete random variable only uses the counting numbers (integers) as possible outcomes. This chapter is dedicated to continuous random variables, which may assume an infinite number of values. The goal is not to calculate the probability of a single value occurring but to establish the probability of an outcome occurring during a given interval. The probability for a continuous variable is measured by the area under a graph, and the probability of any number given value occurring is zero (0). It is impossible to calculate the area under a given value (probability of $X = 30$ or any number is zero).

CONTINUOUS PROBABILITY DISTRIBUTIONS

By Dorit Nevo

In the previous chapter, we introduced the concept of *random variables* with their accompanying *probability distribution.* The probability distribution provides information on the values of the random variable that we might expect to observe. [...] Many important variables, however, are *continuous* and in this chapter we cover some of the common probability distributions of continuous random variables.

Recall our example of the Internet art store in which we used the *binomial* distribution to predict the expected number of shopping cart conversions. Specifically, we defined X as a discrete random variable, counting the number of customers who made the conversion from putting pieces of art into a shopping cart to actually purchasing these art pieces, and we studied the probability of different numbers of customers making purchases from their shopping carts. There are many other variables we may be interested in learning about, such as the amount of time a single website visit lasts or the amount of money spent by each shopper. Both of these are examples of continuous variables.[1]

Suppose you sample one customer at random and measure the amount of money this person spent while shopping at the website. What do you expect this amount to be? If you know that an average customer spends $300 per purchase, then you already have some idea of what to expect in terms of the amount of money a random customer will spend. If you also know the standard deviation of the amount

1 We conceptually treat monetary variables as the result of a continuous measuring process even though, in a physical sense, money is not strictly continuous due to the fact that it is limited by the bills and coins available to us at a point-in-time.

of money spent is $70, then you may have an even better idea of what to expect. But, if only the mean and standard deviation of a random variable are known, many interesting questions cannot be answered, such as: What is the probability that this random customer will spend $400 or more? What is the probability that she will spend between $250 and $450? What is the probability that she will spend exactly $326.76? Questions such as these require knowledge of the *probability distribution* of the variable and this is what Chapter 6 is about. This chapter covers the following topics:

- Continuous Probability Distributions
- The Uniform Distribution
- The Normal Distribution
- The t-Distribution
- The χ^2 Distribution
- The F-Distribution
- Working with the Normal Distribution
- Determining Normal Distribution Probabilities with Excel and with the Standard Normal Distribution Table
- P-Value
- Inverse Probability Calculations

UNIT 1
CONTINUOUS PROBABILITY DISTRIBUTIONS

A ***continuous random variable***, X, can take on any value at a given probability. As in previous chapters, all probabilities must be between zero and one, and the sum of all probabilities is one. In fact, because we are dealing with a continuous variable, the probability of any *specific* value of the variable is practically zero. For example, what is the probability that you will sleep for *exactly* seven hours, five minutes, nine seconds and three milliseconds tonight? Essentially zero! In practice, however, when working with continuous random variables, we usually look at cumulative probabilities across intervals of values (e.g., what is the probability that you will sleep less than seven hours, or more than eight hours, or between seven and nine hours?).

To describe the probability distribution of continuous random variables, we use a line graph that represents the distribution's ***probability density function***. The probability density function, or *density function* for short, describes the likelihood that the values of X, the continuous random variable, fall within a given interval. An example of a density function is shown in Figure 6.1 (page 81).

The total area captured between the line and the x-axis is equal to one, because the sum of all probabilities in a sample space is one. We can compute the probability of X falling in a specific interval along the x-axis by computing the partial area underneath the density function for this interval.

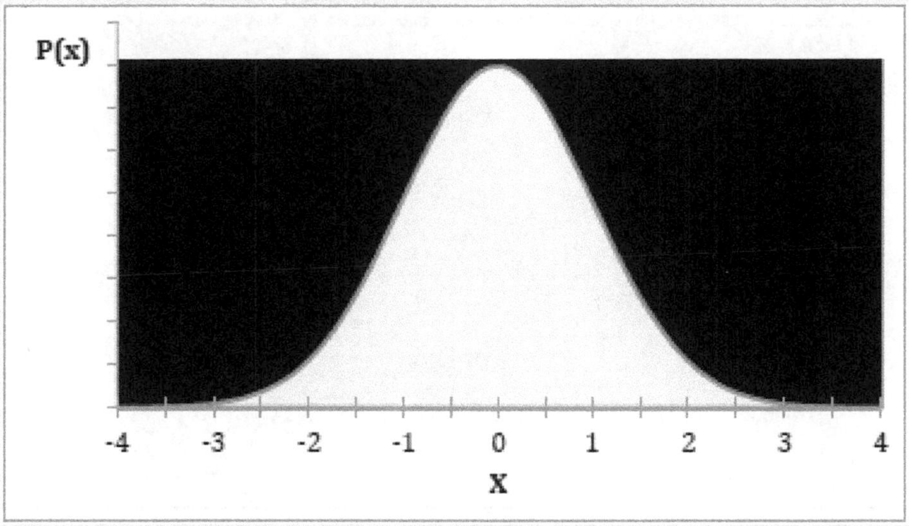

Figure: 6.1 Example of a Probability Density Function

Mathematically, this requires the use of calculus. In practice, and in this book, we use statistical software (specifically, Excel) to derive the values needed in our analyses.

The calculation of probabilities depends on the specific shape of the distribution. We begin this chapter with a review of the most commonly-used probability distributions—the ones that you are likely to use in future analyses. We provide only a general overview of these distributions here and will discuss them again in future chapters that require their use. The remainder of the chapter is then spent on the *normal distribution*, which plays a critical role in many statistical analyses.

THE UNIFORM DISTRIBUTION

Continuing with our Internet art store example, suppose you want to find out the probability that the website will be down (in other words, not available because of technical problems or for maintenance) during a twelve-hour time period between 8am and 8pm. Let us define X, a random variable, as measuring the time of day when the website is down. Let us further assume that X can take on any value in a 24-hour interval (from 12am on one day to 12am on the next day), with equal probabilities for any of the possible values to occur. Here, X follows a ***uniform distribution***[2], which assigns an equal likelihood of occurrence to all possible values of X. This uniform distribution is shown graphically in Figure 6.2 (page 82).

Because the uniform distribution has a rectangular shape, the probability of X taking a specific range of values, i.e., between x_1 and x_2, can be computed as

2 The uniform distribution can also be *discrete,* as in the case of rolling a die (each outcome has the same probability). Here we focus on the *continuous* uniform distribution.

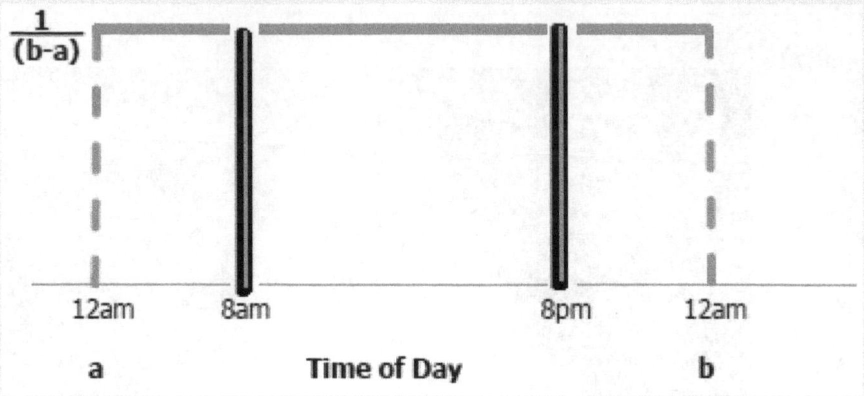

Figure: 6.2 The Uniform Distribution

$$P(x_1 \le X \le x_2) = (x_2 - x_1) * \frac{1}{(b-a)}$$

where x_1 and x_2 define the interval of interest and a and b, respectively, are the lower (0) and upper (24) values of the random variable. Thus, we can compute the desired probability in our example as:

$$P(8am \le X \le 8pm) = \text{(number of hours between 8am and 8pm)} * \frac{1}{24} = \frac{12}{24} = 0.5$$

Given this result, there is a 50% chance that the website will be down during the twelve-hour time period.

THE NORMAL DISTRIBUTION

The ***normal distribution*** is a family of distributions that share the same shape and attributes, but vary in their parameters; namely, the mean and the standard deviation. You may have heard about the normal distribution in your past studies or work and may have heard or seen depictions of the 'bell curve' shown in Figure 6.3 (page 83). The bell curve represents a normal distribution.

The normal distribution is ***symmetric***; that is, each half is a mirror image of the other. The location of its peak is determined by the mean, whereas the standard deviation determines the width of the distribution. Two examples of normally distributed data include: the height of people (the height of women in the US is normally distributed with a mean of 63.8 inches and a standard deviation of 4.25 inches[3]) and the IQ of people (IQ is normally distributed with a mean of 100 and a standard deviation of fifteen).

3 Source: http://www.cdc.gov.

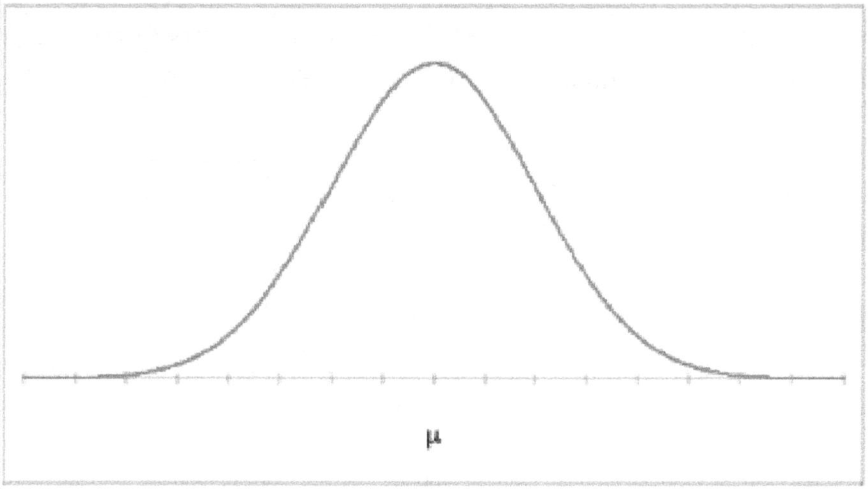

Figure: 6.3 The Normal Distribution Curve

The normal distribution is very important in statistics because its properties enable, or support, a wide range of analytics (that is, there are many different calculations we are able to conduct if we know that a variable is, or is close to being, normally distributed). For this reason, we sometimes use various transformations in attempts to *normalize* a data set. For example, we may take the square root of each data point or the log of each data point, both of which are commonly-used transformations for normalizing data. We will learn how to work with the normal distribution and to compute probabilities in Unit 2 of this chapter, and then build on this knowledge in subsequent chapters.

THE t-DISTRIBUTION

The normal distribution requires either that large samples are available or that the population standard deviation (σ) is known. In most cases, one or both these conditions are not met. In these situations, we work with a similar distribution called the t-distribution. The ***t-distribution*** is similar in shape to the normal distribution (specifically, to a normal distribution with a mean of zero and a standard deviation of one), but its shape also depends on the sample size, n.

More precisely, the shape of the t-distribution depends on a sample's number of ***degrees of freedom***. Degrees of freedom refer to the number of data values that are free to vary in a data set. For each parameter (e.g., μ or σ) that we are estimating, we lose one degree of freedom. In order to better understand what this means, consider the following two examples. First, in the sample X_1, X_2 and X_3 where the Xs can obtain any value possible, we have three degrees of freedom. Now, suppose that $X_1=2$, $X_2=4$, and that *the average of the three values has to be 3*. Given this requirement, the only possible value that X_3 can obtain is 3. Thus, we have lost one degree of freedom. X_1 and X_2 can still obtain any possible value, but X_3 will then be forced to be a value that brings the sample average to 3.

As the sample (and thus the number of degrees of freedom) becomes large, the t-distribution approaches the normal distribution. This is illustrated in Figure 6.4, below.

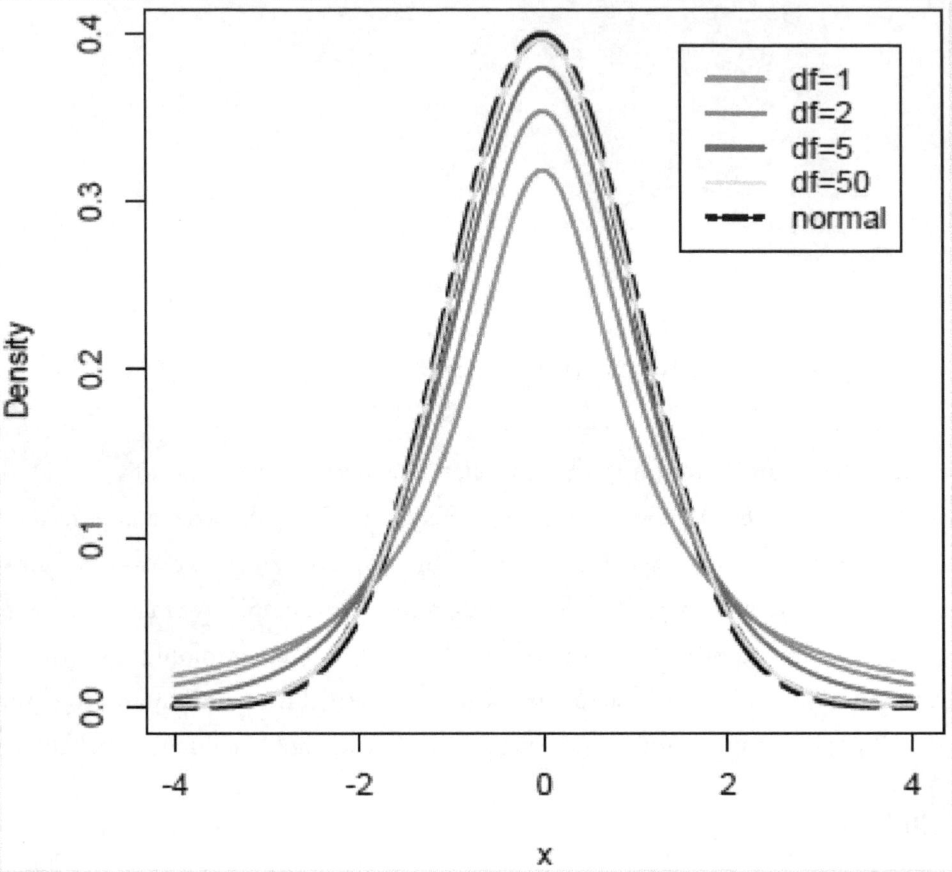

Figure: 6.4 The t-Distribution Curve

The Z and T tables are located in Appendix A.

UNIT 1 SUMMARY

- A **continuous random variable**, X, can take on any value at a given probability. All probabilities must be between zero and one and the sum of all probabilities is one. Because we are dealing with a continuous variable, the probability of any *specific* value of the variable is essentially zero.
- The ***probability density function*** describes the likelihood that the value of X falls within a given interval. Probabilities are expressed as the area between the curve and the x-axis. We use statistical tables and software to compute these probabilities.
- The continuous ***uniform distribution*** assigns an equal likelihood of occurrence to all possible values of X.
- The ***normal distribution***, represented as a bell curve, comprises a family of distributions that share the same shape and attributes, but that vary in their parameters; namely, the mean and the standard deviation. The normal distribution is ***symmetric***; that is, each half is a mirror image of the other.
- The ***t-distribution*** is similar in shape to the normal distribution and used when working with small samples. It can also be used when the population standard deviation (σ) is unknown and we are using the sample standard deviation (s) instead. Its precise shape depends on the number of degrees of freedom. ***Degrees of freedom*** refer to the number of data values that are free to vary in a data set.
- The χ^2 ***distribution*** (chi-squared distribution) is the distribution of the sum of squares of n-1 variables (n being the sample size). The distribution is positively skewed rather than symmetrical. It does not include negative values and its precise shape also depends on the number of degrees of freedom associated with a sample.
- The ***F-distribution*** is the distribution of the ratio of two variances: σ^2_1/σ^2_2. Like the χ^2 distribution, the F-distribution is not symmetrical, can only obtain values that are positive and its precise shape depends on the number of degrees of freedom associated with both the numerator and denominator.

UNIT 1 EXERCISES

1. List five continuous random variables from any domain of interest to you.
2. What can you say about the probability distribution each of these variables is most likely to follow?
3. In your own words, explain what is meant by the term *probability distribution*.
4. What are the key differences between *discrete* and *continuous* probability distributions?
5. In the Olympic Games' 100m freestyle swimming competition, what is the probability of an exact tie between two swimmers?

UNIT 2
WORKING WITH THE NORMAL DISTRIBUTION

We mentioned in the previous section that the normal distribution is a family of distributions, each with its own mean and standard deviation. When a variable, say X, is normally distributed, we denote it as:

$$X \sim N(\text{mean, standard deviation}) \text{ or } X \sim N(\mu,\sigma)$$

Returning to the art store example, an important variable for website store owners is the amount of time that visitors spend on their websites. If we believe that the time a visitor spends on the art store website follows a normal distribution with a mean of five minutes and a standard deviation of one minute, then we would write this as:

$$X \sim N(5,1)$$

Now, suppose we wish to compute the probability that a randomly chosen visitor will spend less than four minutes on the site? Recall that earlier in this chapter we mentioned that probabilities are computed as the area under the probability density curve, which is shown for this example in Figure 6.5. Here, the x-axis is measured in minutes and you can see that the value 5, which we know is the mean value of the distribution, corresponds to the distribution's peak. Also note the area under the curve that is shaded red and that is bounded on the right by the value 4. This shaded area represents

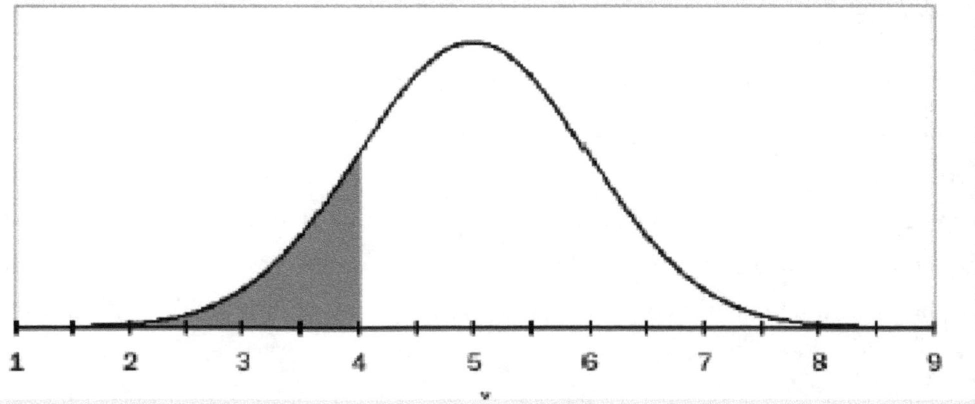

Figure: 6.5 Working with the Normal Distribution

the probability of obtaining a value less than 4 with this distribution. How much of the area under the curve do you think this shaded area represents?

We mentioned earlier in the chapter that calculus is needed to calculate this area, but we can also use statistical software, such as Excel, to compute probabilities. Specifically, Excel's function that allows us to calculate this area (and, hence, the desired probability) is:

=NORMDIST(x,mean,standard_dev,cumulative)

Using the values and parameters from our example, this function would be written

=NORMDIST(4,5,1,1) = 0.1586

where 4 is the value of x we are interested in learning about, 5 is the mean time people spend on the website, 1 is the standard deviation of the time people spend on the website, and the final 1 indicates that we are interested in the cumulative probability (that is, the probability of four minutes or less, depicted as the area shaded red in Figure 6.5)[4].

While Excel enables us to work with any normal distribution using the =NORMDIST() function, it is often easier (especially for someone just learning statistics) to understand how to use the normal distribution if the normal distribution is converted into the *standard normal distribution,* also known as the *Z distribution.*

The ***standard normal distribution*** is the distribution of the random variable Z, which is *normally* distributed with a mean of zero and a standard deviation of one:

$$Z \sim N(0,1)$$

Any normal distribution can be converted into the standard normal distribution by converting a variable X into its corresponding ***Z score*** as follows:

4 If a value of 0 is entered for this fourth parameter, i.e., the *cumulative* argument, Excel will treat the variable as a discrete variable and will return the probability of $X = 4$, rather than the probability of $X \leq 4$. In this book we only work with the cumulative probabilities and thus will always choose 1 for this final argument.

$$Z = \frac{X - \mu}{\sigma}$$

Note that we do not convert the distribution as a whole, but rather individual values of X. This is illustrated by the examples in Table 6.1, which demonstrate how values from different normal distributions are converted into Z scores. The first column provides information on the distribution of X (the mean and standard eviation), the second column is the probability we are interested in finding, and the third column contains the corresponding Z scores.

TABLE 6.1 CONVERTING X VALUES TO Z SCORES

Distribution	*P(x)*	*Corresponding Z Scores*
X~N(10,2)	P(X ≤ 7)	$P\left(Z \le \frac{7-10}{2}\right) = P(Z \le -1.5)$
X~N(3,0.4)	P(X ≥ 3.5)	$P\left(Z \ge \frac{3.5-3}{0.4}\right) = P(Z \ge 1.25)$
X~N(35,5)	P(30 ≤ X ≤ 40)	$P\left(\frac{30-35}{5} \le Z \le \frac{40-35}{5}\right) = P(-1 \le Z \le 1)$
X~N(4,0.2)	P(X ≤ 6)	$P\left(Z \ge \frac{6-4}{0.2}\right) = P(Z \ge 10)$
X~N(50,25)	P(30 ≤ X ≤ 35)	$P\left(\frac{30-50}{25} \le Z \le \frac{35-50}{25}\right) = P(-0.8 \le Z \le -0.6)$

Figure 6.6 (parts a, b and c; page 89) shows the information in the first three rows of Table 6.1 in a graphical form. With each part of the figure, the bottom graphs show the distribution of X with the desired probability shaded in the graph; and, the top graphs show the corresponding standard normal (Z) distributions. As you can see, the only difference between the bottom and top graphs is the labeling of the x-axis, with the bottom graphs centered on the mean value of each respective distribution and *all* top graphs centered on a value of 0 (remember, the Z distribution always has a mean of zero).

Z scores have a special meaning that is important to understand. For each value of X (x_1, x_2, etc.), the corresponding Z score is a measure of *how far*—in terms of the number of (the distribution's) standard deviations—the value of X is from the distribution's mean value. Look at any of the Z distributions in Figure 6.6. Negative values of Z correspond to values of X below (i.e., to the left of) the distribution's mean, while positive values of Z correspond to values of X above (i.e., to the right of) the distribution's mean. Further, a Z score of −1.5 means that the corresponding X value lies exactly 1.5 standard deviations below the mean. Similarly, a Z score of 1.25 means that the corresponding X value lays exactly 1.25 standard deviations above the mean.

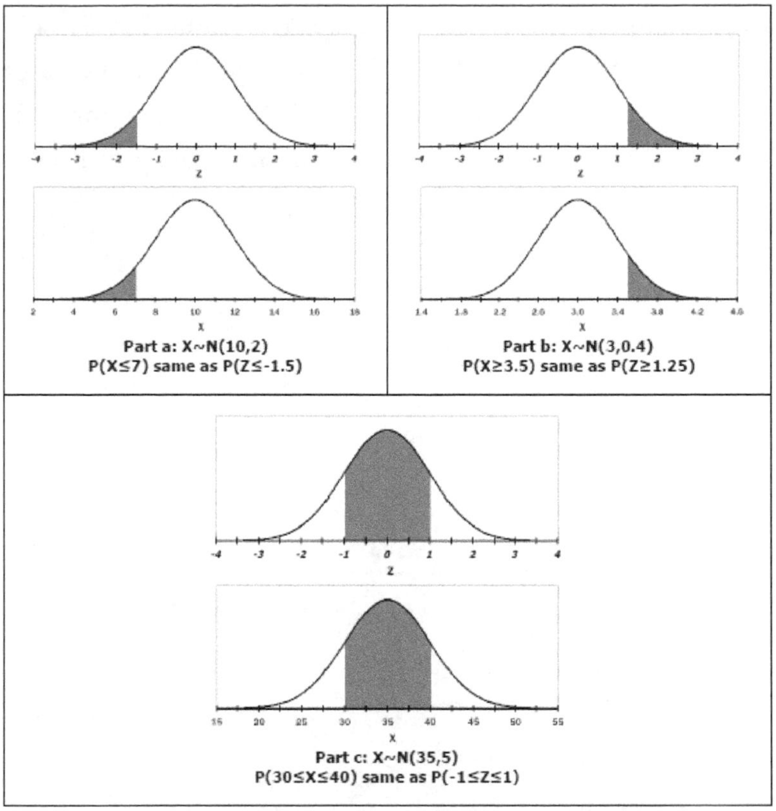

Figure 6.6 Converting X Values to Z Scores

Now, let's return to our Internet art store example. Recall that we were looking for the probability that a customer will spend less than four minutes on the site. The value of a customer visit of four minutes is exactly one standard deviation below the mean (the value of X is 4, the distribution's mean is 5 and the distribution's standard deviation is 1). Indeed, you can calculate that the corresponding Z score for a four minute visit is −1 (that is, one standard deviation *below* the mean):

$$Z = \frac{4-5}{1} = 1$$

The same conversion formula is applied for the examples in Table 6.1. For example, a value of 7 in a distribution with a mean of 10 and standard deviation of 2 is located one and a half standard deviations below the mean and, indeed, the corresponding Z score (first row of Table 6.1) for this value is −1.5.

The reason it is important to understand this meaning of a Z score is because it is essential in understanding how probabilities are derived with a normal distribution. Recalling the *empirical rule* ..., there is a smaller probability of finding values that are farther away from the mean; and, in statistics the most common way to represent how far a value is from its distribution's mean is in terms of the number of standard deviations. Specifically, the empirical rule states that for normal distributions, approximately 68% of all the values in the distribution lie within one standard deviation from the mean. Approximately 95% of all values lie within two standard deviations from the mean, and nearly all values (99.7%) lie within three standard deviations from the mean. This is illustrated graphically in Figure 6.7:

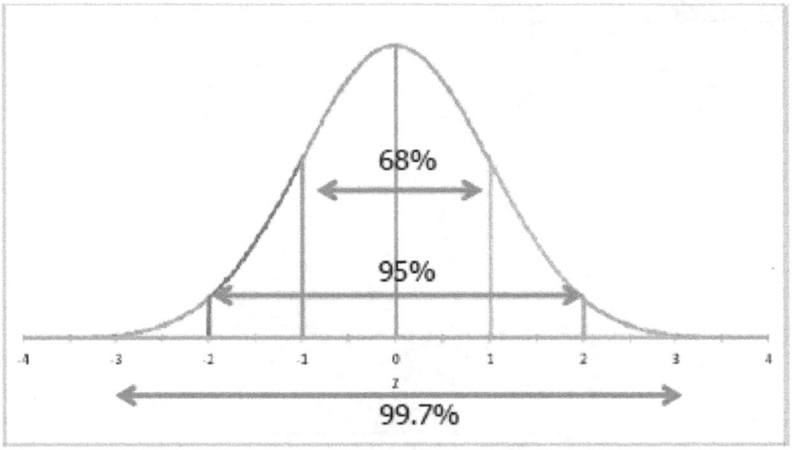

Figure 6.7 The Empirical Rule

DETERMINING NORMAL DISTRIBUTION PROBABILITIES WITH EXCEL AND WITH THE STANDARD NORMAL DISTRIBUTION TABLE

The Excel function =NORMSDIST(z) is the formula for computing any standard normal probability. By default, this function returns the *cumulative probability*, that is: $P(Z \leq z)$. For example, the Excel function =NORMSDIST(0.94) returns a value of 0.8264. In other words, approximately 83% of all possible Z score values are less than or equal to a Z score value of 0.94.

A second way to determine probabilities associated with the normal distribution is to use what is referred to as the standard normal distribution table. This table is provided in this chapter's Excel file in the worksheet titled 'Standard Normal Table'. To match this table with similar tables you might find in other statistics books, it is constructed in two parts: one (the upper part) for the negative side of the standard normal distribution and one (the lower part) for the positive side of the standard normal distribution. [...] The standard normal table provides the probability of commonly-used Z scores and is especially useful when you do not have access to computer software to obtain these probabilities (for example, if you are writing a paper-based exam and are asked to determine probabilities). Both parts of the standard normal distribution table provide the cumulative probability

$$P(Z \leq z)$$

where z corresponds to a particular Z score value.

In the table, the Z score values are shown in the first column and the first row *combined.* For example, in cell A4 you will find the value −2.8. In cell E1 you will find the value 0.03. By combining −2.8 and 0.03, a Z score of −2.83 results, and the probability of a Z score of −2.83 is located in the meeting point of Row 4 and Column E, or in cell E4. As another example, the probability shown in cell C5 (0.0034) is for $P(Z \leq -2.71)$. If you track the row and column that meet at cell C5, you will see that Row 5 refers to the Z value of −2.7 and Column C refers to the value of 0.01. Together these two values comprise a Z score of −2.71, the probability of which is located in cell C5.

Let us return to the examples in Table 6.1, replicated in Table 6.2, to practice finding different Z distribution probabilities in Excel.

TABLE 6.2 FINDING STANDARD NORMAL PROBABILITIES

P(Z)	Convert to	Compute
$P(Z \leq -1.5)$	Leave as is	0.0668
$P(Z \geq 1.25)$	$1 - P(Z \leq 1.25)$	0.1056
$P(-1 \leq Z \leq 1)$	$P(Z \leq 1) - P(Z \leq -1)$	0.6827
$P(Z \geq 10)$	$1 - P(Z \leq 10)$	0
$P(-0.8 \leq Z \leq -0.6)$	$P(Z \leq -0.6) - P(Z \leq -0.8)$	0.0239

Consider the first row in the table:

$$P(Z \leq -1.5)$$

To find this probability, simply type:

=NORMSDIST(−1.5) = 0.0668

This probability can also be obtained from cell B17 within the Excel worksheet labeled 'Standard Normal Table'. Cell B17 is where the Z values of −1.5 (Row 17) and 0.0 (Column B) meet.

Now consider the example in the second row of Table 6.2, also shown in Figure 6.8: $P(Z \geq 1.25)$.

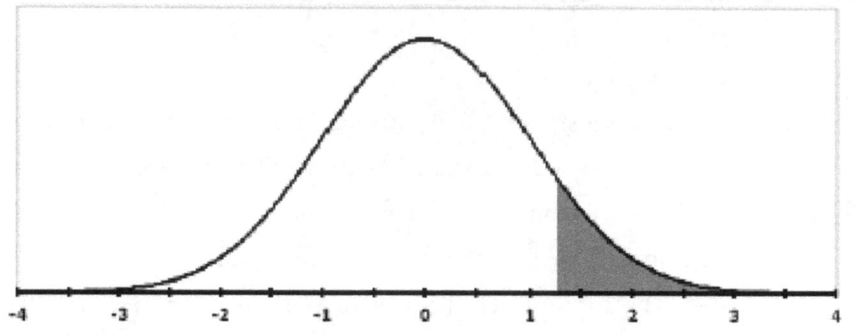

Figure 6.8 The Example in the Second Row of Table 6.2

The area we are looking for is to the *right* of 1.25. Remember, however, that the Excel function provides the *cumulative probability*, or the area to the *left* of 1.25. There are two approaches to determining this probability. First, you can use the complement rule and compute:

$$P(Z \geq 1.25) = 1 - P(Z \leq 1.25)$$

Alternatively, you can use the *symmetry* of the Z distribution to compute

$$P(Z \geq 1.25) = P(Z \leq -1.25)$$

because both sides of the distribution are mirror images of each other. Then, by either applying the Excel function (=NORMSDIST(-1.25)) or by using the standard normal distribution table (cell G20), you will find this probability to be: 0.1056.

Next, consider the example in the third row of Table 6.2, illustrated in Figure 6.9: $P(-1 \leq Z \leq 1)$.

To find the area captured *between* two Z score values (here, between -1 and 1), we subtract one area under the curve from another area under the curve. Specifically, we first find $P(Z \leq 1)$, which covers all the area to the left of the value 1, and we then find $P(Z \leq -1)$, which covers all the area to the left of the value -1. Then, subtracting the second probability from the first probability gives us the sought probability (i.e., just the shaded area of Figure 6.9; page 93):

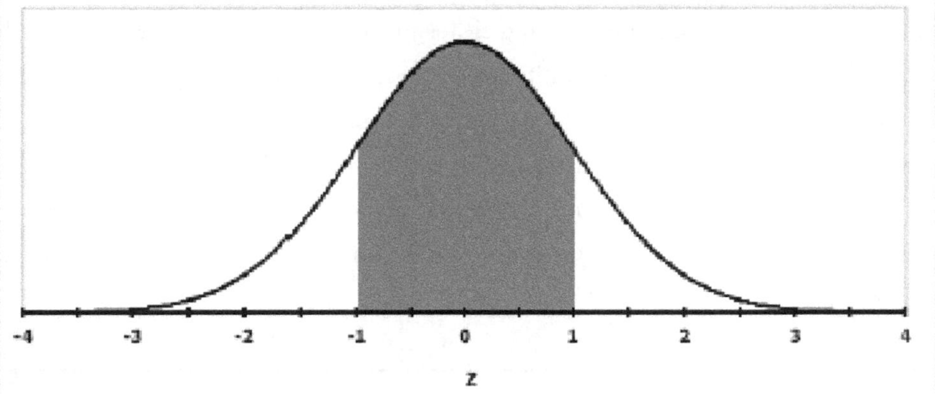

Figure 6.9 The Example in the Third Row of Table 6.2

$$P(-1 \leq Z \leq 1) = P(Z \leq 1) - P(Z \leq -1) = 0.8413 - 0.1587 = 0.6826$$

Again, the cumulative probabilities needed above can be obtained by using either the Excel function or the standard normal distribution table.

We can tie this third example back to the empirical rule, since we calculated that the probability of a value falling within ±1 standard deviations from the mean is about 68%. Can you repeat this exercise to find probabilities that lie within ±2 standard deviations from the mean? Now, recall that the empirical rule also states that practically all values (99.7%) lay within ±3 standard deviations from the mean. You can check the standard normal distribution table to see that, indeed, probabilities beyond Z= ±3 are nearly zero. For this reason, the probability being sought in the example given in the fourth row of Table 6.2, $P(Z \geq 10)$, is practically zero.

We leave it to you to compute on your own the sought probability in the example provided in the fifth row of Table 6.2 to make sure you understand these types of calculations.

P-VALUE

The ***p-value*** is a specific term used to describe a probability that is computed as

$$P(Z \geq |z|)$$

which is the probability of obtaining a Z score value *farther away from the mean* than a *specified* Z score value, shown in the above probability expression as the absolute value of z[5]. Since we are using the

5 The notation |z| refers to the *absolute value* of Z, which measures the distance the number is from zero without regard to direction (positive or negative).

absolute value of z, *farther away* can mean being either to the right of a positive Z score value or to the left of a negative Z score value. This probability is given a special name, i.e., *p-value*, because it plays an important role in the statistical inference tests that are covered in later chapters. We will be discussing the p-value in more depth later, but are introducing it here to describe its computational aspects.

Consider first the left panel of Figure 6.10, which shows a shaded area to the left of the Z score value of −2. Recognizing that what is being sought is a cumulative probability, we can compute the p-value for a Z score of −2 as:

$$P(Z \leq -2) = 0.0228$$

Now consider the right panel of Figure 6.10, which shows a shaded area to the right of the Z value of 1.7. Remembering that the standard normal distribution tables and the associated Excel function provide cumulative probabilities, we use the complement rule to compute the sought p-value as:

$$P(Z \geq 1.7) = 1 - P(Z \leq 1.7) = 0.0446$$

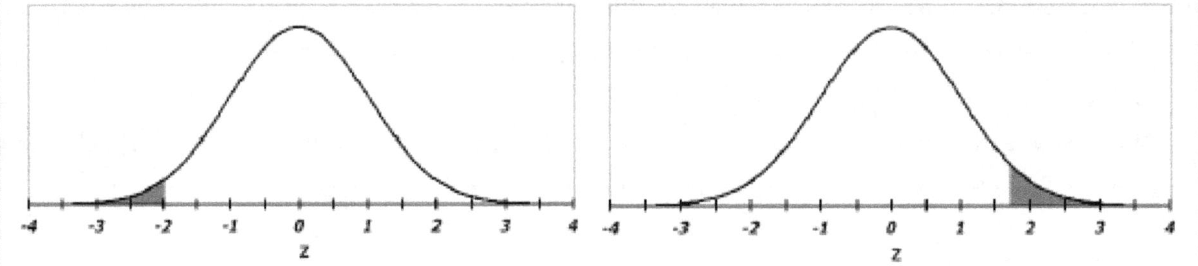

Figure 6.10 P-Value

INVERSE PROBABILITY CALCULATIONS

A final technique we will cover before concluding this chapter is finding the Z score value that corresponds to a given probability. This is referred to as an ***inverse probability calculation*** because we are given a probability value and asked to determine the associated Z score value (i.e., the inverse of being given a Z score value and being asked to determine the associated probability). Specifically, given a probability value

$$P(Z \le z^*) = 0.05$$

what is the value of z*, the sought Z score value?

To find this value, we use the Excel function =NORMSINV(). This function uses a single argument, *probability*, and returns the Z score value for which the following holds:

$$P(Z \le z^*) = \text{probability}$$

It is important to recognize that this probability refers to a *cumulative* probability, i.e., the probability of obtaining a value for Z that is *less than or equal* to z*. For example:

$$=\text{NORMSINV}(0.05) = -1.645.$$

In other words, 5% of the area under the probability distribution curve lies to the left (i.e., the cumulative probability) of a Z score value of −1.645. This is illustrated in the left panel of Figure 6.11.

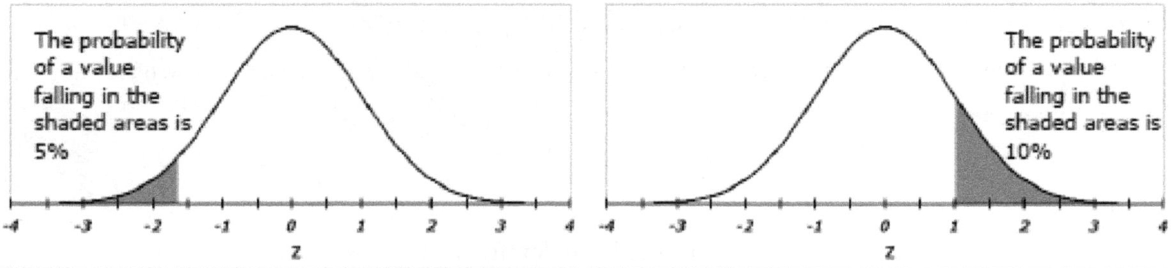

Figure 6.11 Inverse Probability Calculation

As a final example, consider the right panel of Figure 6.11. We are now looking for the Z score value for which 10% of the area under the probability distribution curve lays to the right of the Z score value. In other words, we are looking for the value of z* for which:

$$P(Z \ge z^*) = 0.1$$

We cannot solve this directly, since both Excel and the standard distribution table provide cumulative probability values (i.e., the area under the distribution curve to the left of any given Z score). We can, however, use the complement rule, which tells us that the overall area under the curve should equal one:[6]

$$P(Z \geq z^*) + P(Z \leq z^*) = 1$$

We can rearrange the above to find:

$$P(Z \leq z^*) = 1 - P(Z \geq z^*) = 1 - 0.1 = 0.9$$

Hence, for the same z* value for which $P(Z \geq z^*) = 0.1$ holds, $P(Z \leq z^*) = 0.9$ also holds. This latter probability expression can be easily found using Excel, by typing:

=NORMSINV(0.9) = 1.282

This result indicates that 90% of the area under the probability distribution curve lays to the left of a Z score value of 1.282 and, hence, that 10% of the area under the curve lays to the right of this Z score value.

UNIT 2 SUMMARY

- When a variable X is normally distributed, we denote it as:

$$X \sim N(\mu, \sigma)$$

- The ***standard normal distribution*** is the distribution of Z, which is normally distributed with a mean of zero and a standard deviation of one:

6 Note that it is okay to use ≤ as well as ≥ in this equation, because in continuous distributions the value of P(Z = z*) is zero.

$$Z \sim N(0,1)$$

- Any normal distribution can be converted into the standard normal distribution using the following conversion:

$$Z = \frac{X - \mu}{\sigma}$$

- Z has a special meaning that is important to understand: For each value of X, the corresponding ***Z score*** is a measure of how far *in terms of number of standard deviations* this value is from the mean.
- The ***p-value*** is a term used to refer to the probability of a value falling *farther away from the mean* than a specific z value:

$$P(Z \geq |z|)$$

- We can use ***inverse probability calculations*** to find Z score values that correspond to specific probabilities.

UNIT 2 EXERCISES

1. The eight variables in Table 6.E1 are normally distributed with the means and standard deviations shown in the table.
   a. Use the =NORMDIST function to find the probability $P(X \leq x)$.
   b. Compute the Z scores corresponding to the specific x values in Column 3.

TABLE 6.E1

μ	σ	x	$P(X \le x)$	Z Score
6	0.5	5		
15	5	18		
15	5	21		
40	10	30		
5	0.4	6.2		
100	25	150		
1000	138	743.5		
10	3	10		

2. Find the following probabilities using Excel:
   a. $P(Z \le -2.06)$
   b. $P(Z \ge -0.69)$
   c. $P(Z \le 3.8)$
   d. $P(-2.61 \le Z \le -2.48)$
   e. $P(Z = 1.44)$
   f. $P(Z \le -2.57)$
   g. $P(Z \ge -2.21)$
   h. $P(Z \ge 3.09)$
   i. $P(-1.32 \le Z \le 2.05)$
   j. $P(0.81 \le Z \le 1.68)$
   k. $P(Z \ge 0.85)$
   l. $P(Z \le -2.13 \text{ or } Z \ge 3.06)$
   m. $P(Z \le 0.01)$
   n. $P(-0.64 \le Z \le 0.96)$
   o. $P(0.89 \le Z \le 1.34)$
   p. $P(Z \le -1.96 \text{ or } Z \ge 1.96)$

3. Find the p-value for the following Z scores:
   a. $Z = 2.3$
   b. $Z = -2$
   c. $Z = 1.645$
   d. $Z = -1.96$
   e. $Z = 0$
   f. $Z = 4$
   g. $Z = -1.5$
   h. $Z = -3$

4. Find the Z score values that correspond to the following probabilities:
   a. $P(Z \leq z^*) = 0.1$
   b. $P(Z \leq z^*) = 0.5$
   c. $P(Z \leq z^*) = 0.02$
   d. $P(Z \leq z^*) = 0.9$
   e. $P(Z \geq z^*) = 0.3$
   f. $P(Z \geq z^*) = 0.6$
   g. $P(Z \geq z^*) = 0.95$
   h. $P(Z \geq z^*) = 0.05$
   i. $P(-z^* \leq Z \leq z^*) = 0.68$
   j. $P(-z^* \leq Z \leq z^*) = 0.5$
   k. $P(-z^* \leq Z \leq z^*) = 0.99$

5. In the example of the Internet art store, consider the variable representing time spent on the website. We mentioned that this variable follows a normal distribution with a mean of five minutes and standard deviation of one minute. If a customer is chosen at random, what is the probability that they spend more than three minutes on the site?

6. Weekly demand for a popular art piece on our Internet art store is normally distributed with a mean of 50 and standard deviation of five. The store usually keeps 60 pieces in stock and re-orders them once a week.
   a. What is the probability that average demand will not be met on a given week?
   b. How many of this popular art piece should you keep in inventory to ensure that you do not run short of demand more than 10% of the time?

7. IQ is normally distributed with a mean of 100 and a standard deviation of fifteen. Answer the following questions related to IQ:
   a. MENSA is an organization that accepts people who obtained a score on an IQ test that is within the upper two percent of the population. What is the cut-off IQ score for MENSA?
   b. A gifted child has an IQ of 130 or higher. What is the probability that a randomly selected child is gifted?
   c. If you have a sample of 40 children, what is the probability that four of these children are gifted? (Hint: What is your variable? Is it still normally distributed?)

END-OF-CHAPTER PRACTICE

1. Prior to the 1930s, airports used a two-letter abbreviation. Around 1947, the aviation industry was growing so fast that three letters were needed and *Los Angeles Airport* (LA) became LAX. The letter X has no specific meaning in this identifier, but LAX became one of the busiest airports in the world. The daily number of passengers at LAX is normally distributed with a mean of 163,000 and a standard deviation of 10,000[7].
   a. What is the probability of LAX having over 175,000 passengers on a given day?
   b. What percentage of the time does LAX get between 148,000 and 178,000 daily passengers?

2. Every year, over 9 million Americans are victims to identity theft. The theft amount per person is normally distributed with a mean of $6,383 and a standard deviation of $2,000[8]. Suppose you are a victim of identity theft:
   a. What is the probability that you were robbed of less than $5,000?
   b. You are told your theft incident is in the top 1.5% of thefts in terms of amount stolen. What does this mean?

3. 3% of adults aged 25 to 29 send over 200 text messages per day[9]. If we know that the number of daily text messages sent by adults 25 to 29 is normally distributed with a standard deviation of 50, what is the mean number of daily text messages?

4. Suppose you are working on a pitch for a new project involving multiple hotel properties, and you need to convince your company's investment board that the investment will pay off. Based on company records, the board typically approves projects with at least an 85% chance of profit. If the profit associated with projects is normally distributed with a mean of $1,000,000 and standard deviation of $50,000, what must the minimum projected profit be for approval?

5. Let us take two of the top ten most expensive cities in the world, Tokyo and Moscow, and compare their rent prices. The average cost of a monthly two-bedroom living space (in $US) is $4,436 in Tokyo and $3,600 in Moscow[10]. Suppose rent prices are normally distributed with standard deviations of $200 for Tokyo and $320 for Moscow. Is there a larger probability of rent in Tokyo costing over $4,538 or rent in Moscow costing over $3,740?

7 Source: http://en.wikipedia.org/wiki/Los_Angeles_International_Airport#The_.22X.22_in_LAX.
8 Source: http://visual.ly/identity-theft-facts-and-figures.
9 Source: http://visual.ly/adults-and-mobile-phones.
10 Source: http://visual.ly/most-expensive-cities.

6. With climate change becoming a bigger concern, there is an emphasis on carbon emissions from automobiles. The average car burning one gallon of gas produces twenty cubic pounds of CO_2[11]. If carbon dioxide emissions are normally distributed and it is known that 99% of cars produce more than one cubic pound of CO_2, then:
   a. Find the standard deviation of carbon emissions.
   b. Find the proportion of cars emitting between 20 and 35 cubic pounds per gallon of gas burned.

7. The number of pitches thrown per game by the starting pitcher is normally distributed with a mean of 85 and a standard deviation of ten. The manager decides to take out the starter once he has thrown 100 pitches. What is the probability of this occurring for a randomly selected start for this pitcher?

8. The *Deepwater Horizon* oil spill in April 2010 was one of the largest petroleum accidents in history. It lasted 87 days, claimed eleven lives and has spawned over 130 lawsuits. The average total discharge was estimated at 4.9 million barrels of oil. Assuming that the estimate of total discharge is normally distributed with a standard deviation of 0.16 million barrels[12], what is the probability of the total discharge being under 4.5 million barrels?

9. In Ontario, the per capita household debt in 2012 was normally distributed with a mean of \$17,621 and a standard deviation of \$3,000[13]. What is the probability of a household having a debt of between \$12,000 and \$15,000?

10. The time to fully charge an *Android*-based phone is normally distributed with a mean of 45 minutes and a standard deviation of five minutes.
    a. What is the probability that an *Android*-based phone would be fully charged in less than 30 minutes? Less than 45 minutes? Less than 60 minutes?
    b. What is the probability that it would take more than 50 minutes to fully charge the phone?
    c. What percentage of phones would be fully charged in less than 55 minutes?

---

11 Source: http://visual.ly/automobiles-and-environment.
12 Source: http://www.uscg.mil/foia/docs/dwh/fosc_dwh_report.pdf.
13 Source: http://visual.ly/canadian-debt-infographic-economy-debt-and-you.

11. The lifespan of a refurbished *iPhone 4s* is normally distributed with a mean of 24 months and a standard deviation of one month.
    a. What is the probability that a refurbished *iPhone 4s* you purchased today will last more than two years?
    b. What is the probability that it would last six weeks less than the mean?
    c. What is the probability that it would *die* exactly 730 days from now?
    d. What percentage of refurbished phones would make it past 26 months?

SUMMARY

Chapter 6 introduces continuous random variables and three different distributions. A continuous random variable can assume any value in an interval or set of intervals. Unlike a discrete random variable, which uses only integers as outcomes, continuous random variables can assume any value on a number line. For example, the weight of my Great Dane, Quark, can be 128 pounds or, more precisely, 128.25 lbs. The probability of a continuous random variable and the area under the graph of a given interval are identical. The question is not what the probability of a given X-value is but what is the probability that a given X-value is either less than, greater than, or between two values. The probability of any given X-value occurring is zero (0).

Sampling and Sampling Distributions

7

Chapter 6 presented the normal distribution and the conversion (standardization) of a continuous random variable X into the standard normal variable Z. Chapter 7 applies the normal distribution, not to a given X-value but to a subset of X-values or proportions. The sampling error, which will be dependent on the sample size, will be calculated. The larger the sample size, the closer the standard error approximates the true standard deviation. The standard error calculation will depend on whether or not the population standard deviation is known (or can be estimated) or if it is unknown.

SAMPLING DISTRIBUTIONS

By Jin W. Choi

A sampling distribution refers to the distribution of sample observations and the distribution of their means. Even though we normally do not know the true underlying distribution of the sample observations, statistical theories such as the Central Limit Theorem show that at least the mean of sample observations—the sample mean—follows either a normal Z-distribution or a t-distribution. **If a population standard deviation is known, the sampling distribution of the mean is assumed to follow a normal Z-distribution. If a population standard deviation is unknown, the sampling distribution of the mean is assumed to follow a t-distribution**[1]**.** We shall use this statistical theory extensively without proof throughout the remainder of this book.

This very concept of sampling distributions is the foundation for inferential statistics. **It enables us to examine the likelihood (=probability) of a sample occurring from a known population. It also enables us to infer the likelihood of a unknown population mean occurring from a known sample.** In other words, these two slightly different tasks, arising from two different situations, are the center of inferential statistics.

Because we had studied various sampling methods for collecting primary data in Chapter, we jump right in to the issues of understanding the difference between the distribution of a single sample observation and that of the sample mean. Afterwards, **we will study**

1 This conclusion based on statistical theories is so important that you must memorize and never forget it.

the methods of using Z-and t-distributions to access probability of a sample mean occurring given a known population mean.

A. Definitions to Understand the Sampling Distributions

Even though there are cases where a population mean is known, we will assume herein that it is not known. Therefore, we are to estimate it by a sample mean and utilize the following statistical properties without proof:

1. The population mean, μ, vs. the sample mean, $\bar{X}$
   a. The mean of a sample, $\bar{X}$

   The population mean is estimated by the mean of a sample.

$$X_1, X_2, X_3, etc \Rightarrow \bar{X} \Rightarrow \mu_X \Rightarrow \mu$$

A statistical theory states that a sample mean is an unbiased estimate of a population mean[2] → That is, any sample mean can represent and approximate its population mean $\rightarrow \bar{X} \Rightarrow \mu_X \Rightarrow \mu$.

   b. The mean of sample means, $\bar{\bar{X}}$

$$\bar{X}_1, \bar{X}_2, \bar{X}_3, etc \Rightarrow \bar{\bar{X}} \Rightarrow \mu_{\bar{X}} \Rightarrow \mu$$

The mean of many sample means, which is denoted as $\bar{\bar{X}}$ and often referred as the grand mean, is also an unbiased estimate of a population mean, just like any sample mean, $\bar{X}$, is.

That is, the mean of $\bar{X}'s \Rightarrow \bar{\bar{X}} \Rightarrow \mu_{\bar{X}} \Rightarrow \mu$

Because this is true, there is no need to collect sample after sample. The mean of a single sample will suffice to estimate the population mean without any bias.

2 Recall from Chapter 1 that a (sample) statistic is an estimator of a (population) parameter.

Intuitive Illustration:

Normally, a single sample is taken such as:

$$\text{Sample \#1} \rightarrow 9,\ 10,\ 10,\ 10,\ 11 \rightarrow \bar{X}_1 = 10 \text{ and } S_1 = \sqrt{0.5} = 0.707$$

However, if we assume that 3 additional samples are taken from the same population, we will most likely get different observations in each sample and thus, different means and standard deviations can be calculated as shown below:

$$\text{Sample \#2} \rightarrow 8,\ 9,\ 10,\ 11,\ 12 \rightarrow \bar{X}_2 = 10 \text{ and } S_2 = \sqrt{2.5} = 1.581$$

$$\text{Sample \#3} \rightarrow 7,\ 9,\ 10,\ 12,\ 13 \rightarrow \bar{X}_3 = 10.2 \text{ and } S_3 = \sqrt{5.7} = 2.387$$

$$\text{Sample \#4} \rightarrow 7,\ 8,\ 9,\ 11,\ 14 \rightarrow \bar{X}_4 = 9.8 \text{ and } S_4 = \sqrt{10.53} = 3.245$$

Given these 4 samples above, we note that the mean of these 4 sample means is 10 as shown below:

$$\bar{\bar{X}} = \frac{\bar{X}_1 + \bar{X}_2 + \bar{X}_3 + \bar{X}_4}{4} = \frac{10 + 10 + 10.2 + 9.8}{4} = 10$$

and the sample variance of these means, denoted as $S_{\bar{X}}^2$, is calculated as:

$$S_{\bar{X}}^2 = \frac{0^2 + 0^2 + (0.2)^2 + (-0.2)^2}{3-1} = \frac{0.08}{2} = 0.04$$

And the sample standard deviation of these means, denoted as $S_{\bar{X}}$ and known as the **"sample standard error,"** is calculated as:

$$S_{\bar{X}} = \sqrt{S_{\bar{X}}^2} = \sqrt{0.04} = 0.2$$

If we conduct such an experiment as above repeatedly for numerous times, we will find the grand mean of these sample means to be a number closer to the population mean because sample means are a measure of central tendency and thus, they should gravitate toward the population mean. This property is known as the **"unbiasedness"** of a sample mean → i.e, a sample mean estimates the population mean without any bias.

2. The standard deviation and the standard error

The standard deviation (or the variance) is a measure of dispersion for a single random variable such as X in relation to its mean. The standard error, on the other hand, is a measure of dispersion for the sample means in relation to their grand mean. Therefore, both measure dispersion but the former measures the variability of a single value X whereas the latter measures that of the mean, $\bar{X}$.

We will first review the formula for the standard deviation and the standard error of the population as follows:

a. The population standard deviation of X → $\sigma = \sigma_X$.

$$\sigma = \sigma_X = \sqrt{\sum_{j=1}^{k} P_j \cdot (X_j - \mu)^2} = \sqrt{\frac{\sum_{i=1}^{N} (X_i - \mu)^2}{N}}$$

b. The population standard deviation of $\bar{X}$ = population standard error, $\sigma_{\bar{X}}$.

$$\sigma_{\bar{X}} = \frac{\sigma_X}{\sqrt{n}} = \frac{\sigma}{\sqrt{n}}$$

where n is the number of sample size[3].

3 This formula is for the case of an infinite population. For a finite population, we need to use:

$\sigma_{\bar{X}} = \sqrt{\frac{N-n}{N-1}}\left(\frac{\sigma}{\sqrt{n}}\right)$. However, as the population s size of N approaches an infinity, it does not make a big difference.

c. The intuitive relationship between σ and $\sigma_{\bar{X}}$.

Note that from the variances and the standard deviations of the 4 samples shown above, we can easily understand that the standard deviations (S_i's) of Samples #1 through #4 are larger than the standard deviation of 4 sample means, $S_{\bar{X}}$. This is because given the observations in all 4 samples, the individual X values are dispersed between 7 and 14 whereas their sample means are dispersed between 9.8 and 10.2. That is, the sample means are distributed more compactly near the population mean than individual X values.

This observation intuitively convinces us that individual Xs vary more than their sample means, $\bar{X}'s$ → Therefore, $S_X > S_{\bar{X}}$. More precisely, their theoretical relationship[4] is:

$$S^2 = S_X^2 = n \cdot S_{\bar{X}}^2 \qquad \rightarrow \qquad S_{\bar{X}} = \frac{S_X}{\sqrt{n}} = \frac{S}{\sqrt{n}}$$

This relationship specifically shows that S_X is $\sqrt{n}$ times greater than $S_{\bar{X}}$. This observation can be applied directly to the case between a population standard deviation and a population standard error. That is, we should infer and know that $\sigma_X > \sigma_{\bar{X}}$.

More precisely, their theoretical relationship[5] is defined as:

$$\sigma^2 = \sigma_X^2 = n \cdot \sigma_{\bar{X}}^2 \qquad \rightarrow \qquad \sigma_{\bar{X}} = \frac{\sigma_X}{\sqrt{n}} = \frac{\sigma}{\sqrt{n}}$$

Once again, σ_X is $\sqrt{n}$ times greater than $\sigma_{\bar{X}}$. Also, we note that $\sigma_{\bar{X}}$ discussed above is called the population standard error of the mean, or simply, the **population standard error;** whereas σ_X is called the standard deviation of the population or simply, the **population standard deviation.**

4 We accept this relationship without proof. You must know and memorize this formula.
5 Likewise, we accept this relationship without proof. You must know and memorize this formula.

Important Implication:

In reality, only one sample is taken. However, the statistical theory states that the above relationship between the standard deviation and the standard error is true. Thus, the need to take additional samples does not exist and we simply use the above relationship as the truth in analyzing the distribution of a sample mean.

B. When the Population Mean and Population Standard Deviation are Known

Recall: If a population standard deviation of a normal variable is known, the sampling distribution of its mean follows a normal Z-distribution.

When the population mean and the population standard deviation are known, we can use the following Z formula to standardize a sample mean, $\bar{X}$, into a Z value and analyze the probability of the sample mean occurring:

$$Z = \frac{\bar{X} - \mu}{\sigma_{\bar{X}}} = \frac{\bar{X} - \mu}{\frac{\sigma}{\sqrt{n}}}$$

Note the difference between this Z formula shown above and the Z formula described in Chapter 6. Both are used for standardizing a normal variable. However, **the Z formula shown above standardizes (or normalizes) a sample mean whereas the Z formula in Chapter 6 standardizes a single value of X.**

Always remember that the above Z formula is used when the population standard error or the population standard deviation with the number of observations, n, is known[6].

C. The Comparison of Sampling Distributions of an Individual Value and their Mean

Because statistics is largely a study of samples, everything we do involves samples. In this process, even though an individual sample observation is important and interesting, the sample

6 In business statistics, σ_X or $\sigma_{\bar{X}}$ is often unknown whereas in engineering, they can be known. For example, when an engineer designs a chocolate chip cookie machine, she has to know the tolerance level of how many chocolate chips are acceptable per each cookie being produced. It might be an average number of 5 chocolate chips with a variability of ± 1 chocolate chip per cookie. If this variability is measured by one standard deviation, then $\sigma = 1$. However, in business data such as sales, profits, etc., the population standard deviation or standard error is often unknown. Thus, it needs to be estimated based on a sample.

mean is often the more important and interesting. For example, in order to evaluate the salary level of economics graduates against finance graduates, it is important to know the salary of a single economics and a single finance graduates. However, often, the average salaries based on a large number of economics and finance graduates provide more important and interesting infonnation to a decision maker. That is, the behavior of a sample mean is often more interesting and important.

In a real business world, however, a population mean is either known or unknown. If a population mean is known, we are interested in knowing how likely is the chance that a sample mean is from the population. If it is not known, we are interested in knowing how likely is the chance that the sample mean will represent the unknown population mean.

In this chapter, we will deal with the case of a population mean being known to us. The case of an unknown population mean will be discussed in following chapters[7].

Example 1

Let's assume that you had invested in 5 of the 30 stocks that make up the Dow Jones Industrial Average. If so, we can quickly understand that the population of stocks is made up of 30 stocks (i.e., N=30) and your sample is comprised of 5 stocks that you own (i.e., n=5). Therefore, you will know the population mean by summing all rates of return from 30 stocks and dividing it by 30 and the population standard deviation by using the formula shown above. Suppose that the population mean return is 10% and the standard deviation is 0.6%. Also, you will know the sample mean by summing all rates of return from your 5 stocks and dividing it by 5 and the sample standard deviation by using the formula shown in Chapter 3. Suppose that the sample mean is found to be 10.3% and the sample standard deviation is 0.5%.

1. What is the probability that you could pick **a single stock** in the Dow Jones Industrial Average that would have yielded more than 11%?

Steps to the Answer:

a. Recognize the availability of the population standard deviation → Given both the population and the sample standard deviation in this case, **we choose the population standard deviation because it is superior information to the sample standard deviation.**

7 Obviously, if it is unknown, its estimate must be obtained on the basis of a sample.

b. Because this problem involves **a single stock** and a known population standard deviation, we must use[8]

$$Z = \frac{X - \mu}{\sigma}$$

c. We now formulate the problem as follows and solve:

$$P(X > 11) = P\left(\frac{X-\mu}{\sigma} > \frac{11-\mu}{\sigma}\right) = P\left(Z > \frac{11-10}{0.6}\right)$$
$$= P(Z > 1.67) = 0.0475 \rightarrow 4.75\%$$

That is, there is only 4.75% probability that you could have picked **a stock** that would have yielded a 11% rate of return from the 30 Dow Jones Industrial Average stocks that had yielded 10% as a group.

2. What is the probability that you could pick **a single stock** in the Dow Jones Industrial Average that would have yielded between 9% and 11%?

Answer:

Based on the above procedure, we now formulate the problem as follows and solve:

$$P(9 < X < 11) = P\left(\frac{9-10}{0.6} < Z < \frac{11-10}{0.6}\right) = P(-1.67 < Z < 1.67)$$
$$= 1 - 2 * (0.0475) = 0.905 \rightarrow 90.5\%$$

That is, there is 90.5% probability that you could have picked a stock that would have yielded between 9% and 11%.

3. What is the probability that you could pick 5 stocks in the Dow Jones Industrial Average that would have yielded **an average return** more than 11%?

Steps to the Answer:

a. Recognize that the population standard deviation of 0.6 is given.

8 Recall the procedure we learned in Chapter 6.

b. Because this problem involves an **average** return more than 11% and a known population standard deviation, we must now use the population standard error as follows:

$$Z = \frac{\bar{X} - \mu}{\sigma_{\bar{X}}} \text{ where } \sigma_{\bar{X}} = \frac{\sigma}{\sqrt{n}} = \frac{0.6}{\sqrt{5}} = \frac{0.6}{2.236} = 0.2683$$

c. We now formulate the problem as follows and solve:

$$P(\bar{X} > 11) = P\left(\frac{\bar{X} - \mu}{\sigma_{\bar{X}}} > \frac{11 - 10}{0.2683}\right) = P(Z > 3.73) = 0.0001 \rightarrow 0.01\%$$

That is, there is only 0.01% probability that you could have picked a group of 5 stocks that would have yielded an average of 11% or higher rate of return from the 30 Dow Jones Industrial Average stocks that yielded 10%.

4. What is the probability that you could pick 5 stocks in the Dow Jones Industrial Average that would have yielded **an average return** between 9.8% and 10.5%?

Answer:

Based on the above procedure, we now formulate the problem as follows and solve:

$$P(9.8 < \bar{X} < 10.5) = P\left(\frac{9.8 - 10}{\frac{0.6}{\sqrt{5}}} < Z < \frac{10.5 - 10}{\frac{0.6}{\sqrt{5}}}\right) = P(-0.75 < Z < 1.86)$$

$$= 1 - (0.2266 + 0.0314) = 1 - 0.2580 = 0.7420 \rightarrow 74.2\%$$

That is, there is 74.2% probability that you could have picked a group of 5 stocks that would have yielded between 9.8% and 10.5%.

Example 2

Assume that a national intelligence quotient (IQ) research institute published a data that shows a normal distribution[9] with the mean IQ of 110 for all people tested and a standard deviation of 8.

9 In reality, IQ's are not believed to be normally distributed. This is just an example.

1. John Doe thinks that **he** is smart, having an IQ of 124. What is the probability that John's claim is correct?

Answer:

$$P(X > 124) = P\left(Z > \frac{124-110}{8}\right) = P(Z > 1.75) = 0.0401 \to 4\%$$

Given that only 4% of the people have a higher IQ than he does (or alternatively, 96% of the people have a lower IQ than he does), he can be considered smart.

2. John Doe has signed up for GSB 420 and his classmates all claim that they are smart, too. To verify this claim, Dr. Choi, the GSB 420 instructor, surveyed all 16 students in the class and found that their **average** IQ is 120 with a standard deviation of 10. Can Dr. Choi conclude that he has a "smart" class?

Answer:

$$P(\bar{X} > 120) = P\left(Z > \frac{120-110}{\frac{8}{\sqrt{16}}}\right) = P(Z > 5.00) = 0.00000087 \to 0\%$$

Note 1: Despite the sample standard deviation of 10, the population standard deviation of 8 should be used because the population parameter is always superior to the sample statistic[10] → Thus, use the Z-, not the t-formula.

Note 2: Even though the sample mean of 120 is lower than John's 124, we can definitely conclude that the class is smart because the probability of a sample mean—based on a sample size of 16—being larger than 120 is almost 0.

Note 3: The fact that 110 is the population mean of a normal distribution means that it is also its median[11]. Thus, the probability of finding a group of 16 people whose average IQ is far above the median value of 110 is very unlikely → Thus, the class as a whole is smart.

10 For this reason, often the validity or consistency of a mechanical process is examined by the Z-formula. That is, when a machine is designed to drill a hole, for example, its average diameter and variability have been specified and known. Thus, it is good to use the Z-formula to examine the sample results against this pre-specified mean and standard deviation.

11 This is often not the case for IQ test scores. It tends to show a negative or left-skewness.

D. Examples of When and How to Use the Standard Error

1. Given a population mean of 100 and a population standard deviation of 10, you took a sample of 25 observations.

    a. What is the probability of picking a **sample mean** that is less than 99?

$$P(\bar{X} < 99) = P\left(Z < \frac{99-100}{\frac{10}{\sqrt{25}}} \right) = P(Z < -0.5) = 0.3085$$

Note: Instead of using the Z-table in Chapter 7, one can use the Excel Spreadsheet command of "=normdist(X,μ,σ,True)" where X=99; μ=100; σ=2; and True; to calculate the cumulative probability of Z[12] as follows:

$$\text{"=NORMDIST(99,100,2,TRUE)"} \rightarrow 0.308538$$

    b. What is the probability of picking a **sample mean** that is greater than 100.5?

$$P(\bar{X} > 100.5) = P(Z > 0.25) = 0.4013 \quad \leftarrow \text{the Z table solution}$$

$$= 1 - 0.5987 \quad \leftarrow \text{the Excel solution}$$

$$\text{"= NORMDIST(100.5,100,2,TRUE)"} \rightarrow 0.598706$$

12 The Excel Spreadsheet command always gives the cumulative probability of Z for (X < k)

c. What is the probability of picking a **sample mean** that is between 97 and 104?

$$P(97 < \bar{X} < 104) = P(-1.5 < Z < 2)$$

$$= 1 - (0.0668 + 0.0228) = 0.9104 \quad \leftarrow \text{the Z table solution}$$

$$= 0.9772 - 0.0668 = 0.9104 \quad \leftarrow \text{the Excel solution}$$

0.066807 and 0.97725

2. Given a population mean of 20 and a population standard error of the mean of 3, you took a sample of 100 observations.

a. What is the probability that **the sample mean** will be less than 18?

$$P(\bar{X} < 18) = P\left(Z < \frac{18-20}{3}\right) = P(Z < -0.67) = 0.2514$$

b. What is the probability that **the sample mean** will be greater than 17?

$$P(\bar{X} > 17) = P(Z > -1) = 1 - 0.1587 = 0.8413$$

c. What is the probability that **the sample mean** will be between 21 and 24?

$$P(21 < \bar{X} < 24) = P(0.33 < Z < 1.33)$$

$$= 0.3707 - 0.0918 = 0.2789 \quad \leftarrow \text{the Z table solution}$$

$$= 0.9082 - 0.6293 = 0.2789 \quad \leftarrow \text{the Excel solution}$$

E. Sampling Distribution of the Proportion

When evaluating a probability associated with a proportion, always the Z-distribution is used with the following formulas for the mean and the standard error of a proportion.

1. The Sample Mean Proportion, p

$$p = X/n = (\text{Number of items of interest})/(\text{sample size})$$
$$\text{where } 0 \le p \le 1$$

2. The Standard Error of the Proportion[13]

$$\sigma_p = \sqrt{\frac{\pi(1-\pi)}{n}}$$

where π is the population proportion and n is the number of observations.

3. The Standardized Normal Value for the Proportion, Z[14]

$$Z = \frac{p-\pi}{\sigma_p}$$

4. Example 1

Suppose that 10% of the 1000 taxpayers were audited last year by the IRS.

a. What is the probability that less than 11% will be audited this year, assuming all other things to be unchanged?

$$P(p < 0.11) = P\left(Z < \frac{0.11-0.1}{\sqrt{\frac{0.1(1-0.1)}{1000}}} \right) = P(Z < 1.05) = 0.8531$$

13 When the population proportion, π, is unknown, the sample proportion, p, must be used in place of π to calculate the standard error.
14 When working with a proportion, only the Z-formula and the Z-probability are used.

b. What is the probability that less than 8% will be audited this year?

$$P(p < 0.08) = P\left(Z < \frac{0.08 - 0.1}{\sqrt{\frac{0.1(1-0.1)}{1000}}} \right) = P(Z < -2.11) = 0.0174$$

---

c. What is the probability that between 8% and 11.5% will be audited this year?

$$P(0.08 < p < 0.115) = P(-2.11 < Z < 1.58) = 1 - (0.0174 + 0.0571)$$
$$= 0.9429 - 0.0174 = 0.9255$$

---

5. Example 2

A survey showed that 80% of DePaul MBA students love Dr. Choi. If you ask randomly any 10 students, what is the probability that more than 5 students will love Dr. Choi?

Answer:

Identify $\pi = 0.8; p = \frac{5}{10} = 0.5$; and $n = 10$.

Therefore,

$$P(p > 0.5) = P\left(Z > \frac{0.5 - 0.8}{\sqrt{\frac{0.8(1-0.8)}{10}}} \right) = P(Z > -2.37) = 1 - 0.0089 = 0.9911$$

There is a 99.11% chance that you will find 5 or more students loving Dr. Choi out of 10 that you ask.

6. Example 3

A survey showed that 65% of households in the U.S.A. own a pet animal. If you are to sell door to door a pet-related product to 200 households,

a. what is the probability that more than 70% of the households that you will visit will have a pet animal?

Answer:

Identify $\pi = 0.65$; $p = 0.7$; and $n = 200$.

Therefore,

$$P(p > 0.7) = P\left(Z > \frac{0.7 - 0.65}{\sqrt{\frac{0.65(1-0.65)}{200}}} \right) = P(Z > 1.48) = 1 - 0.9306 = 0.0694$$

There is a 6.94% chance that you will find 70% of the 200 households—that is, 140 households—that will have a pet animal.

b. what is the probability that between 62% and 70% of the households will have a pet animal?

Answer:

Identify $\pi = 0.65$; $p = 0.62$; $p = 0.7$; and $n = 200$, we find:

$$P(0.62 < p < 0.7) = P\left(\frac{0.62 - 0.65}{\sqrt{\frac{0.65(1-0.65)}{200}}} < Z < \frac{0.7 - 0.65}{\sqrt{\frac{0.65(1-0.65)}{200}}} \right) = P(-0.89 < Z < 1.48)$$

$$= 1 - (0.0694 + 0.1867) = 0.9306 - 0.1867 = 0.7439$$

There is a 74.39% chance that you will find between 62% and 70% of the 200 households—that is, between 124 and 140 households—that will have a pet animal.

F. The sample standard deviation vs. the sample standard error

If the population standard deviation is unknown, it has to be estimated on the basis of a sample data by using the following sample standard deviation formula:

a. The sample standard deviation of X → $S = S_X$.

$$S = S_X = \sqrt{\frac{\sum_{i=1}^{n}(X_i - \bar{X})^2}{n-1}}$$

Using the same logic that explained the relationship between σ and $\sigma_{\bar{X}}$, we can obtain the relationship between the sample standard deviation, S, and the sample standard error, $S_{\bar{X}}$, from the sample variances as follows:

$$S_{\bar{X}}^2 = \frac{S^2}{n} \qquad \rightarrow \qquad S_{\bar{X}} = \frac{S}{\sqrt{n}}$$

b. The sample standard error of the mean, $S_{\bar{X}}$

$$S_{\bar{X}} = \frac{S}{\sqrt{n}} = \sqrt{\frac{\sum_{i=1}^{n}(X_i - \bar{X})^2}{n \cdot (n-1)}}$$

In this situation where the sample standard error has to be used in place of a population standard error, we need to use a new t-formula that will standardize (or normalize) the mean of the X variable. It is the same t-formula as studied in Chapter 8 with a small modification on the divisor.

c. The use of the t-formula[15]

The t-formula is used when the population variance or the population standard deviation is UNKNOWN and thus, must be estimated by the sample variance or the sample standard deviation[16]. The t-formula to be used is:

$$t = \frac{\bar{X}-\mu}{S_{\bar{X}}} = \frac{\bar{X}-\mu}{\frac{S}{\sqrt{n}}}$$

However, the use of the t-formula is the same as that of the Z-formula, except that its distribution is subject to the (n – 1) degrees of freedom. This point is best demonstrated by the following examples:

Example 1

Given a population mean of 100 and a sample standard deviation of 10, you took a sample of 25 observations.

1. What is the probability that **the sample mean** will be greater than 103.4218?

$$P(\bar{X} > 103.4218) = P\left(t > \frac{103.4218-100}{\frac{10}{\sqrt{25}}}\right) = P(t > 1.7109) = 0.05$$

[...]

Note: Instead of using the t-table, one can use the Excel Spreadsheet command of "=tdist(X,df,tails)" to calculate the cumulative probability of t at X and (n – 1)

15 Note that these examples are almost identical to the examples shown in Chapter 8. The only and yet, main difference is that we are now assessing the probability of a mean, not an individual value of X. Because we must use the standard error whenever we are to assess the probability of a mean, all of the examples herein use the standard error, not the standard deviation in the divisor of the t-formula.

16 This means, then, whenever the population variance or the population standard deviation or the population standard error is known, the Z-formula must be used. Otherwise, use the t-formula.

degrees of freedom. In this case, because X=1.7109; df=24; and tails=l, the corresponding probability is calculated by Excel as follows[17]:

$$\text{"= TDIST(1.7109, 24,1)"} \rightarrow 0.04999832$$

2. less than 98.6304?

$$P(\bar{X} < 98.6304) = P\left(t < \frac{98.6304 - 100}{\frac{10}{\sqrt{25}}}\right) = P(t < -0.6848) = 0.25$$

$$\text{"= TDIST(0.6848, 24,1)"} \rightarrow 0.250015383$$

Note: Because the t-distribution is symmetrical about the mean, X=0.6848 is used instead of –0.6848 for calculation by Excel Spreadsheet. That is, given the Excel Spreadsheet command of "=tdist(X,df,tails)," X=0.6848; df=24; and tails=l were used.

3. greater than 98.6304?

$$P(\bar{X} > 98.6304) = P\left(t > \frac{98.6304 - 100}{\frac{10}{\sqrt{25}}}\right) = P(t > -0.6848) = 1 - 0.25 = 0.75$$

Note: The probability calculated by the Excel Spreadsheet for P(t > 0.6848) is:

$$\text{"= TDIST(0.6848, 24,1)"} \rightarrow 0.250015383$$

17 The Excel Spreadsheet command always gives the cumulative probability of t for (X > k), which is the opposite of the cumulative probability for Z.

4. greater than 97.3644?

$$P(\bar{X} > 97.3644) = P\left(t > \frac{97.3644 - 100}{\frac{10}{\sqrt{25}}} \right) = P(t > -1.3178) = 1 - 0.10 = 0.90$$

Note: The probability calculated by the Excel Spreadsheet for P(t > 1.3178) is: 0.100005924

5. between 97.3644 and 104.9844?

$$P(97.3644 < \bar{X} < 104.9844) = P(-1.3178 < t < 2.4922) = 1 - 0.1 - 0.01 = 0.89$$

Note 1: The probability calculated by the Excel Spreadsheet for P(t > 2.4922) is: 0.009999099

Note 2: We can graphically visualize this problem and the solution as follows:

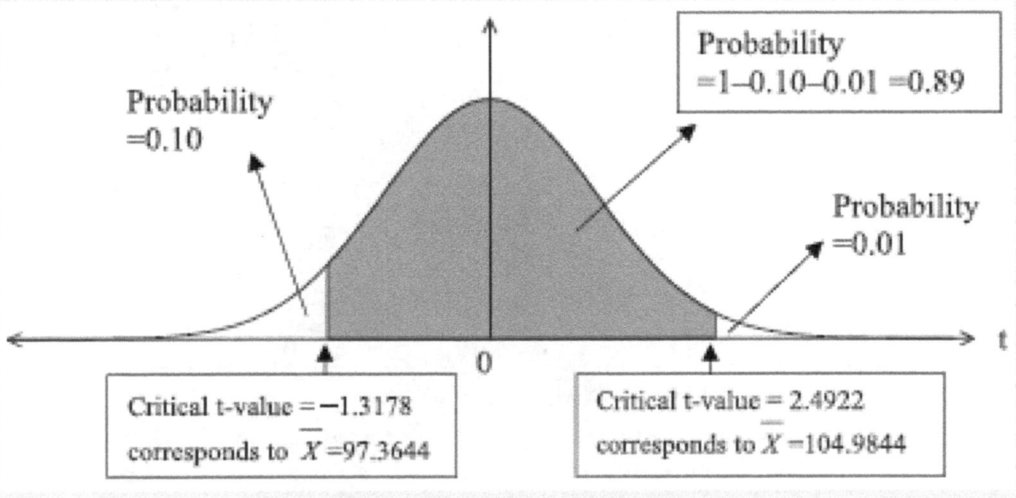

Example 2

Given a population mean of 20 and a sample **standard error** of the mean of 3, you took a sample of 100 observations.

1. What is the probability that **the sample mean** will be less than 16.1297?

$$P(\bar{X} < 16.1297) = P\left(t < \frac{16.1294 - 20}{3}\right) = P(t < -1.2902) = 0.1$$

2. greater than 27.0938?

$$P(\bar{X} > 27.0938) = P(t > 2.3646) = 0.01$$

3. between 17.969 and 24.9812?

$$P(17.969 < \bar{X} < 24.9812) = P(-0.6770 < t < 1.6604) = 1 - 0.25 - 0.05 = 0.7$$

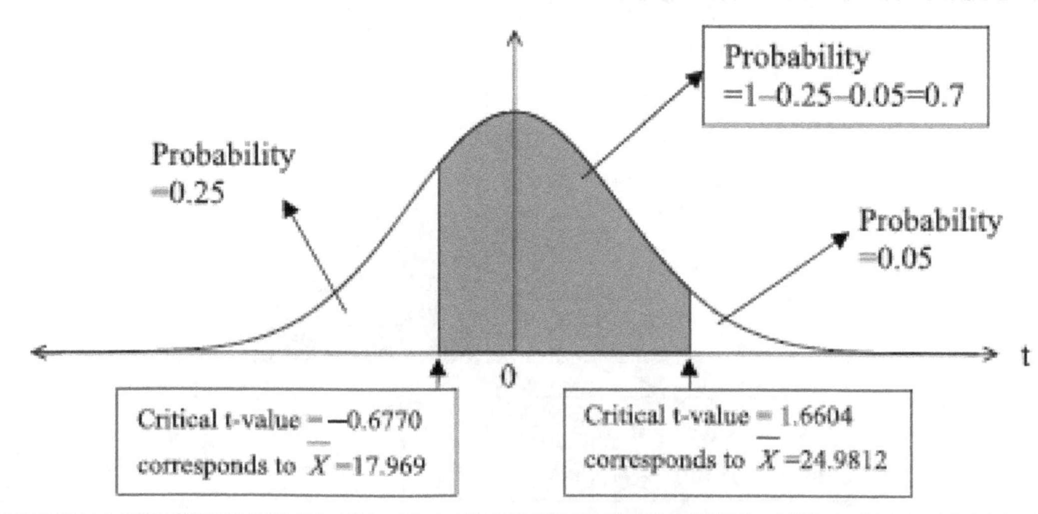

4. between 15 and 23?

(Hint: when table t-values are not available, use the Excel Spreadsheet.)

$$P(15 < \overline{X} < 23) = P(-1.6667 < t < 1) = 1 - 0.0494 - 0.1599 = 0.7907$$

Note 1: $P(t > 1.6667) = 0.049367452$ and $P(t > 1) = 0.159874237$

Note 2: We can graphically visualize this problem and the solution as follows:

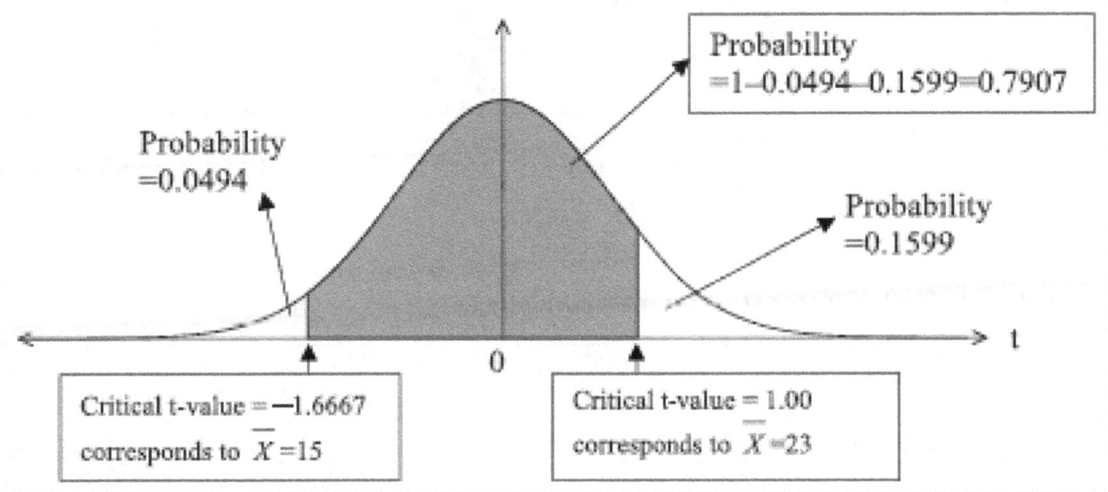

G. The Summary of the Procedures to Identify the Probability

The following steps summarize what we had done so far in assessing a probability associated with a given situation.

Step 1: Identify the nature of the problem by knowing if we are to the probability of an individual X value occurring or a mean of X, $\overline{X}$, occurring?

That is, $P(a \le X \le b) = ?$ or $P(a \le \overline{X} \le b) = ?$

Or $P(a \le X) = ?$ or $P(a \le \overline{X}) = ?$

Step 2: Identify if the problem gives the population standard deviation and asks for a probability of a sample mean occurring or if it deals with a proportion. If so, use the following Z-formula to standardize (or normalize) the $\overline{X}$ value(s):

$$Z = \frac{\overline{X} - \mu_{\overline{X}}}{\sigma_{\overline{X}}} = \frac{\overline{X} - \mu}{\frac{\sigma}{\sqrt{n}}}$$

Step 3: If no population standard deviation is given, use the following t-formula to standardize (or normalize) the $\overline{X}$ value(s):

$$t = \frac{\overline{X} - \mu_{\overline{X}}}{S_{\overline{X}}} = \frac{\overline{X} - \mu}{\frac{S}{\sqrt{n}}}$$

Step 4: Use the Excel Spreadsheet command to identify the probability or look up the probability in the Z- or the t-table.

Summary on the Nature of Problems and Solutions Once More!

Types of Problems concerning an individual X value	Formulas to use	Types of Problems concerning $\overline{X}$	Formulas to use
$P(a < X) = ?$	either $Z=(X-\mu)/\sigma$ or $t=(X-\mu)/S$	$P(a < \overline{X}) = ?$	either $Z = (\overline{X} - \mu) / (\sigma / \sqrt{n})$ or $t = (\overline{X} - \mu) / (S / \sqrt{n})$
$P(X < b) = ?$		$P(\overline{X} < b) = ?$	
$P(a < X < b) = ?$		$P(a < \overline{X} < b) = ?$	

EXERCISE PROBLEMS ON SAMPLING DISTRIBUTIONS

This set of exercise problems has 13 problems, worth a total of 15 points.

1. The population standard error of the mean, $\sigma_{\bar{X}}$, is defined as ______.

   a. $\frac{\sigma_X}{n}$
   b. $\frac{\sigma_X}{n^2}$
   c. $\frac{\sigma_X^2}{n}$
   d. $\frac{\sigma_X}{\sqrt{n}}$
   e. σ_X^2

2. The variance of the sample mean is typically____ the variance of individual observations in a sample.

   a. larger than
   b. smaller than
   c. equal to
   d. less useful than
   e. only (a) and (d) of the above

3. When calculating the Z value for a sample mean, $\bar{X}$, the denominator used is _____.

   a. the variance of the sample mean
   b. the standard error of the population mean
   c. the variance of the population mean
   d. the standard deviation of the population mean
   e. either (a) or (c) of the above

4. Assume that you took a sample of 9 observations from a population whose mean is 50 and standard deviation is 15. What is the probability that the sample mean will be less than 45?

   a. 0.3707
   b. 0.6293
   c. 0.1587
   d. 0.8413
   e. −1

5. The Central Limit Theorem states that as the sample size _____, the resulting distribution of the sample mean becomes almost _____ regardless of the shape of the population probability distribution.

   a. increases; normal
   b. increases; abnormal
   c. decreases; normal
   d. decreases; abnormal
   e. stays the same; normal

6. Even if a population probability distribution is not normal, the standardized normal probability can be used to assess the probability of a mean occurring by invoking ______.
   a. the Chebyshev Rule
   b. the Bayesian Theorem
   c. the Central Limit Theorem
   d. the Law of Averages
   e. God

7. The Law of Large Numbers says that as the sample size, n, increases, the difference between the sample mean and the population mean will approach ______.
   a. a positive infinity
   b. a negative infinity
   c. one
   d. zero
   e. a well-defined positive value such as 1 or 2

8. Given the following sample data,

   20, 24, 28, 30, 22, 26

   the standard deviation is calculated to be ______.
   a. 25
   b. 11.6667
   c. 3.4155
   d. 14
   e. 3.7416

9. Given that a population mean is 20 and a population standard deviation is 5, you collected a sample of 36 observations and found its mean to be 19 and standard deviation to be 4. What is the probability of a single observation having a value greater than 21?
   a. 0.4207
   b. 0.4013
   c. 0.3446
   d. 0.1151
   e. 0.0668

10. Given that a population mean is 20 and a population standard deviation is 5, you collected a sample of 36 observations and found its mean to be 19 and standard deviation to be 4. What is the probability of observing a sample mean smaller than 19?
   a. 0.4207
   b. 0.4013
   c. 0.3446
   d. 0.1151
   e. 0.0668

11. On the basis of 50 people surveyed, a newspaper reported that 30% of them supported the Republican Party. Given this information, what is the probability that the real proportion of Republican Party supporters would be greater than 40%?
   a. 0.25
   b. 0.5
   c. 0.1124
   d. 0.0897
   e. 0.0618

The following problems are worth 2 points each.

12. On the basis of 50 people surveyed, a newspaper reported that 30% of them supported the Republican Party. Given this information, what is the probability that the real proportion of Republican Party supporters would be between 25% and 38%?

a. 0.8907
b. 0.6701
c. 0.5
d. 0.2206
e. 0.1001

13. Given that a population mean is 20 but a population standard deviation is unknown, you collected a sample of 36 observations and found its mean to be 19 and standard deviation to be 4. What is the probability of observing a sample mean between 18.8736 and 21.6251?

a. 0.97
b. 0.94
c. 0.90
d. 0.85
e. 0.55

8 Confidence Intervals

Chapter 7 investigated samples and sampling distributions. One of the goals was to estimate the population parameters using sample data. In some cases, the true population parameters are unknown (for example, anytime there is a process [e.g., manufacturing light bulbs or computers] or the population is so enormous that collecting all of the observations in the data set would be very time consuming). Using sample data to draw conclusions about a population is referred to as statistical inference. A few terms are revisited.

CONFIDENCE INTERVALS

By Andrew Wiesner

Parameter: A summary measure that describes the population. It is fixed, but we rarely know it. Examples include the proportion of American adults who participate in fantasy sports, proportion of NFL home teams who win, the mean height of all NBA players, or the mean attendance for major league baseball games.

Statistic: A summary number that describes the sample. This value is known since it is produced by our sample data, but can vary from sample to sample. For example, if we calculated the proportion of a sample of 1000 American adults who said they participated in fantasy sports last year, this would be the sample proportion. If we took another random sample of 1000 American adults asking the same question, the proportion who said yes for this sample would most likely vary from the proportion of our first sample, since the two samples themselves would consist of different American adults. This fluctuation in sample statistics is called **sampling error**.

Point Estimate: Certain statistics are referred to as point estimates of a parameter. For example, the sample proportion is labeled a point estimate of the population proportion; sample mean is called a point estimate of the population mean. In statistical notation we are saying:

$$\hat{p} \xrightarrow{\text{estimates}} p$$

$$\overline{X} \xrightarrow{\text{estimates}} \mu$$

EXAMPLES

1. A survey is carried out at a university to estimate the proportion of undergraduate students who attended that university's sporting events within the past year. One thousand undergraduate students from that campus are randomly selected and asked whether they attended an on-campus sporting event within the past year. The **population** is all of the undergraduates at that university campus. The **sample** is the group of 1000 undergraduate students selected. The **parameter** is the proportion of all undergraduate students at that university campus who attended an on-campus sporting event within the past year. The **statistic** is the proportion of the 1000 sampled undergraduates who said yes to having attended an on-campus sporting event within the past year.
2. A study is conducted at a university to estimate the mean number of on-campus sporting events that undergraduate students attended within the past year. Five hundred undergraduate students from that campus are randomly selected and asked how many on-campus sporting events they attended within the past year. The **population** is all of the undergraduates at that university campus. The **sample** is the group of 500 undergraduate students selected. The **parameter** is the mean number of on-campus sporting events attended by all undergraduate students at that university campus within the past year. The **statistic** is the mean number of on-campus sporting events attended by the 500 undergraduates sampled.

Ultimately, we will take these statistics and use them to draw conclusions about parameters. This is statistical inference. We begin our discussion with **confidence intervals**. Confidence intervals are primarily used to estimate some unknown parameter by providing a range of values (the interval) with some degree of confidence that the interval correctly contains the parameter. A confidence interval follows the format:

Sample Statistic ± Margin of Error

In this chapter, we discussed margin of error and provided a conservative margin of error for proportions using the equation $1/\sqrt{n}$. In this chapter, we will provide a more exact margin of error for a proportion, plus discuss confidence intervals for a mean. The **margin of error** provides a measure of accuracy of our point estimate in estimating a parameter. The margin of error will consist of two pieces: a multiplier and a standard error. The multiplier will be based on the distribution of the sample statistic, and the standard error will be for that sample statistic. The margin of error, therefore, has this setup:

Margin of Error = Multiplier × Standard Error

8.1 ONE-PROPORTION CONFIDENCE INTERVALS

If $np \geq 15$ **and** $n(1-p) \geq 15$, the sample proportion can be assumed to follow an approximately normal distribution. The problem with this rule as it pertains to the current chapter is that we don't *know* the population parameter, p; we want to estimate it. Because of this, the rule changes by inserting the sample proportion, $\hat{p}$, for p. To simplify this, we recall another prior concept, the binomial random variable [...]. From the binomial, we should recognize that $n\hat{p}$ is the number of "successes" and $n(1-\hat{p})$ is the number of "failures."

When this rule is satisfied, a valid confidence interval for a proportion, p, can use a multiplier from the standard normal (Z) distribution and standard error as follows:

$$S.E. = \sqrt{\frac{\hat{p}(1-\hat{p})}{n}}$$

We just substituted the sample proportion for the population proportion in our standard error equation from Chapter 5.

The multiplier will come from the standard normal distribution. Some common levels of confidence are 90%, 95%, 98%, and 99%, with respective Z-multipliers of 1.65, 1.96, 2.33, and 2.58. To understand how we arrived at these multiplier values, we will examine the 1.96 used for a 95% confidence interval.

From the The Z-Table, we want to find the probability between a negative and positive z-score associated with our level of confidence; for 95% this is 0.95. As Figure 8.1 illustrates, we would find a 0.95 probability between negative and positive 1.96 z-scores. Similar applications would demonstrate the other multipliers. Table 8.1 organizes these multipliers for one-proportion confidence intervals.

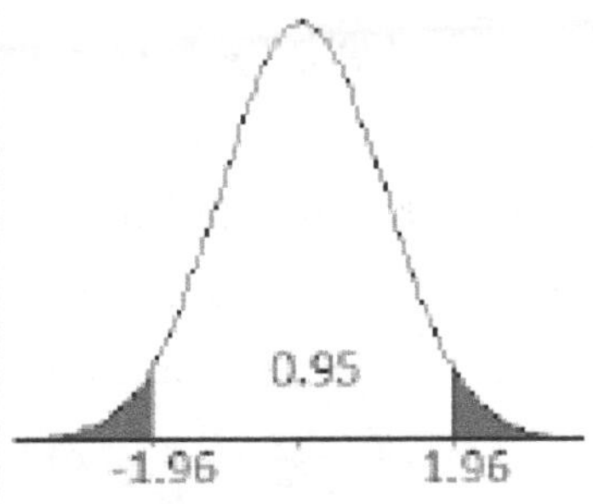

Figure: 8.1 Illustration for z-multiplier being 1.96 for 95% confidence interval.

TABLE 8.1: Z-MULTIPLIERS FOR SPECIFIC LEVELS OF CONFIDENCE.

Confidence	Z Multiplier
90%	1.65
95%	1.96
98%	2.33
99%	2.58

Putting these pieces together, our one-proportion confidence interval takes the form:

$$\hat{p} \pm Z^* \sqrt{\frac{\hat{p}(1-\hat{p})}{n}}$$

where $Z^* \sqrt{\frac{\hat{p}(1-\hat{p})}{n}}$ is the margin of error for the confidence interval.

From these equations and Table 8.1, we should recognize a few general concepts about these intervals, as well as confidence intervals in general:

1. *As the level of confidence increases, the margin of error increases, making our intervals wider.*
2. *As the sample size increases, the standard error decreases, making our intervals narrower.*

Students will sometimes confuse *confidence* with *precision.* Remember that we are trying to estimate with some degree of confidence a range of values for which the parameter will fall. With a wider interval providing more possible outcomes, we in turn are more confident this wider interval is correct in capturing the parameter.

INTERPRETING THE CONFIDENCE INTERVAL

With the primary purpose of our confidence interval being the estimation of a population parameter, our interpretation should reflect this mission. When we say we have 95% confidence or 99% confidence, etc., the meaning relates to how our calculation methods would perform over a long-run series of samples. That is, if we repeated the interval calculation over and over and over, each time using another random sample, we would be confident that 95%, or 99%, or whatever percent of the intervals calculated, would contain the parameter. For instance, if we took a random sample of 1000 subjects from a population, calculated a 95% confidence interval, and repeated this process again and again—say 100 times, we would expect 95 of these 100 confidence intervals to contain the parameter value.

In general, we can build a template of interpreting confidence intervals. This template is:

We are (insert percent) *confident that* (insert parameter and population of interest) *is from* (insert interval bounds).

EXAMPLE 1: WINNING AT HOME IN THE NFL

What is the proportion of NFL teams that win at home? Construct 95% and 99% confidence intervals to estimate this proportion. Using the results of the 2011 NFL season as a sample of all NFL games (see www.repole.com), we find that the home team won 145 of 256 games played.

First, we check to verify that the z-methods can be applied in the calculation of the interval. With 145 "successes" and 111 "failures," both being at least 15, the methods can be used.

Next, we complete our confidence interval equation using 145/256 = 0.57 as our sample proportion and using the appropriate z-multiplier from Table 8.1.

95% Confidence Interval

$$\hat{p} \pm Z^* \sqrt{\frac{\hat{p}(1-\hat{p})}{n}} = 0.57 \pm 1.96^* \sqrt{\frac{0.57(1-0.57)}{256}} = 0.57 \pm 1.96^* 0.031 = 0.57 \pm 0.06$$

Adding and subtracting from 0.57 the margin of error of 0.06, we get a 95% confidence interval of (0.51 to 0.63) or from (51% to 63%). Table 8.2 gives Minitab output for this calculation.

99% Confidence Interval

Here all we need to change is the z-multiplier from 1.96 to 2.58, resulting in a 0.08 margin of error. Adding and subtracting from 0.57 this margin of error of 0.08, we get a 99% confidence interval of (0.49 to 0.65) or from (49% to 65%).

Notice that the 99% confidence interval is *wider* than the 95% confidence interval.

Finally, we need to put into context—give an interpretation of—our resulting confidence interval.

Interpretation: We are 95% confident that the proportion of NFL games won by the home team is from 0.51 to 0.63, or from 51% to 63%. At the 99% level of confidence, this range changes to 0.49 to 0.63, or 49% to 63%.

TABLE 8.2: ANNOTATED MINITAB OUTPUT FOR 95% CONFIDENCE INTERVAL FOR EXAMPLE 1—PROPORTION OF NFL TEAMS WINNING AT HOME.

Variable	X	N	Sample p	95% CI
Home Won	145	256	0.566406	(0.505700, 0.627113)
	↑ Count	↑ Sample Size	↑ Sample Proportion	↑ 95% Confidence Interval Endpoints

EXAMPLE 2: WINNING AT HOME IN COLLEGE FOOTBALL

What is the proportion of college football teams that win at home?[1] Construct a 90% confidence interval to estimate this proportion. Using the results of the 2011 college season (Division 1 or FBS) as a sample of all Division 1 college games (see www.repole.com), we find that the home team won 483 of 748 games played.

1 Home games played at home team's campus stadium. For example, the Georgia-Florida game is played in Jacksonville, so this game was not included.

To start, we check to verify that the z-methods can be applied in the calculation of the interval. With 483 "successes" and 265 "failures," both being at least 15, the methods can be used.

Next, we complete our confidence interval equation, using 483/748 = 0.65 as our sample proportion and using the appropriate z-multiplier from Table 8.1.

90% Confidence Interval

$$\hat{p} \pm Z^* \sqrt{\frac{\hat{p}(1-\hat{p})}{n}} = 0.65 \pm 1.65^* \sqrt{\frac{0.65(1-0.65)}{748}} = 0.65 \pm 1.65^* 0.017 = 0.65 \pm 0.03$$

Adding and subtracting from 0.65 the margin of error of 0.03, we get a 90% confidence interval of (0.62 to 0.68) or from (62% to 68%). Table 8.3 gives annotated Minitab output for this calculation.

Interpretation: We are 90% confident that the proportion of Division 1 college games won by the home team is from 0.62 to 0.68, or from 62% to 68%.

TABLE 8.3: ANNOTATED MINITAB OUTPUT FOR 90% CONFIDENCE INTERVAL FOR EXAMPLE 2—PROPORTION OF COLLEGE FOOTBALL TEAMS WINNING AT HOME.

Variable	X	N	Sample p	90% CI
Home Won	483	748	0.645722	(0.616956, 0.674487)
	↑ Count	↑ Sample Size	↑ Sample Proportion	↑ 90% Confidence Interval Endpoints

EXAMPLE 3: BEATING THE POINT SPREAD IN THE NFL

What is the proportion of NFL home teams beating the point spread? Construct a 98% confidence interval to estimate this proportion. Using the results of the 2011 NFL season as a sample of all NFL games (see www.repole.com), we find that the home covered 123 of 256 games played.

Again, we check to verify that the z-methods can be applied in the calculation of the interval. With 123 "successes" and 133 "failures," both being at least 15, the methods can be used.

Next, we complete our confidence interval equation using 123/256 = 0.48 as our sample proportion and using the appropriate z-multiplier from Table 8.1.

98% Confidence Interval

$$\hat{p} \pm Z^* \sqrt{\frac{\hat{p}(1-\hat{p})}{n}} = 0.48 \pm 2.33^* \sqrt{\frac{0.48(1-0.48)}{256}} = 0.48 \pm 2.33^* 0.031 = 0.48 \pm 0.07$$

Adding and subtracting from 0.48 the margin of error of 0.07, we get a 98% confidence interval of (0.41 to 0.55) or from (41% to 55%). Table 8.4 gives annotated Minitab output for this calculation.

Interpretation: We are 98% confident that the proportion of NFL home teams that cover the spread is from 0.41 to 0.55, or from 41% to 55%.

TABLE 8.4: ANNOTATED MINITAB OUTPUT FOR 98% CONFIDENCE INTERVAL FOR EXAMPLE 3—PROPORTION OF NFL HOME TEAMS THAT BEAT THE POINT SPREAD.

Variable	X	N	Sample p	98% CI
Covered	123	256	0.480469	(0.407826, 0.553112)
	↑ Count	↑ Sample Size	↑ Sample Proportion	↑ 98% Confidence Interval Endpoints

8.2 FINDING SAMPLE SIZE FOR ESTIMATING A POPULATION PROPORTION

When someone begins a study to estimate a population parameter, they typically have an idea of how confident they want to be in their results and within what degree of accuracy—the margin of error. They get started with a set level of confidence and a specified margin of error. We can use these pieces to determine a minimum sample size needed to produce these results by using algebra to solve for n in our margin of error:

$$n = \frac{z^2 \hat{p}(1-\hat{p})}{M.E.^2}$$

Conservative estimate: If we have no preconceived idea of the sample proportion (e.g., previous study results), then a conservative estimate (that is, guaranteeing the largest sample size calculation) is to use 0.5 for the sample proportion. For example, if we wanted to calculate a 95% confidence interval with a margin of error equal to 0.04, then a conservative sample size estimate would be:

$$n = \frac{z^2 \hat{p}(1-\hat{p})}{M.E.^2} = \frac{1.96^2(0.5)(1-0.5)}{0.04^2} = 600.25$$

Since this is the *minimum* sample size and we cannot get 0.25 of a subject, we **round up**. This results in a sample size of 601.

Estimate when proportion value is hypothesized: If we have an idea of a proportion value, then we simply plug that value into the equation. Note that using 0.5 will always produce the largest sample size, and this is why it is called a conservative estimate.

6.3 ONE MEAN CONFIDENCE INTERVALS

Previously, we considered confidence intervals for 1-proportion and our multiplier in our interval used a z-value. But what if our variable of interest is a quantitative variable—points scored, margin of victory, time to complete baseball game—and we want to estimate the population mean? In such a situation, proportion confidence intervals are not appropriate, since our interest is in a **mean** amount and not a proportion.

The solution involves similar techniques for a proportion confidence interval, except we will be interested in estimating the population mean, μ, by using the sample mean, $\bar{X}$. A more significant change comes in choosing our multiplier.

Under certain conditions—population is normally distributed or if sample size is at least 30—the sample mean will approximate a normal distribution. One underlying factor for this application was in knowing the population standard deviation, σ. In practice, knowing the population standard deviation is unlikely. As a result, this, too, is estimated, and we use the sample standard deviation, S or SD. This correction has an effect on the distribution of the sample mean, as this introduces extra error, especially when samples are small. To offset this increased error, we use **t-scores** in place of z-scores. These t-scores come from a t-distribution, which is similar to the standard normal distribution from which we get the z-scores. The similarities are that the t-distribution is symmetrical and centered on 0. A difference is that the standard deviation of the t-distribution is somewhat larger than 1; the standard deviation of the standard normal (Z) distribution. The specific standard deviation value depends on what is called the **degrees of freedom** (**df**). The df will be based on the sample size and are found by **df = n − 1**.

Following our general format for a confidence interval: *Sample Statistic* ± *Margin of Error* and inserting our notation for sample means and using t-scores for multipliers, our confidence interval for one mean will take on the following:

$$\bar{x} \pm t^* \frac{S}{\sqrt{n}}$$

where $t^* \frac{S}{\sqrt{n}}$ is the margin of error for a one-mean confidence intervl and $\frac{S}{\sqrt{n}}$ is the standard error where we replaced the population standard deviation, σ , with the sample standard deviation, *s*.

USING A T-TABLE TO FIND MULTIPLIERS FOR CONFIDENCE INTERVALS ABOUT A MEAN[2]

Below in Figure 8.2 is an portion from the T-table in the appendix. To read this table to find multipliers, we combine the correct degree of freedom (df) row corresponding to the confidence level of interest. For example, if the sample size is 8 and we are interested in a 95% confidence interval for a mean, the correct t-value multiplier would come from matching the df for 7 (from 8 – 1) with the column under 95% confidence level. The corresponding t-value of 2.365 would serve as the multiplier.

T-Table: t Distribution Confidence Interval and Critical Values

	Confidence Level					
	80%	90%	95%	98%	99%	99.8%
	Right Tail Probability					
df	$t_{0.10}$	$t_{0.05}$	$t_{0.025}$	$t_{0.01}$	$t_{0.005}$	$t_{0.001}$
1	3.078	6.314	12.706	31.821	63.657	318.289
2	1.886	2.920	4.303	6.965	9.925	22.328
..	...	...	...	...	...	...
..	...	...	...	...	...	...
7	1.415	1.895	2.365	2.998	3.499	4.785

Figure 8.2: Portion of T-Table.

EXAMPLE 4: AVERAGE POINTS SCORED IN AN NFL GAME

What is the mean number of points scored in an NFL game? Construct 95% and 99% confidence intervals to estimate this proportion. Using the results from a random sample of 25 games played

2 The df in a T-table typical run from 1 to 30 then move up in various increments. This is done as the change in t-values is minimal after reaching sample size of 30. A common practice for df not on the table is to use the closer one without exceeding. As the table indicates, the last row for infinity, ∞, has t-scores that match the Z-table. As sample size increases, the t-distribution approaches the standard normal distribution.

in 2011 as a sample of all NFL games, the sample produced a mean of 50.12 points and standard deviation of 11.71 points.

First, we check to verify that the t-methods can be applied in the calculation of the interval. With a sample size of 25, we would need to assume that the population of points scored in an NFL game were approximately normal, since our sample size is not large enough (at least 30) to apply the Central Limit Theorem.

Next, we complete our confidence interval equation using 50.12 as the sample mean and 11.71 as the sample standard deviation. From the T-table, a portion of which is provided in Figure 8.3, using degrees of freedom (df) of 24, we find the t-multipliers for 95% confidence and 99% confidence are 2.064 and 2.797, respectively.

95% Confidence Interval

$$\overline{x} \pm t^* \frac{S}{\sqrt{n}} = 50.12 \pm 2.064 * \frac{11.71}{\sqrt{25}} = 50.12 \pm 2.064 * 2.342 = 50.12 \pm 4.83$$

Adding and subtracting from 50.12 the margin of error of 4.83, we get a 95% confidence interval of (45.29 to 54.95).

T-Table: t Distribution Confidence Interval and Critical Values

	Confidence Level					
	80%	90%	95%	98%	99%	99.8%
	Right Tail Probability					
df	$t_{0.10}$	$t_{0.05}$	$t_{0.025}$	$t_{0.01}$	$t_{0.005}$	$t_{0.001}$
1	3.078	6.314	12.706	31.821	63.657	318.289
2	1.886	2.920	4.303	6.965	9.925	22.328
..	...	...	...	...	...	...
..	...	...	...	...	...	...
24	1.318	1.711	2.064	2.492	2.797	3.467

Figure 8.3: Portion of T-Table for 95% And 99% Confidence Intervals In Example 4.

99% Confidence Interval

Here all we need to change is the t-multiplier from 2.064 to 2.797, resulting in a 6.55 margin of error. Adding and subtracting from 50.12 this margin of error of 6.55, we get a 99% confidence interval of (43.57 to 56.67). Table 8.5 provides annotated Minitab output for the 95% and 99% confidence intervals.

Notice that the 99% confidence interval is *wider* than the 95% confidence interval.

Finally, we need to put into context—give an interpretation of—our resulting confidence interval.

Interpretation: We are 95% confident that the mean number of points scored in NFL games is from 45.29 to 54.95 points. At the 99% level of confidence, this estimation changes to 43.57 to 56.67 points.

TABLE 8.5: ANNOTATED MINITAB OUTPUT FOR 95% AND 99% CONFIDENCE INTERVAL FOR EXAMPLE 4—MEAN POINTS SCORED IN AN NFL GAME.

Variable	N	Mean	StDev	SE Mean	95% CI	99% CI
Total Points	25	50.12	11.71	2.34	(45.29, 54.95)	(43.57, 56.67)
	↑ Sample Size	↑ Sample Mean	↑ Standard Deviation	↑ Standard Error	↑ Endpoints for 95% Confidence Interval	↑ Endpoints for 99% Confidence Interval

EXAMPLE 5: AVERAGE MARGIN OF VICTORY FOR THE HOME TEAM IN THE NFL

What is the mean margin of victory for the home team in the NFL? Construct a 90% confidence interval to estimate this mean. Using the results of the 2011 NFL season as a sample of all NFL games, we found that the home team won 145 times, with a mean margin of victory of 13.5 points and standard deviation of 10.7 points (see www.nfl.com).

We begin by verifying that the t-methods can be applied in the calculation of the interval. With a sample size of 145, we can assume the sample mean will follow an approximately normal distribution based on the Central Limit Theorem. The t-methods would apply.

Next, we complete our confidence interval equation, using 13.5 as the sample mean and 10.7 as the sample standard deviation. From the T-table, a portion of which is found in Figure 8.4 (page 144), the degrees of freedom (df) are 144. However, since this df value is not listed, we select the closest without exceeding, or df of 100. This gives us a t-multiplier of 1.660 for a 90% confidence interval.

T-Table: t Distribution Confidence Interval and Critical Values

	Confidence Level					
	80%	90%	95%	98%	99%	99.8%
	Right Tail Probability					
df	$t_{0.10}$	$t_{0.05}$	$t_{0.025}$	$t_{0.01}$	$t_{0.005}$	$t_{0.001}$
1	3.078	6.314	12.706	31.821	63.657	318.289
2	1.886	2.920	4.303	6.965	9.925	22.328
..	...	...	...	...	...	...
..	...	...	...	...	...	...
100	1.290	1.660	1.984	2.364	2.626	3.174

Figure 8.4: Portion of T-Table for 90% Confidence Interval in Example 5.

90% Confidence Interval

$$\bar{x} \pm t^* \frac{S}{\sqrt{n}} = 13.5 \pm 1.660 * \frac{10.7}{\sqrt{145}} = 13.5 \pm 1.660 * 0.889 = 13.5 \pm 1.48$$

Adding and subtracting from 13.5 the margin of error of 1.48, we get a 90% confidence interval of (12.02 to 14.98). Table 8.6 offers annotated Minitab output of this interval.

Interpretation: We are 90% confident that the mean margin of victory for NFL home teams is from 12.02 to 14.98 points.

TABLE 8.6: ANNOTATED MINITAB OUTPUT FOR 95% CONFIDENCE INTERVAL FOR EXAMPLE 5—MEAN MARGIN OF VICTORY FOR NFL HOME TEAMS.

Variable	N	Mean	StDev	SE Mean	90% CI
Win Margin	145	13.50	10.70	0.889	(12.029, 14.971)
	↑ Sample Size	↑ Sample Mean	↑ Standard Deviation	↑ Standard Error	↑ Endpoints for 90% Confidence Interval

EXAMPLE 6: HOW FAR DO THE TOP COLLEGE RECRUITS TRAVEL IN SELECTING A COLLEGE?

What is the mean driving distance between the ESPN Top 150 football recruits and their chosen college? Using the top 36 players listed as ESPN Top 150 recruits for 2012 and www.travelmath.com, the mean driving distance between the recruit's hometown and college was 439.4 miles, with a standard deviation of 542.4 miles. Calculate a 98% confidence interval for this mean.

As always, we check to verify that the t-methods can be applied in the calculation of the interval. With a sample size of 36, we can assume the sample mean will follow an approximately normal distribution based on the Central Limit Theorem. The t-methods would apply.

Next, we complete our confidence interval equation using 439.4 as the sample mean and 542.4 as the sample standard deviation. From the T-table, a portion of which is provided in Figure 8.5, the degrees of freedom (df) are 35. This gives us a t-multiplier 2.438 for a 98% confidence interval.

T-Table: t Distribution Confidence Interval and Critical Values

	Confidence Level					
	80%	90%	95%	98%	99%	99.8%
	Right Tail Probability					
df	$t_{0.10}$	$t_{0.05}$	$t_{0.025}$	$t_{0.01}$	$t_{0.005}$	$t_{0.001}$
1	3.078	6.314	12.706	31.821	63.657	318.289
2	1.886	2.920	4.303	6.965	9.925	22.328
..	...	...	...	...	...	...
..	...	...	...	...	...	...
35	1.306	1.690	2.030	2.438	2.724	3.340

Figure 8.5: Portion of T-Table for 98% confidence interval in Example 6.

98% Confidence Interval

$$\bar{x} \pm t^* \frac{s}{\sqrt{n}} = 439.4 \pm 2.438 * \frac{542.4}{\sqrt{36}} = 439.4 \pm 2.438 * 90.4 = 439.4 \pm 220.4$$

Adding and subtracting from 439.4 the margin of error of 220.4, we get a 98% confidence interval of (219.0 to 659.8). Table 8.7 gives annotate Minitab output for this calculation.

Interpretation: We are 98% confident that the mean driving distance between ESPN Top 150 football recruits and their chosen college is from 219 to 659.8 miles.

TABLE 8.7: ANNOTATED MINITAB OUTPUT FOR 98% CONFIDENCE INTERVAL FOR EXAMPLE 6—MEAN DISTANCE TOP COLLEGE FOOTBALL RECRUITS TRAVEL TO SELECTED COLLEGE.

Variable	N	Mean	StDev	SE Mean	98% CI
Distance	36	439.4	542.4	90.4	(219.0, 659.8)
	↑ Sample Size	↑ Sample Mean	↑ Standard Deviation	↑ Standard Error	↑ Endpoints for 98% Confidence Interval

6.4 FINDING SAMPLE SIZE FOR ESTIMATING A POPULATION MEAN

Calculating sample size for estimating a population mean is similar to that for estimating a population proportion: We solve for n in our margin for error. However, since the t-distribution is not as neat as the standard normal distribution, the process can be iterative. This means that we would solve, reset, solve, reset, etc., until we reached a conclusion. Yet, we can avoid this iterative process if we employ an approximate method based on the t-distribution, approaching the standard normal distribution as the sample size increases. This approximate method invokes the following formula:

$$n = \left(\frac{Z * \sigma}{M.E.} \right)^2$$

where σ is a population standard deviation possibly based on prior studies or knowledge, and Z comes from the z-multipliers in Table 8.1. Another possible way to estimate this standard deviation is to consider the Empirical Rule, where almost all observations fall within three standard deviations of the mean. Here, we could use an educated guess on the range of the data and divide by 4 to get a suitable value for σ.

Example: What sample size would be needed to estimate the mean recruiting distance in Example 3 if we wanted a margin of error of 300 miles with a 95% level of confidence? Before figuring this out, think of what sample size you would guess is required: maybe 20, or 50, possibly more? The longest driving distance in the continental United States is about 3500 miles from the southern tip of Florida to Washington State. Dividing 3500 by 4, we get a crude guess of 875 miles for σ. For a 95% level of confidence:

$$n = \left(\frac{1.96 * 875}{300} \right)^2 = 5.72^2 = 32.7 \text{ or } 33.$$

A surprisingly small sample! How was your guess?

EXPRESSIONS AND FORMULAS

1. Formula for a one-proportion confidence interval is:

   $\hat{p} \pm Z^* \sqrt{\frac{\hat{p}(1-\hat{p})}{n}}$ where "Z" is a multiplier based on the level of confidence. Some common confidence levels and corresponding multipliers are:

Confidence	Z Multiplier
90%	1.65
95%	1.96
98%	2.33
99%	2.58

2. The margin of error for a one-proportion confidence interval is:

$$Z^* \sqrt{\frac{\hat{p}(1-p)}{n}}$$

3. To find the sample size required for a specific margin of error and confidence level for a one-proportion confidence interval (use 0.5 as a conservative estimate of is one is not provided):

$$n = \frac{z^2 \hat{p}(1-\hat{p})}{M.E.^2}$$

4. Formula for a one-mean confidence interval is:

   $\bar{x} \pm t^* \frac{S}{\sqrt{n}}$ where "t" is a t-multiplier from the T-table.

5. DF stands for "degrees of freedom" and is found by n – 1.
6. The margin of error for a one-mean confidence interval is:

$$t^* \frac{S}{\sqrt{n}}$$

7. To find the sample size required for a specific margin of error and confidence level for a one-mean confidence interval:

$$n = \left(\frac{Z * \sigma}{M.E.}\right)^2$$ where "z" can come from the z-multipliers provided in No. 1 and σ is the population standard deviation which can be estimated by taking the range and dividing by 4.

9 Hypothesis Testing

Hypothesis testing is the evaluation of a statement and claim about a population. It is one example of statistical inference. Whether or not we reject (or fail to reject) the statement comes from information contained in the sample. Hypothesis testing is not an absolute science. It is possible that a hypothesis may or may not be rejected, given a certain sample, but if another sample is taken and the hypothesis is retested, a different conclusion could be reached. Chapter 9 explores the process of hypothesis testing of a single population as well as testing whether or not two populations have the same mean.

HYPOTHESIS TESTING

By Justin Bateh and Bert G. Wachsmuth

***Preview**: It is one thing to develop a hypothesis but quite another to actually prove it beyond a reasonable doubt. Your intuition may lead you to believe that men and women who are obese are more likely to die early than those who are of normal weight. While that conclusion may seem logical, you cannot simply assume that it is true. In order to prove or disprove the hypothesis, you must first develop a series of experiments to determine the truth or falsehood of your assumption. You might look at the distributions of weight across a given population and compare that information to mortality statistics. In the case of early mortality and excess weight, the purpose of the study is to find out whether obese individuals do in fact have shorter life spans than their thinner counterparts. When developing a statistical test, we introduce a null hypothesis, which refers to the status quo, and a competing alternative hypothesis. We then gather data that in turn will support either the null or the alternative hypothesis. If we find sufficient evidence to support the alternative, we reject the null hypothesis. In the case outlined earlier, the null hypothesis would mean there is no difference in longevity between obese individuals and nonobese ones, whereas the alternative one is that nonobese people would live longer. We will develop statistical tests for a mean, a difference of means test, and a test for a proportion.*

Learning Objectives: At the conclusion of this chapter, you should be able to:

1. Describe the basic principles of hypothesis testing
2. Use hypothesis testing to test for a mean, a difference of means, and a proportion

3. Evaluate the assumptions of each hypothesis-testing procedure
4. Avoid the pitfalls involved in hypothesis testing
5. Describe the ethical issues involved in hypothesis testing

INTRODUCTION

In the previous chapter we investigated how to provide estimates for population parameters based on sample data, complete with error estimation. Now we want to handle "Yes or No" questions such as "Is the average weight of a bag of chips really 450 gr?" or "Is new medication X better than medication Y?"; of course we want to include an error estimate with our answer. The technical term for what we will describe in this chapter is "hypothesis testing."

INNOCENT UNTIL PROVEN GUILTY: HYPOTHESIS TESTING AS A TRIAL BY JURY

Consider the following case: A company is labeling their product to weigh, on average, 10 oz. However, the last time we bought that product it only weighed 8.5 oz, so either we were unlucky to get one of the rare but possible cases where the weight differs a lot from the listed mean or the manufacturer is cheating and puts less product in the package than they are claiming on the label. We suspect that the company is indeed cheating and want to determine whether our suspicion is true or not.

If the company was correct in saying that their packages weigh 10 oz on average, it does not mean that each and every package weighs exactly 10 oz. However, it is likely that most packages weigh *close* to 10 oz and only a few weigh a lot less or more. Conversely, if I found a package that weighs a lot more or a lot less than 10 oz, then it seems likely that the company's claim may be wrong. In fact, the chances that the original claim is incorrect are higher the more the weights of our sample differ from 10 oz.

As another example, we suppose a new medical drug claims to work better in lowering a person's cholesterol level than currently existing drugs. From past experiments we know that the existing drugs lower cholesterol levels by 10 percent, on average. We want to determine whether the new drug is really more effective than the existing ones.

To check the assumption that the new drug works better than old drugs, we could test it on a sample of, say, 100 patients. If we find that the drug for these 100 patients lowers the cholesterol level by more than 10 percent it seems likely that it indeed works better than the other drugs. In fact, the higher the difference to 10 percent, the more likely it seems that the drug is really better. The question is: What exactly do we mean when we say that the difference should be higher than 10 percent. Is 11 percent already good enough? Or should we require a difference of 20 percent before conceding that the new drug is better than the old ones.

In general, we are interested in testing a particular hypothesis and we want to decide whether it is true or not. Moreover, we want to associate a probability with our decision so that we know how certain (or uncertain) we are about our decision.

We will approach this problem like a trial. Recall that in a standard trial in front of a judge or jury there are two mutually exclusive hypotheses: The defendant is either guilty or not guilty.

During the trial evidence is collected and weighed either in favor of the defendant being guilty or in favor of the defendant being not guilty. At the end of the trial the judge (or jury) decides between the two alternatives and either convicts the defendant (if he/she was assumed to be proven guilty beyond a reasonable doubt) or lets them go (if there was sufficient doubt in the defendant's guilt). Note that if the judge (or jury) decides a defendant is not guilty, it does not necessarily mean he/she is innocent. It simply means there was not enough evidence for a conviction. Now we will formalize this procedure.

Definition: A statistical test involves four elements.

- **Null Hypothesis** (written as H_0): The "tried and true situation," "the status quo," or "innocent until proven guilty."
- **Alternative Hypothesis** (written as H_a): This is what you *suspect* is *really* true, the new situation, "guilty beyond a reasonable doubt"—in general, it is the opposite of the null hypothesis.
- **Test Statistics**: Collect evidence—in our case we usually select a random sample and compute some number based on that sample data.
- **Rejection Region**: Do we reject the null hypothesis (and therefore accept the alternative, which was the opposite of null hypothesis) or do we declare our test inconclusive? Moreover, if we do decide to reject the null hypothesis, what is the probability that our decision is correct?

Please note that our final conclusion is *always one of two options*: We either *reject* the null hypothesis or we declare the test *inconclusive*. We never conclude anything else, such as accepting the null hypothesis.

- Rejecting the null hypothesis when in fact it is true is called *type-1 error*. It should, of course, be small so that we can be confident in our decision to reject the null hypothesis.
- Accepting the null hypothesis when in fact it is false is called a *type-2 error*. This type of error is not covered by our procedure since we will never accept the null hypothesis; we instead declare our test inconclusive if necessary.

Most importantly, your conclusion should always be stated in terms that are easy to understand for anyone, even if they had no statistical training, and it is preferable using the terms of the original hypothesis.

Example: A new antihypertensive drug is tested. It is supposed to lower blood pressure more than other drugs. Other drugs have been found to lower the pressure by 10 mmHg on average, but we suspect (or hope) that our new drug will work better. To collect evidence, we select a random sample of size $n = 62$ (say), administer the new drug, and find a sample mean of 11.3 and a sample standard deviation of 5.1. Is the new drug better than the old drugs, that is, does the new drug lower blood pressure more than other drugs?

Since the sample mean is 11.3, which is more than other drugs, it looks like this sample mean supports the claim (because the mean from our sample is indeed bigger than 10). But the question is whether that difference is so big that it could not have happened by chance if the null hypothesis was true. In other words, we want to know if the difference is *statistically significant.* To find out, we set up the four components of a statistical test.

- The null hypothesis H_0 is the "tried and true" assumption that all drugs are about the same and the new drug has about the same effect as all other drugs. Thus, the null hypothesis is that the average decrease in blood pressure (the population mean) is 10 mmHg, just as for all other drugs. Thus H_0: $\mu = 10$.
- The alternative hypothesis H_a is what we hope to be true, that is, the new drug results in a higher decrease than the traditional dugs. Thus, the alternative hypothesis is that the average decrease in blood pressure (the population mean) is different from 10 mmHg. Hence H_a: $\mu \neq 10$.
- For our test statistics we collect evidence in the form of a random sample. We found that for this random sample the sample mean is 11.3 mmHg, the sample standard deviation is 5.1 mmHg, and the sample size N is 62. These figures convert into a standard z-score of $z = 2.007$ (as we will soon see).
- Rejection region: Finally we use the test statistics $z = 2.007$ to compute the probability p that this could happen due to chance if the null hypothesis was true. This p is the probability of committing an error in deciding to reject the null hypothesis when in fact it was true (the type-1 error). If that error is small, we do indeed decide to reject the null hypothesis; otherwise we will declare the test to be inconclusive. It turns out that $p = 0.044$ or 4.4 percent (see the following text for the computation).

So, if we decide to reject the null hypothesis, this decision is invalid with a probability of about 4 percent. That is an acceptable risk for us, so we indeed decide to *reject the null hypothesis* and thus accept the alternative. This means, in terms of our original problem, that there is sufficient evidence to conclude that the new drug is better than the existing drugs in lowering blood pressure. In fact, our alternative hypothesis is that the new drug is different from the old drugs, but since the sample mean is indeed bigger, the difference must be that the new drug works better.

TESTING HYPOTHESIS FOR MEAN

In this section we will answer the question: Is the population mean μ equal to a particular number or not? We will follow the outline of a statistical test as described in the previous section, but adjust the four elements of the test to our situation of testing for a population mean. It turns out that such a test is slightly different depending on the sample size *n*.

LARGE SAMPLE SIZE ($n > 30$)

Our first test is a test for a sample mean when the sample size is relatively large:

- Null hypothesis: H_0: $\mu = \mu_0$ where μ_0 is a fixed number
- Alternative hypothesis: H_a: $\mu \neq \mu_0$
- Test statistics: $z_0 = \dfrac{\overline{x} - \mu_0}{(s / \sqrt{n})}$
- Rejection region: $p = 2P(z > |Z_0|) = 2(1 - NORMDIST(ABS(z_0), 0.1, true))$. If p is small, reject the null hypothesis; otherwise the test is inconclusive.

In other words, we compute the *z*-score to help us decide between null and alternative hypotheses. This makes sense, since we know that sample means are normal by the Central Limit Theorem if the sample size is large. Thus, assuming the null hypothesis is true, the distribution of sample means itself has mean μ_0 with standard deviation $s / \sqrt{n}$. Therefore, the difference between the actually measured sample mean $\overline{x}$ and the assumed population mean μ_0 being large would be unlikely, so that if that difference *was indeed large* the null hypothesis could not be true and we are inclined to reject it. Converting to *z*-scores enables us to compute the actual probability p that the sample mean could be as far away from μ_0 as has been measured, assuming the null hypothesis was true.

In most cases you pick a predetermined number α, called the *level of significance*, *before* you start any calculations, that specifies the maximum error you are willing to accept. Then you conduct the test as described and reject the null hypothesis if $p < \alpha$; if not, the test was inconclusive. Typically, $\alpha = 0.1$, $\alpha = 0.05$, or $\alpha = 0.01$ (compare this to a 90 percent, 95 percent, or 99 percent confidence interval, respectively).

Let us review the previous example, now that we have introduced the appropriate formulas.

Example: A new antihypertensive drug is tested. It is supposed to lower blood pressure more than other drugs. Other drugs have been found to lower the pressure by 10 mmHg on average, so we suspect (or hope) that our drug will lower blood pressure by more than 10 mmHg. To collect evidence, a random sample of size $n =$ 62 was selected (say), which was found to have a sample mean of 11.3 and a sample standard deviation of 5.1. Conduct a test at the $\alpha = 0.05$ level of significance.

The two competing hypotheses are:

$$H_0: \mu = 10.0$$
$$H_a: \mu \neq 10.0.$$

The test statistics is:

$$z_0 = \frac{x - \mu_0}{(s / \sqrt{n})} = \frac{11.3 - 10.0}{5.1 / \sqrt{62}} = \frac{1.3}{0.6477} = 2.007.$$

The rejection region is:

$$p = 2P(z > |z_0|) = 2(1 - NORMDIST(ABS(2.007), 0, 1, true)) = 2 * 0.022 = 0.044.$$

Since $0.044 = p < \alpha = 0.05$, we reject the null hypothesis and accept the alternative. Thus, the new drug is more effective than the old one with an error of 4.4 percent.

COMMENTS

- The null hypothesis for this test is that the population mean is equal to a particular number. That number is usually thought of as the "default value," the "status quo," or the "best guess" value. It is usually mentioned explicitly somewhere in the problem.
- The alternative hypothesis could actually be split into two cases: a so-called two-tailed test where $\mu \neq \mu_0$ or a one-tailed test where either $\mu > \mu_0$ or $\mu < \mu_0$. However, for simplicity we will restrict ourselves to the more conservative two-tailed case here while discussing one-tailed tests in a later section.
- Please note that even if we reject a null hypothesis and hence accept the alternative it is still possible that the null hypothesis is true. However, the probability with which that can happen is p, which is small if we choose this answer (smaller than our predetermined comfort level α). This error of rejecting the null hypothesis even though it is true is called a *type-1 error*.
- In our statistical language there are two outcomes for a test: reject H_0 or inconclusive test. For real problems, however, you should always phrase your conclusion in terms that are relevant for the particular problem and easy to understand even if you knew nothing about statistics.

After all this talk it is high time for another example.

Example: Bottles of ketchup are filled automatically by a machine that must be adjusted periodically to increase or decrease the average content per bottle. Each bottle is supposed to contain 18 oz. It is important to detect an average content significantly above or below 18 oz so that the machine can be adjusted; too much ketchup per bottle would be unprofitable, while too little would be a poor business practice and open the company up to law suits about invalid labeling. We select a random sample of 32 bottles filled by the machine and compute their average weight to be 18.24 with a standard deviation of 0.7334. Should we adjust the machine? Use a comfort level of 5 percent.

We can see right away that the average weight of our sample, being 18.24 oz, is indeed different from what it is supposed to be (18 oz), but the question is whether the difference is statistically significant (or "large enough" so that it would be unlikely if the null hypothesis was true). Our statistical test for the mean will provide the answer. The two competing hypotheses are:

$$H_0: \mu = 18.0$$
$$H_a: \mu \neq 18.0.$$

The test statistics is:

$$z_0 = \frac{\overline{x} - \mu_0}{(s / \sqrt{n})} = \frac{18.24 - 18.0}{0.7334 / \sqrt{32}} = \frac{0.24}{0.1296} = 1.852.$$

The rejection region is defined via:

$$p = 2P(z > |z_0|) = 2(1 - NORMDIST(1.852,\ 0,1,\ true)) = 0.064.$$

This time we have $0.064 = p > \alpha = 0.05$ so that our test is *inconclusive*. For our example, this means that we do not know conclusively if the machine works correctly or not. In particular, we would not adjust the machine at this time.

Example: In a nutrition study, 48 calves were fed "factor X" exclusively for six weeks. The weight gain was recorded for each calf, yielding a sample mean of 22.4 lb and a standard deviation of 11.5 lb. Other nutritional supplements are known to cause an average weight gain of about 20 lb in six weeks. Can we conclude from this evidence that, in general, a six-week diet of "factor X" will yield an average weight gain of 20 lb or more at the 1 percent level of significance? In other words, is "factor X" feed significantly better than standard supplements?

Null hypothesis: H_0: $\mu = 20$, that is, there is no improvement, everything is as it has always been.

Alternative hypothesis: H_a: $\mu \neq 20$ (we actually want to know whether "factor X" results in *higher* average weight gains, so that our alternative hypothesis really should be H_a: $\mu > 20$ but that would be a one-tailed test, which we will not conduct.

Test statistics: Sample mean is 22.4, standard deviation is 11.5, and sample size is 48. That makes the *z*-score $z_0 = \frac{22.4 - 20.0}{11.5 / \sqrt{48}} = 1.446.$

We finally use Excel to compute $p = 2 * (1 - NORMSDIST(1.446)) = 0.148$ or 14.8 percent. This probability is relatively large: If we reject the null hypothesis, the probability that we make a mistake is 14.8 percent. This is larger than our comfort level of 1 percent, so our conclusion is: The test is inconclusive, which means there is not enough evidence to decide whether "factor X" feed is better (or worse) than the regular feed.

Example: A group of secondary education student teachers were given 2.5 days of training in interpersonal communication group work. The effect of such a training session on the dogmatic nature of the student teachers was measured as the difference of scores on the "Rokeach dogmatism test" given before and after the training session. The difference "post minus pre score" was recorded as follows:

$$-16, -5, 4, 19, -40, -16, -29, 15, -2, 0, 5, -23, -3,$$
$$16, -8, 9, -14, -33, -64, -33.$$

Can we conclude from this evidence that the training session makes student teachers less dogmatic (at the 5 percent level of significance)?

We can easily compute (using Excel) that the sample mean is -10.9 and the standard deviation is 21.33. The sample size is $N = 20$, which is a problem, since N should be at least 30 to use the procedure introduced earlier. So, we need to define the procedure to test for a sample mean if the sample size is small before we can continue.

SMALL SAMPLE SIZE ($N \leq 30$)

In this section we will adjust our statistical test for the population mean to apply to small sample situations. Fortunately (sic!), this will be easy—in fact, once you understand one statistical test, additional tests are easy since they all follow a similar framework.

The only difference in performing a "small sample" statistical test for the mean as opposed to our "large sample" test is that we do not use the normal distribution as prescribed by the Central Limit theorem, but instead the more conservative t-distribution introduced earlier.

Fix an error level you are comfortable with (as usual, something like 10 percent, 5 percent, or 1 percent is most common) and denote that "comfortable" error level by α (our *level of significance*). Then set up the test as follows:

- Null hypothesis: H_0: $\mu = \mu_0$, where μ_0 is a fixed number
- Alternative hypothesis: H_a: $\mu \neq \mu_0$

- Test statistics: $t_0 = \dfrac{\overline{x} - \mu_0}{(s / \sqrt{n})}$

- Rejection region: $p = 2P(t > |t_0|) = TDIST(ABS(t_0),df,2)$, where $df = n - 1$. If $p < \alpha$, reject the null hypothesis; otherwise the test is inconclusive.

Note that the null and alternative hypothesis for this test are the same as before; the calculation of the test statistics is the same as well, but the result is called t_0 instead of z_0. The final probability p, however, is computed using the t-distribution. To see how this works, let us reconsider our last example.

Example: A group of secondary education student teachers were given 2.5 days of training in interpersonal communication group work. The effect of such a training session on the dogmatic nature of the student teachers was measured as the difference of scores on the "Rokeach dogmatism test" given before and after the training session. The difference "post minus pre score" was recorded as follows:

$$-16, -5, 4, 19, -40, -16, -29, 15, -2, 0, 5, -23, -3, 16,$$
$$-8, 9, -14, -33, -64, -33.$$

Can we conclude from this evidence that the training session makes student teachers less dogmatic at the 5 percent level of significance?

We have already computed the mean $\overline{x} = -10.9$ and the standard deviation s=21.33. The sample size is N=20, so our test goes as follows:

- Null hypothesis: H_0: $\mu = 0$,
- Alternative hypothesis: H_a: $\mu \neq \mu_0$

- Test statistics: $t_0 = \dfrac{\overline{x} - \mu_0}{(s / \sqrt{n})} = \dfrac{-10.9 - 0}{21.33 / \sqrt{20}} = \dfrac{10.9\sqrt{10}}{21.33} = -2.285$

- Rejection region: $p = 2P(t > 2.285) = TDIST\,(2.285, 20 - 1, 2) = 0.034$. Since $0.034 = p < \alpha = 0.05$, we reject the null hypothesis and conclude that the training indeed had an impact.

To be picky, we do not want to know whether the training had an impact ($\mu \neq 0$) but we really want to know if the training made the student teachers *less* dogmatic ($\mu < 0$). Technically this amounts to a one-tailed test, which we will cover a little later in this chapter. Here is one more example.

Examples: Suppose GAP, the clothing store, wants to introduce their line of clothing for women to another country. But their clothing sizes are based on the assumption that the average size of a woman is 162 cm. To determine whether they can simply ship the clothes to the new country they select five women at random in the target country and determine their heights as follows:

149, 165, 150, 158, 153.

Should they adjust their line of clothing or they ship them without change? Make sure to decide at the 0.05 level.

By now statistical testing is second nature:

- Null hypothesis: H_0: $\mu = 162$
- Alternative hypothesis: H_a: $\mu \neq 162$
- Test statistics: $t_0 = \dfrac{\overline{x} - \mu_0}{(s / \sqrt{n})} = \dfrac{155 - 162}{6.59 / \sqrt{3}} = -2.37$
- Rejection region: $p = 2P(t > 2.37) = TDIST(2.37,5 - 1,2) = 0.077$. Since $0.077 = p > \alpha = 0.05$, the test is inconclusive.

Note that our test is inconclusive, which does not mean that we accept the null hypothesis. Thus, we do not recommend *anything* to GAP. Using common sense, however, we could suggest that GAP conduct a new study but this time with a random sample of (much) larger size, something like 100 or more. Hopefully the new study will provide statistically significant evidence.

DIFFERENCE OF MEANS TEST

Our next test applies to differences of means. Such tests are common when you conduct a study involving two groups. In many medical trials, for example, subjects are randomly divided into two groups: One group receives a new drug and the second receives a placebo (sugar pill). Then a researcher measures any differences between the two groups to check the efficacy of the new medication.

While our test for a single mean used the sample size to distinguish between two slightly different procedures, a test for the difference of two means uses the variances of the two underlying populations to distinguish between two different procedures. We use the ratio of sample variances s_1^2 / s_2^2 to decide which case to use:

If the ratio of sample variances s_1^2/s_2^2 is between 0.5 and 2 we assume that the population variances are approximately equal and use the procedure for equal variances, otherwise that for unequal variances.

EQUAL VARIANCES

Suppose that two independent samples with sizes n_1 and n_2, are selected from two populations that have approximately the same population variances.

Compute the *pooled standard deviation* $S_p = \sqrt{\dfrac{(n_1 - 1)s_1^2 + (n_2 - 1)s_2^2}{n_1 + n_2 - 2}}$ as well as *joint standard error* $SE = S_p\sqrt{\dfrac{1}{n_1} + \dfrac{1}{n_2}}$. Then a two-sample test about the difference of means goes as follows:

- Null hypothesis: H_0: $\mu_1 - \mu_2 = c$, where c is some constant
- Alternative hypothesis: H_a: $\mu_1 - \mu_2 \neq c$
- Test statistics: $t_0 = \dfrac{\bar{x}_1 - \bar{x}_2 - c}{SE}$, where SE is the joint standard error (see earlier)
- Rejection region: $p = 2P(t > |t_0|) = TDIST(ABS\ (t_0), df, 2)$. with $df = n_1 + n_2 - 2$. If p is small, reject the null hypothesis; otherwise the test is inconclusive.

As in previous test, "p is small" means that $p < \alpha$ for some fixed number α, typically 0.1, 0.05, or 0.01.

Example: Two procedures to determine the amylase in human body fluids were studied. The "original" method is considered to be an acceptable standard method, while the "new" method uses a smaller volume of water, making it more convenient as well as more economical. Proponents of the new method claim that the amylase values obtained by the new method yields better results, on average, than the original method. A test using the original method was conducted on 14 subjects and the test with the new method on 15 subjects, giving the data displayed in Table 9.1. Test the claim at the 1 percent level.

TABLE 9.1 DATA FOR AMYLASE ANALYSIS EXAMPLE

Original	38	48	58	53	75	58	59	46	69	59	81	44	56	50	
New	46	57	73	60	86	67	65	58	85	74	96	55	71	63	74

Using Excel we find the means and standard deviations of the two variables as:

$$n_1 = 14,\ \bar{x}_1 = 56.714 \text{ and } s_1 = 11.932$$

$$n_1 = 15,\ \bar{x}_2 = 68.667 \text{ and } s_2 = 13.281$$

Note that $\frac{s_1^2}{s_2^2} = \frac{11.932^2}{13.281^2} = 0.8$, which is between 0.5 and 2 so that we can indeed use the procedure for equal variances. The test for the difference of means therefore is:

- Null hypothesis: $\mu_1 - \mu_2 = 0$, where c is some constant
- Alternative hypothesis: $\mu_1 - \mu_2 \neq 0$
  - Pooled standard deviation:

$$S_p = \sqrt{\frac{(n_1 - 1)s_1^2 + (n_2 - 1)s_2^2}{n_1 + n_2 - 2}} = \sqrt{\frac{13 \cdot 11.932^2 + 14 \cdot 13.281^2}{14 + 15 - 2}} = 12.649$$

  - Joint standard error:

$$SE = s_p \sqrt{\frac{1}{n_1} + \frac{1}{n_2}} = 12.649 \cdot 0.3716 = 4.7005$$

- Test statistics: $t_0 = \frac{56.714 - 68.667}{4.7005} = \frac{-11.952}{4.7005} = -2.5427$
- Rejection region: $p = 2P(t > |t_0|) = TDIST(2.5427, 27, 2) = 0.017$. Since p is (just barely) larger than 0.01, our test is inconclusive at the 1 percent level.

This means that there is not enough evidence to conclude that the two methods of checking amylase are different. In particular, neither method can be called better than the other. Now it is tempting to change the value of α to 0.05, because at that level the test *would* be conclusive. But that is *not* correct. The value of α should be chosen carefully prior to starting your experiment. Presumably whatever reason made you decide on a 1 percent value has not changed. Adjusting α after the fact amounts to fixing the data to support whatever conclusion you want to come out.

UNEQUAL VARIANCES

Suppose we have two independent samples with sizes n_1 and n_2, selected from populations with *unequal variances*. Compute the *joint standard error* $SE = \sqrt{\frac{s_1^2}{n_1} + \frac{s_2^2}{n_2}}$. Then a two-sample test about the difference of means goes as follows:

- Null hypothesis: H_0: $\mu_1 - \mu_2 = c$, where c is some constant
- Alternative hypothesis: H_a: $\mu_1 - \mu_2 \neq c$
- Test statistics: $t_0 = \frac{\bar{x}_1 - \bar{x}_2 - c}{SE}$, where SE is the joint standard error defined earlier
- Rejection region: $p = 2P(t > |t_0|) = TDIST(ABS(t_0), df, 2))$.

  with degree of freedom $df = \frac{\left(\frac{s_1^2}{n_1} + \frac{s_2^2}{n_2}\right)^2}{\frac{\left(\frac{s_1^2}{n_1}\right)^2}{n_1 - 1} + \frac{\left(\frac{s_2^2}{n_2}\right)^2}{n_2 - 1}}$. (use the nearest integer). If p is small, reject the null hypothesis; otherwise the test is inconclusive.

As usual, "p is small" means that $p < \alpha$ for some fixed number α, typically 0.1, 0.05, or 0.01.

Example: The data file employeenumeric-split.xls contains the salaries for the Acme Widget Company, separated by sex. Use that data to test the hypothesis that women make at least $10,000 less on average than men at that company.
www.betterbusinessdecisions.org/data/employeenumeric-split.xls

---

Since we have the raw data we could use the appropriate test procedure from the Analysis ToolPak (which you should try as practice—see the following text), but we will first use the manual procedure outlined earlier. First, we need to find the mean and standard deviations for the two samples of our data.

	Mean ($)	Standard deviation ($)	N
Males	41,442	19,499.21	258
Females	26,032	7,558.02	216

Next, we need to decide if the variances are equal or not by checking the ratio of the sample variances:

$$\frac{s_1^2}{s_2^2} = \frac{19{,}499.21^2}{7{,}558.02^2} = 6.65.$$

This ratio is greater than 1, so we need to use the "unequal variance" procedure. Now we can proceed with our two-sample test as usual:

- Null hypothesis: H_0: $\mu_1 - \mu_2 \neq \$10{,}000$
- Alternative hypothesis: H_a: $\mu_1 - \mu_2 \neq \$10{,}000$
  - Joint standard error:

$$SE = \sqrt{\frac{s_1^2}{n_1} + \frac{s_2^2}{n_2}} = \sqrt{\frac{19499.21^2}{258} + \frac{7558.02^2}{216}} = 1318.4$$

- Degree of freedom $df = \dfrac{\left(\dfrac{s_1^2}{n_1} + \dfrac{s_2^2}{n_2}\right)^2}{\dfrac{\left(\dfrac{s_1^2}{n_1}\right)^2}{n_1 - 1} + \dfrac{\left(\dfrac{s_2^2}{n_2}\right)^2}{n_2 - 1}} = 344.26$ (closest integer) so that $df = 344$

- Test statistics: $t_0 = \dfrac{(41442 - 26032) - 10000}{1318.4} = 4.103$

- Rejection region: $p = 2P(t > 4.103) = TDIST(4.103{,}344{,}2) = 0.00005$. Since $p < 0.01$, we reject the null hypothesis and accept the alternative.

Thus, the difference in average salary between men and women at the Acme Widget Company is at least \$10,000 and we are very sure that this answer is correct (since $p = 0.00005$). Note that our test actually confirms that the difference is *not equal to* \$10,000, but looking at the actual values of the means as computed by Excel we can clearly conclude that the difference must be more than \$10,000 (it is certainly not less). In fact, a one-tailed test would be more appropriate here (see the "One-Tailed and Two-Tailed Tests" section), which would show indeed that men make at least \$10,000 more than women.

t-test: Two-Sample assuming Equal Variances		
	Original	New
Mean	56.71429	68.66667
Variance	142.3736	176.381
Observations	14	15
Pooled Variance	160.0071	
Hypothesized Mean Difference	0	
Degrees of Freedom df	27	
t-Statistic	−2.5427	
P(T<=t) one-tail	0.008522	
t Critical one-tail	1.703288	
P(T<=t) two-tail	0.017045	
t Critical two-tail	2.051831	

t-test: Two-Sample assuming Unequal Variances		
	Male	Female
Mean	41441.78	26031.92
Variance	3.8E+08	57123688
Observations	258	216
Hypothesized Mean Difference	10000	
Degrees of Freedom df	344	
t-Statistic	4.103352	
P(T<=t) one-tail	2.54E-05	
t Critical one-tail	1.649295	
P(T<=t) two-tail	5.09E-05	
t Critical two-tail	1.966884	

Figure 9.1 ***Output of Analysis ToolPak two-sample t-test with equal variance (amylase example, left) and with unequal variances (salary example, right)***

Excel actually provides several procedures in the Analysis ToolPak to help conduct this test, including the "t-test assuming unequal variances" and the "t-test assuming equal variances." We leave the details to you, but the output Excel produces for the last two examples is shown in Figure 9.1.

TESTING HYPOTHESIS FOR PROPORTION

Finally, let us introduce one more test, namely, testing for a proportion. This will be useful because it works on non-numerical variables whereas our previous tests required numerical ones. Recall that a proportion p is the number of successes divided by the total number of tries in a Bernoulli trial that has only two outcomes called success or failure. Our goal is to decide what the (unknown) probability of success might be, or—to phrase it in terms appropriate for a test—whether the probability of success equals a specific value or not. The test has the form:

- Null hypothesis: H_0: $\pi = p_0$
- Alternative hypothesis: H_0: $\pi \neq p_0$
- Test statistics: $z_0 = \dfrac{\hat{p} - p_0}{SE}$, where $SE = \sqrt{\dfrac{p_0 \cdot (1 - p_0)}{n}}$
- Rejection region: $p = 2(1 - NORMDIST(ABS(z_0),0,1,true))$; reject the null hypothesis if $p < \alpha$

Here $\hat{p} = \dfrac{x}{n}$ is the ratio of the number of successes divided by the total number of trials. This procedure is valid as long as there are at least 10 successes and 10 failures in our sample. Note that we use the standard normal distribution to compute the p-value. This is only an approximation, actually, and we could compute p exactly. However, the added accuracy is negligible, so we will not bother.

Example: Providing municipal services costs money; in order to cover the rising costs, a municipality could raise taxes or cut services. The town conducts a survey, asking 200 randomly selected people if taxes should go up; it turns out that 108 vote to increase taxes and 92 vote no. If you were hired by the town as statistical consultant, how would you advise the town?

Of course at first glance it looks like the town should increase taxes, since 108 out of 200, or 54 percent, voted yes. But that is only 54 percent of the sample asked whereas we need to infer the proportion of the *entire town* from that. In fact, we need to figure out whether the population proportion is 50 percent or not, based on the sample. So, we set up our hypothesis as follows:

Null hypothesis H_0: $\pi = 0.5$
Alternative hypothesis H_a: $\pi \neq 0.5$.

If our test lets us reject the null hypothesis we would accept the alternative where $\pi \neq 0.5$. But our sample ratio of 0.54 would then imply that $\pi > 0.5$ so that we could conclude that the majority of *all* people in the town want to see taxes raised. The other outcome would be that the test is is inconclusive so that we would not recommend any course of action to the town.

Once set up, the calculations are straightforward. First, let us fix our level of significance $\alpha = 0.05$. Then:

- $\hat{p} = \dfrac{108}{200} = 0.54$ and

$$SE = \sqrt{\frac{p_0 \cdot (1 - p_0)}{n}} = \sqrt{\frac{0.5 \cdot (1 - 0.5)}{200}} = 0.0354$$

- Test statistics: $z_0 = \dfrac{\hat{p} - p_0}{SE} = \dfrac{0.54 - 0.5}{0.0354} = 1.13$

- Rejection region: $p = 2(1 - NORMDIST(1.13{,}0{,}1{,}true)) = 0.2585$

Since $0.2585 = p > \alpha = 0.05$, our test is inconclusive. Thus, 108 out of a sample of 200 is not enough "yes" votes to convince us that the majority of the entire town is for raising taxes. Of course the town could decide to raise taxes after all, but if they claimed that based on this survey the majority of people were for raising taxes, their margin of error would be 25 percent, which should be way too high to feel comfortable about.

The preceding example is interesting because at first it seems unclear what the null hypothesis should be. Other examples are more straightforward.

Example: The General Social Science Survey from 2008 includes data provided by a random sample of adults in the United States. You will find, among many other variables, answers to the question "Did the universe begin with a huge explosion?" Based on that sample data, does the majority of people in the United States believe that this is false? Use a level of significance $\alpha = 0.01$.
www.betterbusinessdecisions.org/data/gss2008-short-2.xls

After loading that data file you will find the variable in column AJ. As we learned earlier, a pivot table can be used to find the ratio of true/false answers for this survey. It turns out that 606 out of 1,088 subjects responded negatively, while 482 agreed. The example clearly asked whether $\pi = 0.5$, so setting up this test should be straightforward.

We defined "success" if someone answered "no" to the question of whether the universe began with a huge explosion. Then our test works as follows:

- Null hypothesis: H_0: $\pi = 0.5$
- Alternative hypothesis: H_a: $\pi \neq 0.5$

- $SE = \sqrt{\dfrac{0.5 \cdot (1-0.5)}{1088}} = 0.0151$

- Test statistics: $Z_0 = \dfrac{\dfrac{606}{1033} - 0.5}{0.0151} = 3.7739$

- Rejection region: $p = 2(1 - NORMDIST(3.7739,0,1,true)) = 0.00016$.

Since $0.00016 = p < \alpha = 0.01$, our test is conclusive. Therefore, we reject the null hypothesis and accept the alternative. In words this means that over 50 percent of the U.S. population does *not* believe that the universe started with a huge explosion.

Note: It is generally accepted today that the universe did start with the "Big Bang" (a huge explosion) some 13.798 ± 0.037 billion years ago (according to Wikipedia). Note that the age of the universe is an estimate just [...].

ONE-TAILED AND TWO-TAILED TESTS

All of our tests so far tested whether a parameter was equal to a fixed value or not. In many cases, however, we are interested more specifically if the parameter is bigger than a fixed value, or perhaps smaller, not just unequal.

Example: For each of the following situations, determine the null and alternative hypotheses that best reflect the question:

1. Do bottles of ketchup contain less than the indicated weight of 16 oz?
2. Does the new feed for cows result in higher weight gain than the average of 100 lb per week when using standard feeds?
3. Is the effect of a new hypertension drug different from that of the traditional drug?

1. We want to test for the mean weight of ketchup. Let x be the weight of the contents of a ketchup bottle and μ be the (unknown) population average. Then:

$$H_0: \mu = 16$$
$$H_a: \mu < 16.$$

2. We know that old feed for cows results in a weight gain of 100 lb per week on average. Let x be the weight gain for cows getting the new feed and μ be the population average. Then:

$$H_0: \mu = 100$$
$$H_a: \mu > 100.$$

3. Hypertension drugs are supposed to lower blood pressure. If μ_1 denotes the average blood pressure of patients on the new drug and μ_2 that of patients on the traditional drug, we want to test:

$$H_0: \mu_1 = \mu_2$$
$$H_a: \mu_1 \neq \mu_2.$$

Examples 1 and 2 are called one-tailed tests, whereas Example 3 is a two-tailed test. A two-tailed test at a level of significance α allocates half of that alpha to testing the statistical significance in one direction and half of the alpha to testing statistical significance in the other direction. A one-tailed test, on the other hand, concentrates the entire alpha on one of the tails of the distribution. Thus, a one-tailed test has a slightly different rejection region.

- One-tailed test for the mean (large sample size):

  If $H_a: \mu > \mu_0$ then $p = P(z > z_0) = 1 - NORMDIST(z_0,0,1,true)$.
  If $H_a: \mu < \mu_0$ then $p = P(z < z_0) = NORMDIST(z_0,0,1,true)$.

- One-tailed test for the mean (small sample size):

  If $H_a: \mu > \mu_0$ then $p = P(t > t_0) = TDIST(t_0,df,1)$ if $t_0 > 0$. If $H_a: \mu < \mu_0$ then $p = P(t < t_0)$ $= TDIST(-t_0,df,1)$ if $t_0 < 0$.

- One-tailed test for the difference of two means—compute *df* as usual:

  If $H_a: \mu_1 - \mu_2 > c$ then $p = P(t > t_0) = TDIST(t_0,df,1)$ if $t_0 > 0$. If $H_a: \mu_1 - \mu_2 < c$ then $p = P(t < t_0)$ $= TDIST(-t_0,df,1)$ if $t_0 < 0$.

Example: We suspect that bottles of ketchup contain less than the indicated weight of 16 oz. We collect a sample of 100 bottles and find that the sample mean is 15.5 oz with $s = 2.6$ oz. Decide at the $\alpha = 0.05$ level.

This is a one-tailed test; here we go:

$$H_0: \mu = 16.0$$

$$H_a: \mu < 16$$

$$z_0 = \frac{15.5-16}{2.6/\sqrt{100}} = \frac{-0.5}{2.6} * 10 = -1.9231$$

$$p = P(z < -1.9231) = NORMDIST(-1.9231, 0, 1, true) = 0.0272.$$

Thus, since $p = 0.0272 < \alpha = 0.05$, we reject the null hypothesis and thus we think that the bottles indeed contain too little content.

Note: Had we used a two-tailed test we would have found that $p = 2 * 0.0272 = 0.0544 > \alpha = 0.05$, so that a two-tailed test would come out inconclusive. This is no coincidence: A one-tailed test is more powerful than a two-tailed test; it is possible that a two-tailed test is inconclusive but the corresponding one-tailed test results in rejecting the null hypothesis. On the other hand, if a one-tailed test is inconclusive then the corresponding two-tailed test will also be inconclusive. Thus, if we only consider two-tailed tests we might decide that a test is inconclusive when it actually might be significant (as a one-tailed test) but we will never call a test significant when in fact it is not.

Note: If we conduct a one-tailed test $H_a: \mu < \mu_0$ and the sample mean comes out *bigger* than μ_0, then the one-tailed test will always be inconclusive. That makes sense: If we suspect a population mean to be less than, say, 10, but our sample mean comes out bigger than 10, this can never support the alternative hypothesis. Thus, the test is inconclusive. Mathematically we have that if $\bar{x} > 10$ then $z_0 > 0$ so that $p = NORMDIST(z_0, 0, 1, true) > 0.5$ for $z_0 > 0$. A similar argument applies if we test the alternative hypothesis $H_a: \mu > \mu_0$ and the sample mean $\bar{x} < \mu_0$: this test, too, is inconclusive.

RELATIONSHIP BETWEEN CONFIDENCE INTERVALS AND HYPOTHESIS TESTING

While confidence intervals and hypothesis testing are used for different purposes, they are related. For example, to decide whether a population mean equals a certain value μ_0 you would naturally conduct a test for a mean. However, you could also compute a confidence interval as long as you interpret the answer properly:

- If a 95 percent confidence interval about the mean *includes* the number μ_0, the test whether the mean equals μ_0 would be inconclusive at the $\alpha = 0.05$ level.
- If a 95 percent confidence interval about the mean *excludes* the number μ_0, we would reject the null hypothesis that $\mu = \mu_0$ and accept the alternative that $\mu \neq \mu_0$ at the $\alpha = 0.05$ level.

Example: To equip soldiers with properly fitting helmets it is important to know the average head size of all soldiers. A study selected 80 soldiers at random and measured their head size. It turns out that the sample has an average head size of 56 cm with a standard deviation of 1.36 cm. Find a 95 percent confidence interval for the population mean and use it to decide if the population mean could be 56.3.

To compute a 95 percent confidence interval (for large N), we need to find $\bar{x} \pm 1.96 \frac{S}{\sqrt{n}} = 56 \pm 1.96 \frac{1.36}{\sqrt{80}} = 56 \pm 0.298$ so that the 95 percent confidence interval goes from 55.702 to 56.298. This interval does not include the hypothesized mean of 56.3 so that according to our discussion the population mean could not be 56.3 (within our alpha level of 0.05).

Let us conduct a proper test to see if we get the same answer. Our null hypothesis would be H_0: $\mu = 56.3$ with the alternative H_a: $\mu \neq 56.3$. We compute the *z*-score $z_0 = \frac{56.3 - 56}{1.36 / \sqrt{80}} = 1.973$. Finally we compute the value of $p = 2 * (1 - NORMDIST(1.973,0,1,true)) = 0.485$. This is smaller than alpha so that we indeed reject the null hypothesis and conclude that the population mean indeed cannot be equal to 56.3.

Note that the hypothesized mean of 56.3 is *barely* outside the 95 percent confidence interval. That corresponds to the *p*-value being *just* smaller than 0.05. If we checked for a number well outside the 95 percent confidence interval, the corresponding *p*-value would be much smaller than 0.05.

SUMMARY

Hypothesis testing lets you decide which of two mutually exclusive situations is true and provides an error estimate for your answer. Each test has four components: (1) a null hypothesis H_0, (2) an alternative hypothesis H_a, (3) test statistics, and (4) a rejection region where you compute a probability

p and decide to reject H_0 (and accept H_a) if $p < \alpha$; otherwise the test is inconclusive. The number α is called level of significance and is typically 0.1, 0.05, or 0.01. We covered the following tests.

- **Test for a mean**: (1) H_0: $\mu = \mu_0$ and (2) H_a: $\mu \neq \mu_0$; (3) test statistics $z_0 = \dfrac{\overline{x} - \mu_0}{s / \sqrt{n}}$; and (4) probability

  $p = 2(1 - NORMDIST(ABS(z_0),0,1,true))$ for large samples ($n > 30$) or $p = TDIST(ABS(t_0),N - 1,2)$ for small samples ($n \leq 30$).

- **Test for a difference of means (equal variances)**:
  (1) H_0: $\mu_1 - \mu_2 = c$ and (2) H_a: $\mu_1 - \mu_2 \neq c$; (3) test statistics $t_0 = \dfrac{(\mu_1 - \mu_2) - c}{SE}$, where

  $S_p = \sqrt{\dfrac{(n_1 - 1)s_1^2 + (n_2 - 1)s_2^2}{n_1 + n_2 - 2}}$ and $SE = S_p\sqrt{\dfrac{1}{n_1} + \dfrac{1}{n_2}}$; and (4) probability $p = TDIST(ABS(t_0)$,

  $n_1 + n_2 - 2,2)$

- **Test for a difference of means (unequal variances)**:
  (1) H_0: $\mu_1 - \mu_2 = c$ and (2) H_a: $\mu_1 - \mu_2 \neq c$; (3) test statistics $t_0 = \dfrac{(\mu_1 - \mu_2) - c}{SE}$, where

  $SE = \sqrt{\dfrac{s_1^2}{n_1} + \dfrac{s_2^2}{n_2}}$; and (4) probability $p = TDIST(ABS(t_0), df, 2)$, where $df = \dfrac{\left(\dfrac{s_1^2}{n_1} + \dfrac{s_2^2}{n_2}\right)^2}{\dfrac{\left(\dfrac{s_1^2}{n_1}\right)^2}{n_1 - 1} + \dfrac{\left(\dfrac{s_2^2}{n_2}\right)^2}{n_2 - 1}}$

  (use the nearest integer).

- **Test for proportion**: (1) H_0: $p = p_0$ and (2) H_a: $p \neq p_0$; (3) test statistics $z_0 = \dfrac{\hat{p} - p_0}{SE}$, where

  $SE = \sqrt{\dfrac{p_0 \cdot (1 - p_0)}{n}}$; and (4) $p = 2(1 - NORMDIST(ABS(z_0),0,1,true))$.

While the preceding tests list are all *two-tailed* tests, they also come in a *one-tailed* variety, in which case the computation of the p-value is slightly different.

EXCEL DEMONSTRATION

Company P, the large manufacturer of paper products, has the business objective of developing an improved process for fulfilling orders during the 12 p.m. to 1 p.m. lunch period. The management decides to first study the fulfillment and delivery time in the current process in the plant. The fulfillment time is defined as the number of minutes that elapses from when the order enters the plant until the product is packed and ready to ship. The data collected from a random sample are presented from two assembly lines within the company. Assuming that the population variances from both lines are unequal, is there evidence of a difference in the mean fulfillment time between the two lines, using alpha = 0.05?

Step 1: Enter the fulfillment times into Excel in Column A and create a corresponding identifying label in Column B (see Figure 9.2):
Assembly Line 1: 4.22, 5.56, 3.01, 5.14, 4.78, 2.35, 3.53, 3.21, 4.49, 6.11, 0.39, 5.13, 6.47, 6.20, 3.80
Assembly Line 2: 9.77, 5.91, 8.01, 5.78, 8.72, 3.81, 8.02, 8.36, 10.48, 6.69, 5.67, 4.09, 6.18, 9.90, 5.48.

Step 2: Click on "Data," then "Data Analysis," and choose "t-Test: Two-Sample Assuming Unequal Variances."

Note: In this example we were told the variances are unequal, which is why we chose the tool we did. If you are not told, you must first check whether the variances are equal in both groups, which determines the type of t-test to perform (one that assumes equal variances or one that does not make that assumption). A conservative approach is to always assume unequal variances.

Step 3: For "Variable Range 1," enter or select the range of numbers for Assembly Line 1 in column A. For "Variance Range 2," enter or select the range of numbers for Assembly Line 2, column A.

	A	B	C
1	Fulfillment Time		
2	4.22	Assembly Line 1	
3	5.56	Assembly Line 1	
4		...	
17	9.77	Assembly Line 2	
18	5.91	Assembly Line 2	
19		...	

Figure 9.2 Fulfillment data in Excel (excerpt)

Step 4: Since we did not use labels in the first row, we do not need to check the "Labels" box. The alpha level is set by default to 0.05, which is what we wanted to use. Compare with Figure 9.3; then Click OK.

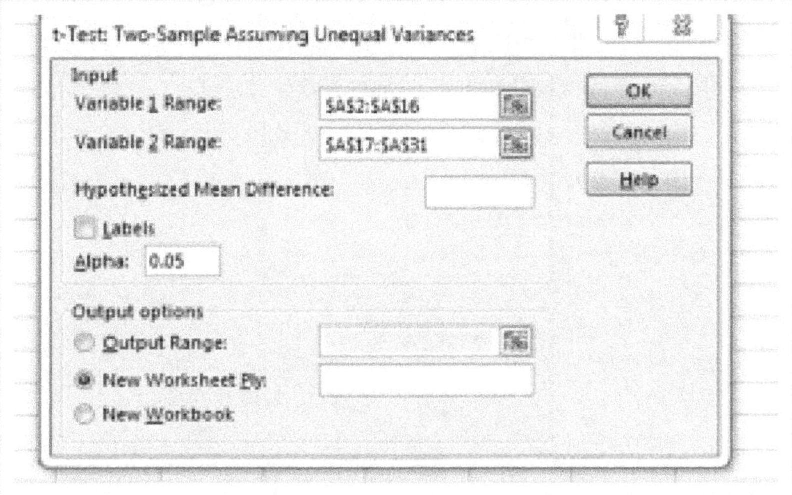

Figure 9.3 The parameters for the "t-Test: Two-Sample Assuming Unequal Variances"

The procedure should produce the following output.

t-Test: Two-Sample Assuming Unequal Variances		
	Variable 1	**Variable 2**
Mean	4.292666667	7.124666667
Variance	2.688206667	4.356940952
Observations	15	15
Hypothesized Mean Difference	0	
Df	27	
t Stat	−4.132318902	
P(T <= t) one-tail	0.000155796	
t Critical one-tail	1.703288446	
P(T <= t) two-tail	0.000311591	
t Critical two-tail	2.051830516	

This relates to our problem as follows.

- *Null hypothesis*: There is no difference (the two means are equal) in fulfillment time between Assembly Line 1 and Assembly Line 2.
- *Alternative hypothesis*: There is a difference (the two means are not equal) in fulfillment time between Assembly Line 1 and Assembly Line 2.

- *Results*: We have a two-tailed *p*-value of 0.0003. This is less than our alpha value, so we reject the null hypothesis and conclude that there is difference (the two means are not equal) in fulfillment time between Assembly Line 1 and Assembly Line 2.

Even though we used a two-tailed test, that is, we do not care which mean is larger, it is clear that the means are different because Assembly Line 1 has a smaller mean than line 2. Since Company P wishes to reduce fulfillment times within their manufacturing plant, the management should try to identify why there is a difference and consider implementing the work practices of Assembly Line 1 across all assembly lines as best practice.

10 Analysis of the Variance

Analysis of Variance, or ANOVA for short, refers to the use of statistical models and procedures to test the differences among more than two independent group means. ANOVA analysis allows statisticians to evaluate the variation within each group and how each group's variance varies from the total variance of all observations. Chapter 10 will explore ANOVA, including the set of hypothesis, the analysis, and conclusions.

ANALYSIS OF VARIANCE

By Justin Bateh and Bert G. Wachsmuth

Preview: *Testing for the differences between two means is a relatively straightforward exercise, but what happens when there are three or more groups? These multiple groups may have means that differ significantly from one another, which makes the comparison process much more complicated. Fortunately, there is a way to test the means no matter how many groups are involved. For example, if a researcher wanted to study the impact of listening to music on student test scores, she could randomly divide the class into three groups of students. One group would listen to popular music while they study or do homework. The second group would listen to classical music while studying and the third group would study in silence. At the conclusion of the study period, the performance of students in each group is evaluated. The analysis of variance (ANOVA) procedure is then used to determine whether there is a significant difference among a group of means, and Excel will do all calculations for you automatically.*

Learning Objectives: At the conclusion of this chapter, you should be able to:

1. Use a factor to partition an experiment into multiple groups
2. Understand the assumptions to check before using a one-way ANOVA
3. Use the one-way ANOVA to test for differences among the means of several groups
4. Understand how to obtain information about two-factor ANOVA

INTRODUCTION

We have already introduced a test for the difference of (two) means. But in many cases there are three or more groups whose means may or may not differ significantly.

Example: Many parents complain that students listen to pop music while they study. To test the impact of music on students' concentration levels, we divide 40 students randomly into three groups: Group A does not listen to any music, group B listens to pop music, and group C listens to classical music. All students study a text for 30 min and then they take a test about their understanding of the text.

There are two types of variables in this example: the performance of students on a test and the type of music students listen to. The first variable (quiz_score) is numerical, while the second (music_type) is categorical and is used to partition the first variable into three groups. This, as it turns out, is typical for an ANOVA test to compare multiple means. Note that to decide whether multiple means of various groups are different from each other, we could use multiple difference of means tests between pairs of means, but that would quickly escalate.

- For three groups we would need three comparisons: $m_1 \neq m_2$, $m_1 \neq m_3$, and $m_2 \neq m_3$.
- For four groups we would need six comparisons: $m_1 \neq m_2$, $m_1 \neq m_3$, $m_1 \neq m_4$, $m_2 \neq m_3$, $m_2 \neq m_4$, and $m_3 \neq m_4$.
- For five groups we would need 10 comparisons, and so on.

This quickly becomes a lot of work. In addition—and perhaps more important—each time we conduct a difference of means test we accept an error, typically 5 percent. These errors add up, approximately, so that checking three group means would add up to an error of 15 percent. Thus, we need a new procedure that keeps the error at a constant level even if we are comparing quite a number of means.

Definition: The ANOVA procedure is used to test for a significant difference among a group of means. The null hypothesis is: H_0: $m_1 = m_2 = \ldots = m_k$ and the alternative is that at least two means differ significantly: H_a: $m_j \neq m_i$.

Note that in case the ANOVA procedure is used for only *two* means it should reduce to a difference of means test. It might sound strange for a procedure that claims to test for differences of *means* to be called

ANOVA. However, it turns out that we can analyze the variances yet draw conclusions about any difference of means.

The procedure works by comparing the variance SS_B *between* group means against the variance SS_W *within* groups to determine whether the groups are all part of one larger population (no difference between means) or separate populations with different characteristics (at least two means differ significantly).

ONE-FACTOR ANOVA

Suppose we have quiz scores of students in a statistics course as follows:

2 (male), 5 (female), 1 (male), 3 (male), 6 (female), 7 (female).

We want to know if there is a difference in mean scores between males and females. Since these represent two samples only, we could use our familiar difference of means test (which incidentally results in a *t*-value of $t = -4.0$ and a *p*-value of $p = 0.016$) but we want to use a different method that will readily extend to more than two groups and their means. First, we use sex to divide the scores into two groups, as follows.

Male	Female
2	6
1	5
3	7

Definition: The variable we are interested in analyzing is called the *dependent* variable, while the variable we use to divide the dependent variable into groups is called the *independent* variable or *factor*. For ANOVA, the dependent variable should be numerical while the factor should be categorical. A *single-factor* ANOVA uses *one* factor to divide the dependent variable into groups.

For a single-factor ANOVA we will assume that all groups are approximately normal with roughly the same standard deviations. In the preceding example we are using one factor (sex) to define the groups; consequently we will perform a single-factor ANOVA. Both groups have sample variances of 1, as you can readily compute. The samples are really too small to check for normality but for this example we will simply assume everything is normal. If the variable used as factor had more values (categories), it would result in that many groups; still it would be a single-factor ANOVA.

We now compare the variance of our overall data with the variances of each group. In fact, since the variance is a function of the square difference of each point to the respective mean, we compute only the sum of the square differences to the mean instead of the full variance (see Table 10.1).

As you can see, the means for the two groups are quite different. The sums of square differences within each group are 2. Adding them together, we get $SS_W = 4$. If we ignore group membership and compute the total sum of square differences SS_T based on the overall mean 4, we get $SS_T = 28$. In other words, the variance (aka sums of squares) SS_W within the groups is much smaller than the total variability SS_T, which indicates that the means are indeed different.

More precisely, under the null hypothesis that there are no mean differences between groups in the population, we would expect only minor random fluctuation in the means of the two groups. Therefore, under the null hypothesis, it turns out that the variance SS_W *within* groups divided by the degree s of freedom *within* groups should be about the same as the variance SS_B *between* groups divided by the degrees of freedom *between* groups. We can compare those expressions via the F distribution and test whether their ratio is significantly greater than 1. Here is the formal definition of a single-factor ANOVA.

TABLE 10.1 GROUP AND TOTAL VARIANCES OR SUM OF SQUARE (*SS*) DIFFERENCES TO THE MEAN

	Male	Female
Data	2	6
	1	5
	3	7
Mean	**2**	**6**
***Group* SS**	$(2-2)^2 + (1-2)^2 + (3-1)^2 = 2$	$(6-6)^2 + (5-6)^2 + (7-6)^2 = 2$
Total mean	4	
***Total* SS**	$(2-4)^2 + (1-4)^2 + (3-4)^2 + (6-4)^2 + (5-4)^2 + (7-4)^2 = 28$	

Definition: Suppose we have k groups and each group contains n_j measurements, $1 \le j \le k$. Assume that all groups are approximately normal and that their standard deviations are approximately the same. The four components of a single-factor ANOVA are:

$$H_0\colon m_1 = m_1 = \ldots = m_k,$$
$$H_a\colon m_i \neq m_j \text{ for some } i, j.$$

Test statistics: $f_0 = \left(\dfrac{SS_B}{df_B}\right) \Big/ \left(\dfrac{SS_W}{df_W}\right)$, where $df_B = k - 1$, $df_W = (n_1 - 1) + (n_2 - 1) + \ldots + (n_k - 1)$, sum of squares within groups $SS_W = SS_1 + SS_2 + \ldots + SS_k$, the total sum of squares SS_T, and the sum of squares between groups $SS_B = SS_T - SS_W$.

Rejection region: Reject H_0 if $p = P(f > f_0) < a$, where $P(f > f_0) = FDIST(f_0, df_B, df_W)$ using the F distribution.

Now we can finish the preceding example: $df_B = 2 - 1 = 1$, $df_W = (3 - 1) + (3 - 1) = 4$, $SS_T = 28$, $SS_W = 2 + 2 = 4$, $SS_B = SS_T - SS_W = 28 - 4 = 24$. At this point we know the variance within groups SS_W as well as the variance between groups SS_B so that $f_0 = \left(\frac{24}{1}\right) / \left(\frac{4}{4}\right) = 24$ and $p = P(f > f_0) = FDIST(24,1,4) = 0.008$.

Hence, assuming as usual that $a = 0.05$, we reject the null hypothesis and conclude that there *is* a difference between the means. Incidentally, this would have been our conclusion had we used the difference of means procedure. Now we are ready for a true ANOVA, that is, for an example with more than two groups.

Example: We want to determine if a new drug is effective in lowering blood pressure, and what dosage might work best. So we give three different levels of the drug (zero drugs, low amount, high amount) to 20 patients and measure the difference in blood pressure before and 30 min after administering the drug. The 20 people were randomly assigned to receive one of the three dosages. The results are:

Zero dosage: 4, 1, 7, 8, 2, 10
Low dosage: 11, 15, 12, 13, 18, 16, 14
High dosage: 15, 17, 12, 13, 10, 11, 10.

Is there a significant difference between the three averages? Test at the $a = 0.05$ level.

The computations for our ANOVA test are as follows:

$$\bar{x}_1 = 5.333, \bar{x}_2 = 14.14, \bar{x}_3 = 12.57, \bar{x}_{total} = 10.95$$

$$SS_1 = (4 - 5.333)^2 + (1 - 5.333)^2 + \cdots + (10 - 5.333)^2 = 63.33$$
$$SS_2 = (11 - 14.14)^2 + (15 - 14.14)^2 + \cdots + (14 - 14.14)^2 = 34.85$$
$$SS_3 = (15 - 12.57)^2 + (17 - 12.57)^2 + \cdots + (10 - 12.57)^2 = 41.71$$
$$\text{so that } SS_W = SS_1 + SS_2 + SS_3 = 139.90$$
$$SS_T = (4 - 10.95)^2 + (1 - 10.95)^2 + \cdots + (11 - 10.95)^2 + (10 - 10.95)^2 = 418.95$$
$$\text{so that } SS_B = SS_T - SS_W = 418.95 - 139.9 = 279.065$$
$$df_B = 2,\ df_W = 17 \text{ so that, finally:}$$

$$f_0 = \left(\frac{SS_B}{df_1}\right) \Big/ \left(\frac{SS_W}{df_2}\right) = 139.52/8.229 = 16.95 \text{ and therefore}$$

$$p = FDIST(16.95,2,17) = 0.0000085 \text{ and } p < a = 0.05.$$

Thus, we reject the null hypothesis and accept the alternative, that is, there is a significant difference between (at least two of) the means.

This is a lot of work and it is very easy to make mistakes. Fortunately, Excel has a procedure to perform these calculations automatically.

Exercise: Given the data from the previous example, use Excel to perform an ANOVA to decide whether the means differ significantly.

---

zero	low	high
4	11	15
1	15	17
7	12	12
8	13	13
2	18	10
10	16	11
	14	10

Figure 10.1 Data entered in columns for each group

First, we enter the data into Excel in three columns, one column per group (see Figure 10.1).

Next, click on the "Data Analysis" on the Data ribbon, select "ANOVA: Single factor," and define as input range the data you entered, including the data labels in the first row. Make sure that "Labels in First Row" is checked and hit OK. The output of the ANOVA procedure is shown in Figure 10.2.

The SUMMARY block in Figure 10.2 shows the means and variances of the three groups. In the more interesting

Anova: Single Factor

SUMMARY

Groups	*Count*	*Sum*	*Average*	*Variance*
zero	6	32	5.333333	12.666667
low	7	99	14.142857	5.809524
high	7	88	12.571429	6.952381

ANOVA

Source of Variation	*SS*	*df*	*MS*	*F*	*P-value*	*F crit*
Between Groups	279.04524	2	139.522619	16.953565	0.000089	3.591531
Within Groups	139.90476	17	8.229692			
Total	418.95	19				

Figure 10.2 Output of single-factor ANOVA routine

ANOVA section we can see that $SS_B = 279.04$ and $SS_W = 139.90$. It lists the degrees of freedom next and finally shows the f_0 value of 16.95 together with the associated probability $p = 0.000089$, computed using the F distribution. Our conclusion is, just as before, to reject the null hypothesis and accept that some means differ significantly from each other.

We will show another, carefully worked out problem in the last section of this chapter; you can check that if you have any questions. You might want to work out that example manually, as we did earlier, and compare your answers.

But the idea of the ANOVA is even more powerful and applies to more complex experiments.

TWO-WAY ANOVA

As we mentioned, a one-factor ANOVA uses one categorical variable called factor to divide the dependent variable into groups. But complex situations often depend on more factors, which will result in two-way ANOVA or higher. As it turns out, the ANOVA procedure cannot only decide on whether means are different but detect *interaction effects* between variables, and therefore can be used to test more complex hypotheses about reality. As it turns out, in many areas of research five-way or higher interactions are not that uncommon.

However, this discussion is difficult and, while most certainly useful, is beyond the scope of this text. Thus, we will refer the reader to more advanced statistical textbooks, or better yet, appropriate online resources and we will not discuss two-way (or higher) ANOVA here. For more information, the reader can check:

- *Introduction to Probability and Statistics* by Mendenhall, Beaver, and Beaver
- *Introduction to ANOVA/MANOVA* at www.statsoft.com/Textbook/ANOVA-MANOVA
- *Analysis of variance* at http://en.wikipedia.org/wiki/Analysis_of_variance

EXCEL DEMONSTRATION

Company S, the accounting firm, has an HR department that has suggested managers learn different leadership styles to help decrease employee stress levels. An experiment was conducted to determine if leadership styles (*transformational* and *transactional*) in management significantly impacted employee stress levels compared to no intervention. An employee

TABLE 10.2 DATA FOR STRESS LEVELS

Transformational	Transactional	Control
0	2	6
7	5	5
3	3	8
5	0	9
2	1	5

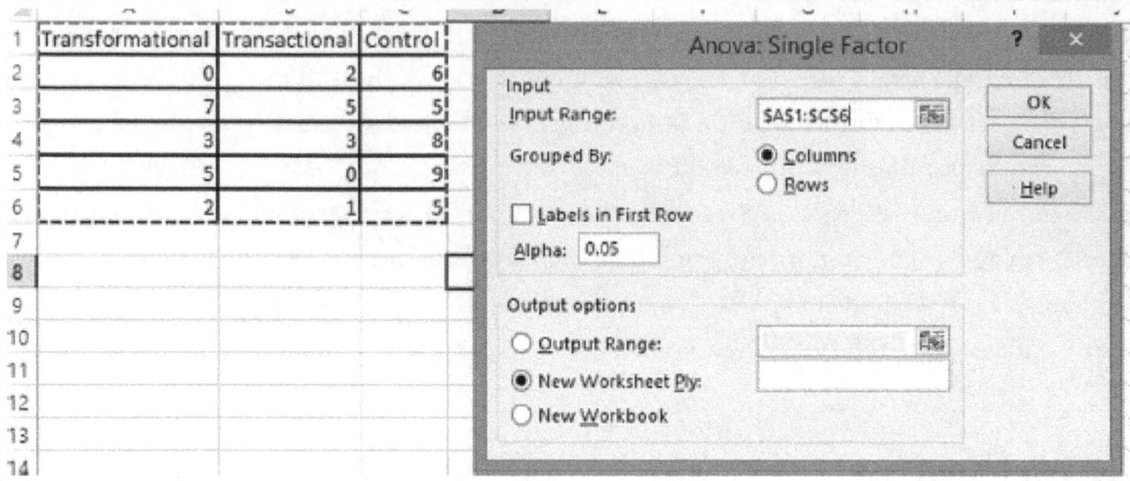

Figure 10.3 Data for stress levels of employees together with ANOVA dialog

	A	B	C	D	E	F	G
1	Anova: Single Factor						
2							
3	SUMMARY						
4	*Groups*	*Count*	*Sum*	*Average*	*Variance*		
5	Transformational	5	17	3.4	7.3		
6	Transactional	5	11	2.2	3.7		
7	Control	5	33	6.6	3.3		
8							
9							
10	ANOVA						
11	*Source of Variation*	*SS*	*df*	*MS*	*F*	*P-value*	*F crit*
12	Between Groups	51.73333333	2	25.86666667	5.426573427	0.020960972	3.885293835
13	Within Groups	57.2	12	4.766666667			
14							
15	Total	108.9333333	14				
16							
17							

Figure 10.4 Output of the single-factor ANOVA procedure

survey was given to three groups: one group under a manager who started using a transformational motivation technique, one group under a manager who began using a transactional motivation technique, and then a control group with no new technique used. Stress levels were self-reported by the employees as shown in Table 10.2 (page 185). Use alpha = 0.05.

Step 1: Start a new Excel worksheet and enter the preceding data (see Figure 10.3 above).

Step 2: Click on DATA, then Data Analysis, and then ANOVA: Single Factor. We are choosing Single Factor because we have only one dependent variable (stress level) that defines three categories of independent variables (transformational, transactional, control).

Step 3: In the dialog that comes up, select all of the data including the labels at once as shown in Figure 10.3. Check the box called "Labels in First Row." Notice that Alpha is automatically set to 0.05. Click OK. The output of this procedure is shown in Figure 10.4.

In a review of the *p*-value in the between groups row, we see a $p = 0.02$ that is less than our alpha level of 0.05, so we know there is a significant difference in stress levels between the groups.

Now that we know there is a general difference between all the groups, we would like to run a post hoc test to determine if there is a significant difference between certain groups, like between transformational and control; or between control and transactional; and so on. In Excel, it is difficult to do this. However, a quick and easy way is to run a two-sample t-test between the two groups that you wish to check (only do this if you have determined that there is a significant difference between all groups).

11 Simple and Multiple Linear Regression

Simple linear regression is a process used to evaluate the relationship between two quantitative variables. Regression analysis can be used to understand how changes in the independent variable(s) (X) influence the dependent variable (Y) and how much of the variation in the dependent variable is explained by one or more independent variables. The chapter will explain the process of Ordinary Least Squares (OLS) and will expand discussion to multiple linear regression toward the end of the chapter. The last part of the chapter will discuss some complications with using multiple linear regression.

THE ORDINARY LEAST SQUARES (OLS) REGRESSION MODEL

By J. Holton Wilson, Barry P. Keating, and Mary Beal

PREVIEW

When you have completed reading this chapter you will be able to:

- Know the difference between a dependent variable and an independent variable.
- Know what portion of a regression equation (model) represents the intercept (or constant) and how to interpret that value.
- Know what part of the regression equation represents the slope and how to interpret that value.
- Know that for business applications the slope is the most important part of a regression equation.
- Know the ordinary least squares (OLS) criterion for the "best" regression line.
- Know four of the basic statistical assumptions underlying regression analysis.
- Know how to perform regression analysis in Excel.

THE REGRESSION EQUATION

[In this chapter, you will see] examples of what is sometimes called "simple" linear regression. The term "simple" in this context means that only two variables are used in the regression. However, the mathematics and statistical foundation are not particularly simple. Two example regression equations discussed [... are listed below]:

1. Women's clothing sales (WCS) as a function of personal income (PI)

$$WCS = 1{,}187.123 + 0.165(PI)$$

2. Basketball team's conference winning percentage (WP) as a function of the team's successful field goal attempt percentage (FG)

$$WP = -198.9 + 5.707(FG)$$

In both of these regression equations, there are just two variables. While you use Excel to get these equations, the underlying mathematics can be relatively complex and certainly time consuming. Excel hides all those details from us and performs the calculations very quickly.

THE DEPENDENT (Y) AND INDEPENDENT VARIABLES (X)

In the simplest form of regression analysis, you have only the variable you want to model (or predict) and one other variable that you hypothesize to have an influence on the variable you are modeling. The variable you are modeling (WCS or WP in the examples above) is called the **dependent variable**. The other variable (PI or FG) is called the **independent variable**. Sometimes the independent variable is called a "causal variable" because you are hypothesizing that this variable *causes* changes in the variable being modeled.

The dependent variable is often represented as Y, and the independent variable is represented as X. The relationship or model you seek to find could then be expressed as:

$$Y = a + bX$$

This is called a *bivariate* linear regression (BLR) model because there are just two variables: Y and X. Also, because both Y and X are raised to the first power the equation is linear.

THE INTERCEPT AND THE SLOPE

In the expression above, a represents the intercept or constant term for the regression equation. The intercept is where the regression line crosses the vertical, or Y, axis. Conceptually, it is the value that the dependent variable (Y) would have if the independent variable (X) had a value of zero. In this context, a is also called the constant because no matter what value bX has a is always the same, or constant. That is, as the independent variable (X) changes there is no change in a.

The value of b tells you the slope of the regression line. The slope is the rate of change in the dependent variable for each unit change in the independent variable. Understanding that the slope term (b) is the rate of change in Y as X changes will be helpful to you in interpreting regression results. If b has a positive value, Y increases when X increases and Y decreases when X decreases. On the other hand, if b is negative, Y changes in the opposite direction of changes in X. The slope (b) is the most important part of the regression equation, or model, for business decisions.

THE SLOPE AND INTERCEPT FOR WOMEN'S CLOTHING SALES

You might think about a and b in the context of the two examples you have seen so far. First, consider the women's clothing sales model:

$$\text{WCS} = 1{,}187.123 + 0.165(\text{PI})$$

In this model, a is 1,187.123 million dollars. Conceptually, this means if personal income in the United States drops to zero women's clothing sales would be $1,187,128,000. However, from a practical perspective you realize this makes no sense. If no one has any income in the United States you would not expect to see over a billion dollars being spent on women's clothing. Granted there is the theoretical possibility that even with no income people could draw on savings for such spending, but the reality of this happening is remote. It is equally remote that personal income would drop to zero.

Figure 2.2 is reproduced on page 194 as Figure 12.1. The line drawn through the scattergram represents the regression equation for these data. You see that the regression line would cross the Y-axis close to the intercept value of $1,187.123 if extended that far from the observed data. You also see that the origin ($Y = 0$ and $X = 0$) is very far from the observed values of the data.

The slope, or b, in the women's clothing sales example is 0.165. This means that for every one unit increase in personal income women's clothing sales would be estimated to increase by 0.165 units. In this example, personal income is in billions of dollars and women's clothing sales is in millions of dollars. Therefore, a one billion dollar increase in personal income would increase women's clothing sales by 0.165 million dollars ($165,000).

THE SLOPE AND INTERCEPT FOR BASKETBALL WINNING PERCENTAGE

For the basketball WP model discussed in Chapter 2, the model is:

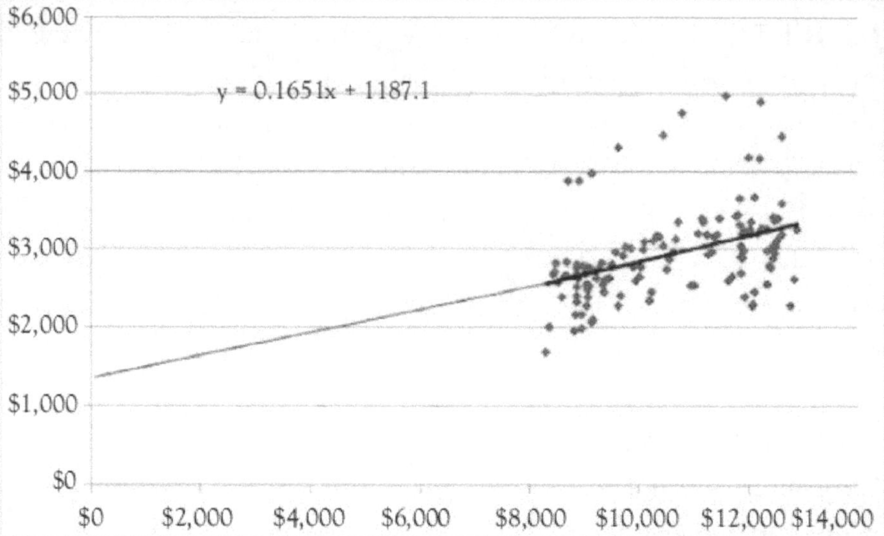

Figure 12.1 Scattergram of women's clothing sales versus personal income. Women's clothing sales is on the vertical (Y) axis and personal income is on the horizontal (X) axis[1]

$$WP = -198.9 + 5.707(FG)$$

In this example, the intercept a is negative (–198.9). Because the intercept just positions the height of the line in the graph, and because the origin is usually outside of the range of relevant data whether the intercept is positive, negative, or zero is usually of no concern. It is just a constant to be used when applying the regression model. It certainly cannot be interpreted in this case that if a team had a zero success rate for FG attempts the percentage of wins would be negative.

For the slope term the interpretation is very useful. The number 5.707 tells you that for every 1 percent increase in the percentage of FGs that are made the team's WP would be estimated to increase by about 5.7 percent. Similarly, a drop of 1 percent in FG would cause the WP to fall by about 5.7 percent. This knowledge could be very useful to a basketball coach. In later chapters, you will see how other independent variables can affect the WP of basketball teams.

1 The equation written in the scattergram is the way you would get it from Excel. In this format, the slope times the independent variable is the first term and the intercept or constant is the second term. Mathematicians often use this form but the way the equation is presented in this book is far more common in practice. By comparing the two forms of the function you can see they give the same result.

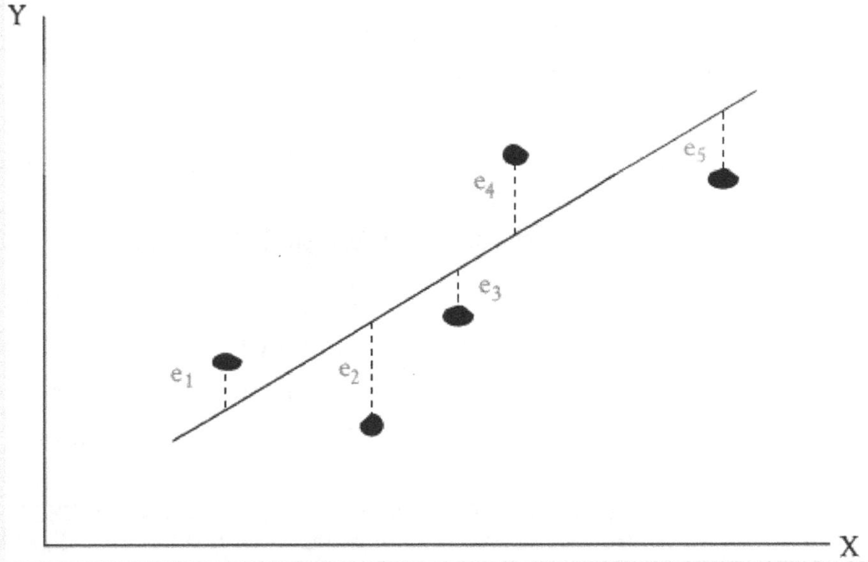

Figure 12.2 The ordinary least squares regression line for *Y* as a function of *X*. Residuals (or deviations or errors) between each point and the regression line are labeled e_i

HOW CAN YOU DETERMINE THE BEST REGRESSION LINE FOR YOUR DATA?

The most commonly used criterion for the "best" regression line is that the sum of the squared vertical differences between the observed values and the estimated regression line be as small as possible. To illustrate this concept, Figure 12.2 shows five observations of the relationship between some *Y* variable and some *X* variable. You can see from the scattering of points that no straight line would go through all of the points. You would like to find the one line that does the "best" job of fitting the data. Thus, there needs to be a common and agreed upon criterion for what is best.

This criterion is to **minimize the sum of the squared vertical deviations of the observed values from the regression line.** This is called "ordinary least squares" (OLS) regression.

The vertical distance between each point and the regression line is called a deviation.[1] Each of these deviations is indicated by e_i (where the subscript *i* refers to the number of the observation). A regression line is drawn through the points in Figure 12.2. The deviations between the actual data points and the estimates made from the regression line are identified as e_1, e_2, e_3, e_4, and e_5. Note that some of the deviations are positive (e_1 and e_4), while the others are negative (e_2, e_3, and e_5). Some errors are fairly large (such as e_2), while others are small (such as e_3).

By our criterion, the best regression line is that line which minimizes the sum of the squares of these deviations (min $\sum(e_i)^2$). This regression method (OLS) is the most common type of regression.

2 The deviations from the regression line (e_i) are also frequently called residuals or errors. You are likely to see the term residuals used in printouts from some computer programs that perform regression analysis, such as in Excel.

If someone says they did a regression analysis you can assume it was OLS regression unless some other method is specified. In OLS regression, the deviations are squared so that positive and negative deviations do not cancel each other out as we find their sum. The single line that gives us the smallest sum of the squared deviations from the line is the best line according to the OLS method.

AN EXAMPLE OF OLS REGRESSION USING ANNUAL VALUES OF WOMEN'S CLOTHING SALES

The annual values for women's clothing sales (AWCS) are shown in Table 12.1. To get a linear trend over time, you can use regression with AWCS as a function of time. Usually time is measured with an index starting at 1 for the first observation. In Table 12.1, the heading for this column is "Year."

TABLE 12.1 ANNUAL DATA FOR WOMEN'S CLOTHING SALES WITH REGRESSION TREND PREDICTIONS. THIS OLS MODEL RESULTS IN SOME NEGATIVE AND SOME POSITIVE ERRORS WHICH SHOULD BE EXPECTED[2]

Date	Year	AWCS (annual data)	Trend predictions for AWCS (annual data)	Error (actual-predicted)
2000	1	31,480	31,483	−3
2001	2	31,487	32,257	−770
2002	3	31,280	33,031	−1,751
2003	4	32,598	33,805	−1,207
2004	5	34,886	34,579	307
2005	6	37,000	35,353	1,647
2006	7	38,716	36,127	2,589
2007	8	40,337	36,901	3,436
2008	9	38,351	37,675	676
2009	10	35,780	38,449	−2,669
2010	11	36,969	39,223	−2,254

The OLS regression equation for the women's clothing sales trend on an annual basis (AWCS) is shown in Figure 12.3 (page 197). The OLS regression equation is[3]:

$$\text{AWCS} = 30{,}709.200 + 773.982(\text{Year})$$

2 You should enter the data in Table 3.1 into Excel and use it for practice with regression. You can compare your results with those shown here.

3 This type of regression model is often called a trend regression. Some people would call the independent variable "Time" rather than "Year."

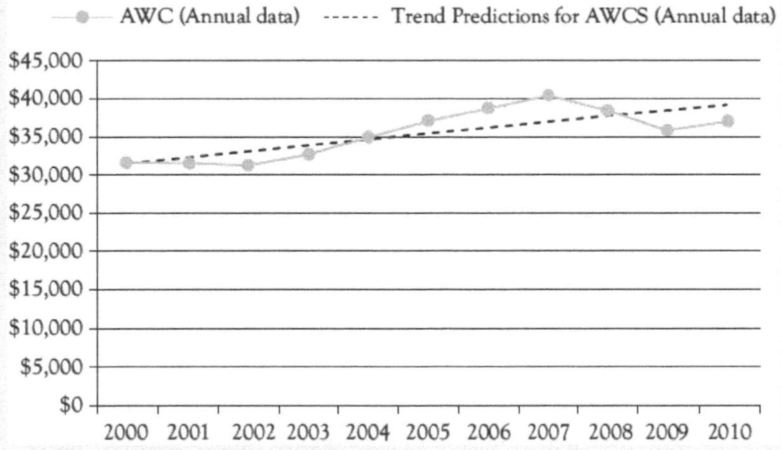

Figure 12.3 The OLS regression trend for annual women's clothing sales (M$). Here you see that for 2000, the regression trend was almost perfect and that the biggest error is for 2007

In Figure 12.3, you see that for 2000 the model is almost perfect, having a very small error and that the error is the largest for 2007. Overall, the dotted line showing the predicted values is the "best" regression line using the OLS criterion.

THE UNDERLYING ASSUMPTIONS OF THE OLS REGRESSION MODEL

There are certain mathematical assumptions that underlie the OLS regression model. To become an expert in regression you would want to know all of these, but our goal is not to make you an expert. The goal is to help you be an informed user of regression, not a statistical expert. However, there are four of these assumptions that you should be familiar with in order to appreciate both the power and the limitations of OLS regression.

THE PROBABILITY DISTRIBUTION OF *Y* FOR EACH *X*

First for each value of an independent variable (X) there is a probability distribution of the dependent variable (Y). Figure 12.4 shows the probability distributions of Y for two of the possible values of X (X_1 and X_2). The means of the probability distributions are assumed to lie on a straight line, according to the equation: $Y = a + bX$. In other words, the mean value of the dependent variable is assumed to be a linear function of the independent variable (note that the regression line in Figure 12.4 is directly under the peaks of the probability distributions for Y).

THE DISPERSION OF *Y* FOR EACH *X*

Second, OLS assumes that the standard deviation of each of the probability distributions is the same for all values of the independent variable (such as X_1 and X_2). In Figure 12.4 (page 198), the "spread" of

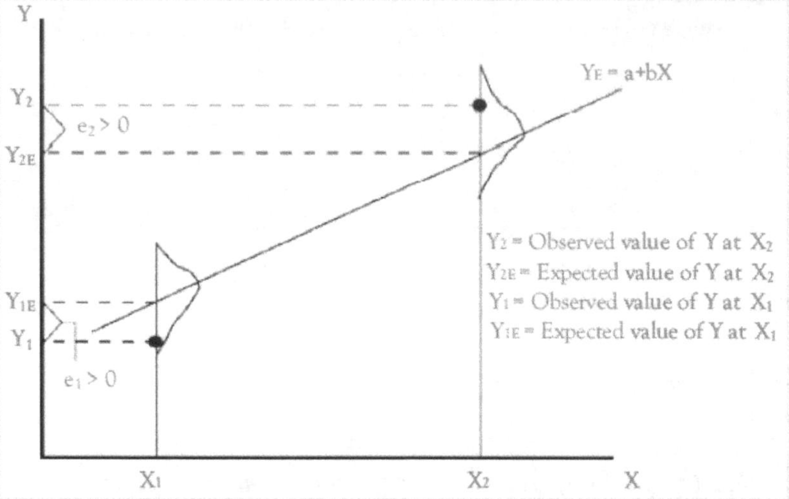

Figure 12.4 Distribution of *Y* values around the OLS regression line. For any *X*, the possible values of *Y* are assumed to be distributed normally around the regression line. Further, the errors or residuals (e_i) are assumed to be normally distributed with a mean of zero and a constant standard deviation

both of the probability distributions shown is the same (this characteristic of equal standard deviations is called homoscedasticity).

VALUES OF *Y* ARE INDEPENDENT OF ONE ANOTHER

Third, the values of the dependent variable (*Y*) are assumed to be independent of one another. If one observation of *Y* lies below the mean of its probability distribution, this does not imply that the next observation will also be below the mean (or anywhere else in particular).

THE PROBABILITY DISTRIBUTION OF ERRORS FOLLOW A NORMAL DISTRIBUTION

Fourth, the probability distributions of the errors, or residuals, are assumed to be normal. That is, the differences between the actual values of *Y* and the expected values (from the regression line) are normally distributed random variables with a mean of zero and a constant standard deviation.

THEORY VERSUS PRACTICE

These four assumptions may be viewed as the ideal to which one aspires when using regression. While these underlying assumptions of regression are sometimes violated in practice, they should be followed closely enough to ensure that estimated regression equations represent true relationships between variables. For the practitioner, it is important to note that if these four assumptions are not at least closely approximated, the resulting OLS regression analysis may be flawed. Summary statistics that are used with regression analysis allow us to check compliance with these assumptions. These statistics are described later, as are the likely outcomes of violating these assumptions.

DOING REGRESSION IN EXCEL

To do regression analysis in Excel, you need to use the "Data Analysis" tools of Excel. How you get to "Data Analysis" depends on the version of Excel you are using. [...] Once you get to the "Data Analysis" dialog box, the process of doing regression is the same in all versions of Excel. What follows is based on screen shots for Excel 2013 but the process within "Data Analysis" will work in all versions of Excel.

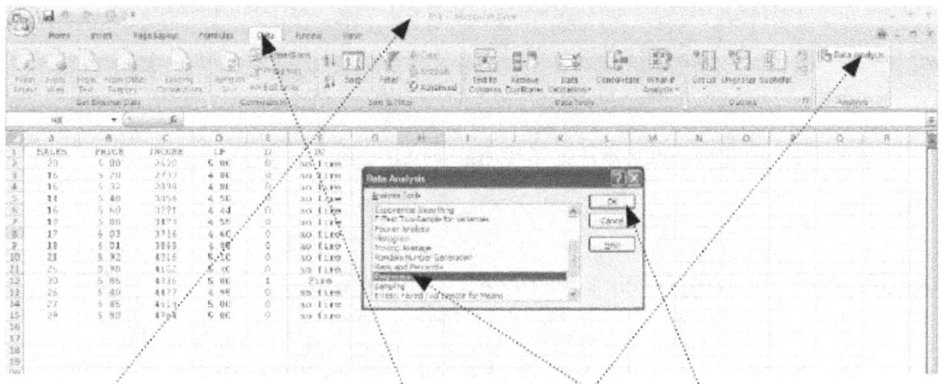

1. Start by entering data or opening a data file. Here, an example file is opened.
2. Click on Data and then select "Data Analysis".
3. In the "Data Analysis" box select Regression.
4. Then click on OK.

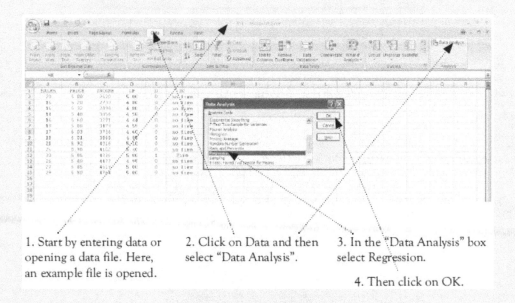

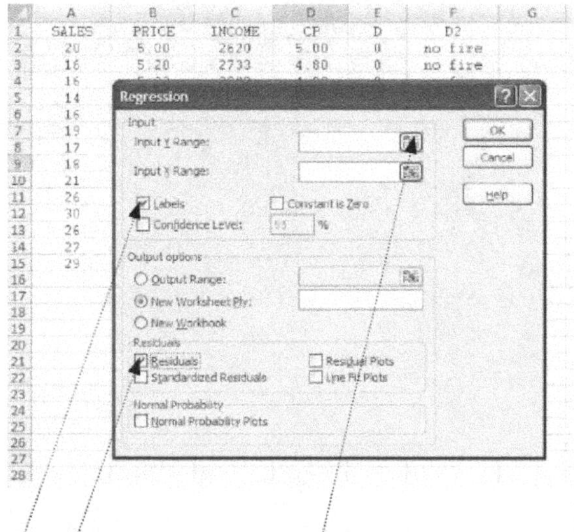

5. Check labels and residuals

6. Next click on the square in the Input Y Range box.

Then, drag over the range for the *Y* (dependent) variable(s). This is shown below. You see that the column for sales has a dashed line around it to indicate it has been selected and the range is shown in the small dialog box. To complete the selection of *Y* click here.

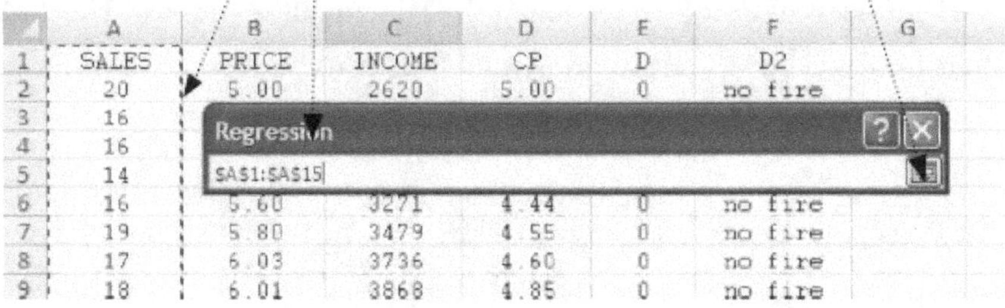

7. Next click on the square in the Input *X* Range box, which is right below the Input *Y* Range box.

Then, drag over the range for the *X* (independent) variable(s). If you have more than one independent variable they should be in adjacent columns. This is shown below. You see that the columns for price, income, CP, and D have a dashed line around them to indicate they have been selected and the range is shown in the dialog box. Sometimes you may need to move columns around a bit so that all independent variables are in contiguous columns.

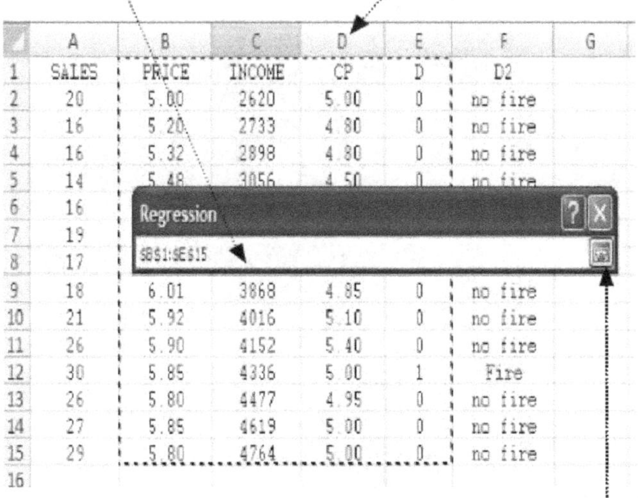

To complete the selection of the *X* variables click here.

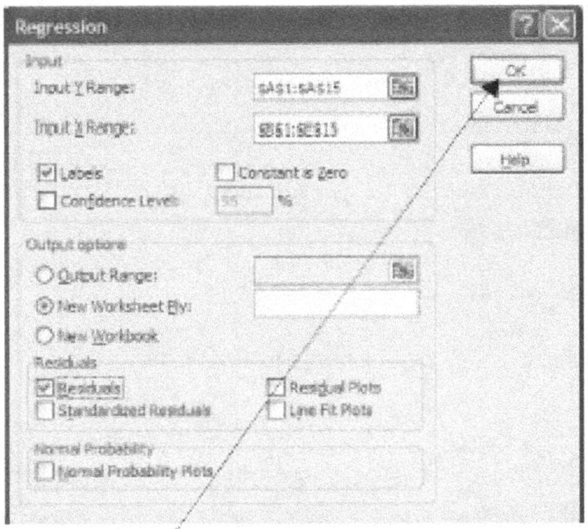

This brings you back to the main regression dialog box. You are now ready for Excel to calculate the regression equations so click on OK.

The results will appear on a new sheet, as shown below. You will probably want to delete some of this output and reformat the column widths and cells, especially reducing the number of decimal points shown.

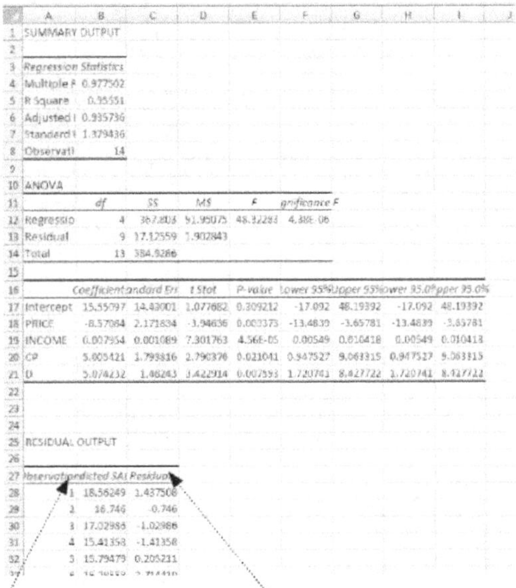

	A	B	C	D	E	F	G	H	I
1	SUMMARY OUTPUT								
2									
3	*Regression Statistics*								
4	Multiple R	0.977502							
5	R Square	0.95551							
6	Adjusted I	0.935736							
7	Standard I	1.379436							
8	Observati	14							
9									
10	ANOVA								
11		*df*	*SS*	*MS*	*F*	*gnificance F*			
12	Regressio	4	367.803	91.95075	48.32283	4.38E-06			
13	Residual	9	17.12559	1.902843					
14	Total	13	384.9286						
15									
16		*Coefficient*	*andard Err*	*t Stat*	*P-value*	*Lower 95%*	*Upper 95%*	*ower 95.0%*	*pper 95.0%*
17	Intercept	15.55097	14.43001	1.077682	0.309212	-17.092	48.19392	-17.092	48.19392
18	PRICE	-8.57084	2.171834	-3.94636	0.003373	-13.4839	-3.65781	-13.4839	-3.65781
19	INCOME	0.007954	0.001089	7.301763	4.56E-05	0.00549	0.010418	0.00549	0.010418
20	CP	5.005421	1.793816	2.790376	0.021041	0.947527	9.063315	0.947527	9.063315
21	D	5.074232	1.48243	3.422914	0.007593	1.720741	8.427722	1.720741	8.427722
22									
23									
24									
25	RESIDUAL OUTPUT								
26									
27	*Observation*	*redicted SA*	*Residuals*						
28	1	18.56249	1.437508						
29	2	16.746	-0.746						
30	3	17.02986	-1.02986						
31	4	15.41358	-1.41358						
32	5	15.79479	0.205211						

You can copy the predicted values then paste them in a column next to your original Y values to make it easy to generate a graph and to illustrate how the actual and predicted values compare.

For time series data, you will need to program in the Durbin–Watson formula. The Residuals column contains the necessary data (the residuals are often called the errors). The Durbin–Watson formula is given in Chapter 4.

To obtain the correlation coefficients for the independent variables:

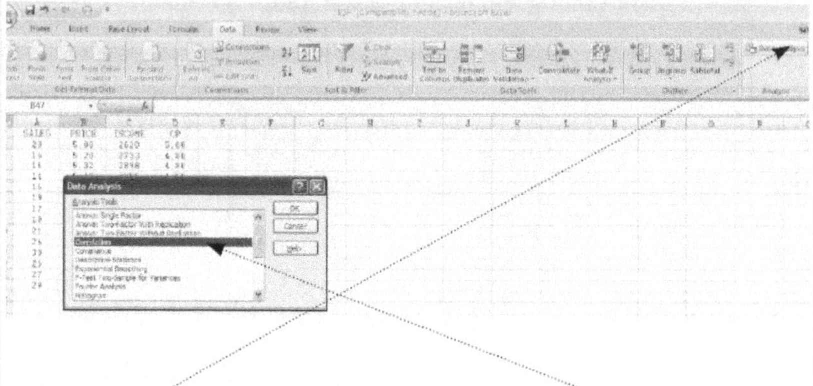

Select "Data Analysis"

In the "Data Analysis" box select Correlation.

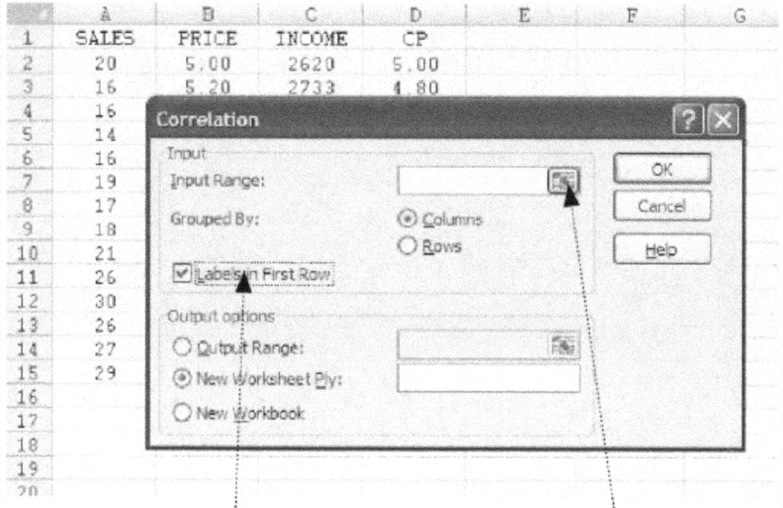

Check Labels in First Row

Click on the square in the Input Range box.

Then, drag over the range for the independent variables. This is shown below. You see that the columns for price, income, and CP have a dashed line around them to indicate they have been selected and the range is shown in the dialog box. Then click here.

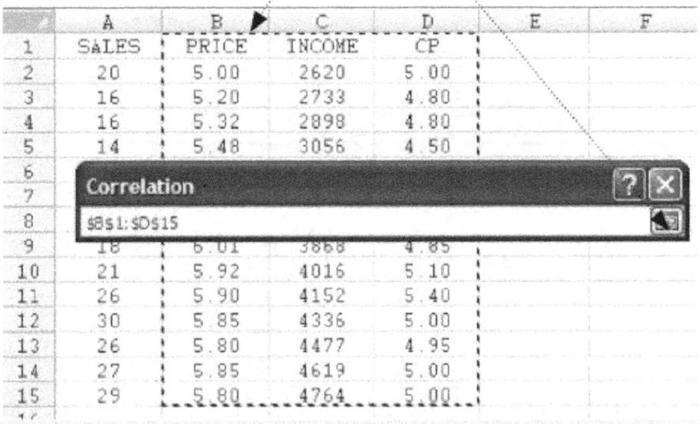

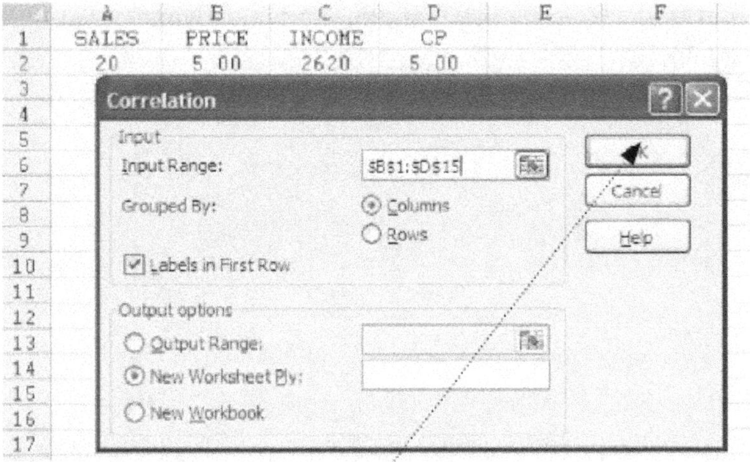

This brings you back to the main Correlation dialog box. You are now ready for Excel to calculate the correlation coefficients so click on OK.

The results will appear on a new sheet, as shown below.

	PRICE	*INCOME*	*CP*
PRICE	1		
INCOME	0.794293	1	
CP	0.165771	0.477671	1

WHAT YOU HAVE LEARNED IN CHAPTER 11

- You know the difference between a dependent variable and an independent variable.
- You know what portion of a regression equation (model) represents the intercept (or constant) and how to interpret that value.
- You know what part of the regression equation represents the slope and how to interpret that value.
- You know that for business applications the slope is the more important part of a regression equation.
- You know the ordinary least squares (OLS) criterion for the "best" regression line.
- You know four of the basic statistical assumptions underlying regression analysis.
- You know how to perform regression analysis in Excel.

Appendix

By Priscilla Chaffe-Stengel and Donald N. Stengel

STANDARD NORMAL TABLE (*Z*)

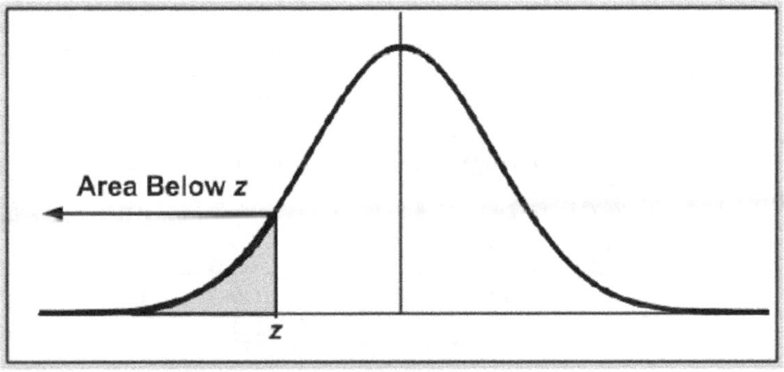

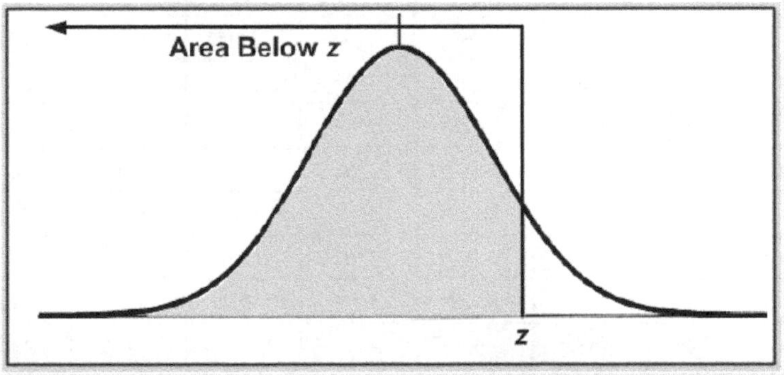

z	.00	.01	.02	.03	.04	.05	.06	.07	.08	.09
−3.8	.0001	.0001	.0001	.0001	.0001	.0001	.0001	.0001	.0001	.0001
−3.7	.0001	.0001	.0001	.0001	.0001	.0001	.0001	.0001	.0001	.0001
−3.6	.0002	.0002	.0001	.0001	.0001	.0001	.0001	.0001	.0001	.0001
−3.5	.0002	.0002	.0002	.0002	.0002	.0002	.0002	.0002	.0002	.0002
−3.4	.0003	.0003	.0003	.0003	.0003	.0003	.0003	.0003	.0003	.0002
−3.3	.0005	.0005	.0005	.0004	.0004	.0004	.0004	.0004	.0004	.0003
−3.2	.0007	.0007	.0006	.0006	.0006	.0006	.0006	.0005	.0005	.0005

z	.00	.01	.02	.03	.04	.05	.06	.07	.08	.09
−3.1	.0010	.0009	.0009	.0009	.0008	.0008	.0008	.0008	.0007	.0007
−3.0	.0013	.0013	.0013	.0012	.0012	.0011	.0011	.0011	.0010	.0010
−2.9	.0019	.0018	.0018	.0017	.0016	.0016	.0015	.0015	.0014	.0014
−2.8	.0026	.0025	.0024	.0023	.0023	.0022	.0021	.0021	.0020	.0019
−2.7	.0035	.0034	.0033	.0032	.0031	.0030	.0029	.0028	.0027	.0026
−2.6	.0047	.0045	.0044	.0043	.0041	.0040	.0039	.0038	.0037	.0036
−2.5	.0062	.0060	.0059	.0057	.0055	.0054	.0052	.0051	.0049	.0048
−2.4	.0082	.0080	.0078	.0075	.0073	.0071	.0069	.0068	.0066	.0064
−2.3	.0107	.0104	.0102	.0099	.0096	.0094	.0091	.0089	.0087	.0084
−2.2	.0139	.0136	.0132	.0129	.0125	.0122	.0119	.0116	.0113	.0110
−2.1	.0179	.0174	.0170	.0166	.0162	.0158	.0154	.0150	.0146	.0143
−2.0	.0228	.0222	.0217	.0212	.0207	.0202	.0197	.0192	.0188	.0183
−1.9	.0287	.0281	.0274	.0268	.0262	.0256	.0250	.0244	.0239	.0233
−1.8	.0359	.0351	.0344	.0336	.0329	.0322	.0314	.0307	.0301	.0294
−1.7	.0446	.0436	.0427	.0418	.0409	.0401	.0392	.0384	.0375	.0367
−1.6	.0548	.0537	.0526	.0516	.0505	.0495	.0485	.0475	.0465	.0455
−1.5	.0668	.0655	.0643	.0630	.0618	.0606	.0594	.0582	.0571	.0559
−1.4	.0808	.0793	.0778	.0764	.0749	.0735	.0721	.0708	.0694	.0681
−1.3	.0968	.0951	.0934	.0918	.0901	.0885	.0869	.0853	.0838	.0823
−1.2	.1151	.1131	.1112	.1093	.1075	.1056	.1038	.1020	.1003	.0985
−1.1	.1357	.1335	.1314	.1292	.1271	.1251	.1230	.1210	.1190	.1170
−1.0	.1587	.1562	.1539	.1515	.1492	.1469	.1446	.1423	.1401	.1379
−0.9	.1841	.1814	.1788	.1762	.1736	.1711	.1685	.1660	.1635	.1611
−0.8	.2119	.2090	.2061	.2033	.2005	.1977	.1949	.1922	.1894	.1867
−0.7	.2420	.2389	.2358	.2327	.2296	.2266	.2236	.2206	.2177	.2148
−0.6	.2743	.2709	.2676	.2643	.2611	.2578	.2546	.2514	.2483	.2451
−0.5	.3085	.3050	.3015	.2981	.2946	.2912	.2877	.2843	.2810	.2776
−0.4	.3446	.3409	.3372	.3336	.3300	.3264	.3228	.3192	.3156	.3121
−0.3	.3821	.3783	.3745	.3707	.3669	.3632	.3594	.3557	.3520	.3483
−0.2	.4207	.4168	.4129	.4090	.4052	.4013	.3974	.3936	.3897	.3859
−0.1	.4602	.4562	.4522	.4483	.4443	.4404	.4364	.4325	.4286	.4247
−0.0	.5000	.4960	.4920	.4880	.4840	.4801	.4761	.4721	.4681	.4641
0.0	.5000	.5040	.5080	.5120	.5160	.5199	.5239	.5279	.5319	.5359
0.1	.5398	.5438	.5478	.5517	.5557	.5596	.5636	.5675	.5714	.5753
0.2	.5793	.5832	.5871	.5910	.5948	.5987	.6026	.6064	.6103	.6141
0.3	.6179	.6217	.6255	.6293	.6331	.6368	.6406	.6443	.6480	.6517

z	.00	.01	.02	.03	.04	.05	.06	.07	.08	.09
0.4	.6554	.6591	.6628	.6664	.6700	.6736	.6772	.6808	.6844	.6879
0.5	.6915	.6950	.6985	.7019	.7054	.7088	.7123	.7157	.7190	.7224
0.6	.7257	.7291	.7324	.7357	.7389	.7422	.7454	.7486	.7517	.7549
0.7	.7580	.7611	.7642	.7673	.7704	.7734	.7764	.7794	.7823	.7852
0.8	.7881	.7910	.7939	.7967	.7995	.8023	.8051	.8078	.8106	.8133
0.9	.8159	.8186	.8212	.8238	.8264	.8289	.8315	.8340	.8365	.8389
1.0	.8413	.8438	.8461	.8485	.8508	.8531	.8554	.8577	.8599	.8621
1.1	.8643	.8665	.8686	.8708	.8729	.8749	.8770	.8790	.8810	.8830
1.2	.8849	.8869	.8888	.8907	.8925	.8944	.8962	.8980	.8997	.9015
1.3	.9032	.9049	.9066	.9082	.9099	.9115	.9131	.9147	.9162	.9177
1.4	.9192	.9207	.9222	.9236	.9251	.9265	.9279	.9292	.9306	.9319
1.5	.9332	.9345	.9357	.9370	.9382	.9394	.9406	.9418	.9429	.9441
1.6	.9452	.9463	.9474	.9484	.9495	.9505	.9515	.9525	.9535	.9545
1.7	.9554	.9564	.9573	.9582	.9591	.9599	.9608	.9616	.9625	.9633
1.8	.9641	.9649	.9656	.9664	.9671	.9678	.9686	.9693	.9699	.9706
1.9	.9713	.9719	.9726	.9732	.9738	.9744	.9750	.9756	.9761	.9767
2.0	.9772	.9778	.9783	.9788	.9793	.9798	.9803	.9808	.9812	.9817
2.1	.9821	.9826	.9830	.9834	.9838	.9842	.9846	.9850	.9854	.9857
2.2	.9861	.9864	.9868	.9871	.9875	.9878	.9881	.9884	.9887	.9890
2.3	.9893	.9896	.9898	.9901	.9904	.9906	.9909	.9911	.9913	.9916
2.4	.9918	.9920	.9922	.9925	.9927	.9929	.9931	.9932	.9934	.9936
2.5	.9938	.9940	.9941	.9943	.9945	.9946	.9948	.9949	.9951	.9952
2.6	.9953	.9955	.9956	.9957	.9959	.9960	.9961	.9962	.9963	.9964
2.7	.9965	.9966	.9967	.9968	.9969	.9970	.9971	.9972	.9973	.9974
2.8	.9974	.9975	.9976	.9977	.9977	.9978	.9979	.9979	.9980	.9981
2.9	.9981	.9982	.9982	.9983	.9984	.9984	.9985	.9985	.9986	.9986
3.0	.9987	.9987	.9987	.9988	.9988	.9989	.9989	.9989	.9990	.9990
3.1	.9990	.9991	.9991	.9991	.9992	.9992	.9992	.9992	.9993	.9993
3.2	.9993	.9993	.9994	.9994	.9994	.9994	.9994	.9995	.9995	.9995
3.3	.9995	.9995	.9995	.9996	.9996	.9996	.9996	.9996	.9996	.9997
3.4	.9997	.9997	.9997	.9997	.9997	.9997	.9997	.9997	.9997	.9998
3.5	.9998	.9998	.9998	.9998	.9998	.9998	.9998	.9998	.9998	.9998
3.6	.9998	.9998	.9999	.9999	.9999	.9999	.9999	.9999	.9999	.9999
3.7	.9999	.9999	.9999	.9999	.9999	.9999	.9999	.9999	.9999	.9999
3.8	.9999	.9999	.9999	.9999	.9999	.9999	.9999	.9999	.9999	.9999

Source: The cumulative normal probablilities were generated in Excel.

STUDENT'S *T*-DISTRIBUTION

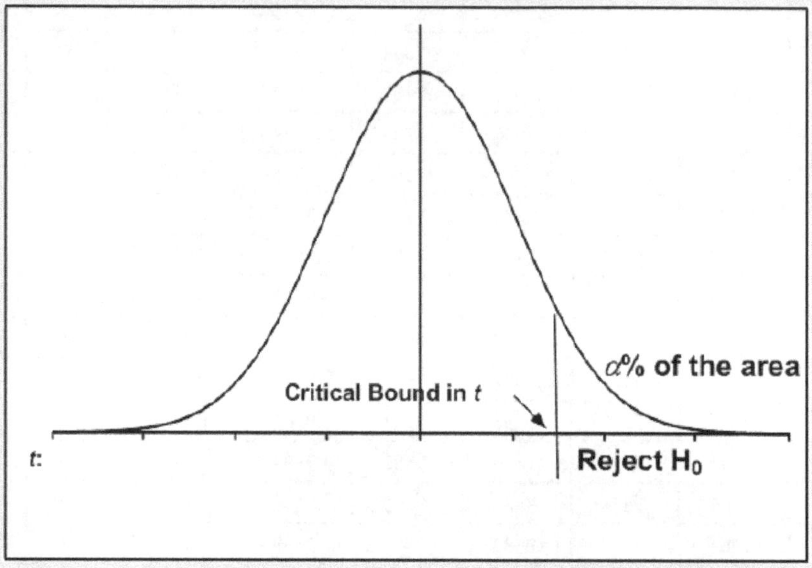

α = / df =	0.10	0.05	0.025	0.01	0.005
1	3.078	6.314	12.706	31.821	63.657
2	1.886	2.920	4.303	6.965	9.925
3	1.638	2.353	3.182	4.541	5.841
4	1.533	2.132	2.776	3.747	4.604
5	1.476	2.015	2.571	3.365	4.032
6	1.440	1.943	2.447	3.143	3.707
7	1.415	1.895	2.365	2.998	3.499
8	1.397	1.860	2.306	2.896	3.355
9	1.383	1.833	2.262	2.821	3.250
10	1.372	1.812	2.228	2.764	3.169
11	1.363	1.796	2.201	2.718	3.106
12	1.356	1.782	2.179	2.681	3.055
13	1.350	1.771	2.160	2.650	3.012
14	1.345	1.761	2.145	2.624	2.977
15	1.341	1.753	2.131	2.602	2.947
16	1.337	1.746	2.120	2.583	2.921

$\alpha =$	0.10	0.05	0.025	0.01	0.005
17	1.333	1.740	2.110	2.567	2.898
18	1.330	1.734	2.101	2.552	2.878
19	1.328	1.729	2.093	2.539	2.861
20	1.325	1.725	2.086	2.528	2.845
21	1.323	1.721	2.080	2.518	2.831
22	1.321	1.717	2.074	2.508	2.819
23	1.319	1.714	2.069	2.500	2.807
24	1.318	1.711	2.064	2.492	2.797
25	1.316	1.708	2.060	2.485	2.787
26	1.315	1.706	2.056	2.479	2.779
27	1.314	1.703	2.052	2.473	2.771
28	1.313	1.701	2.048	2.467	2.763
29	1.311	1.699	2.045	2.462	2.756
30	1.310	1.697	2.042	2.457	2.750
31	1.309	1.696	2.040	2.453	2.744
32	1.309	1.694	2.037	2.449	2.738
33	1.308	1.692	2.035	2.445	2.733
34	1.307	1.691	2.032	2.441	2.728
35	1.306	1.690	2.030	2.438	2.724
36	1.306	1.688	2.028	2.434	2.719
37	1.305	1.687	2.026	2.431	2.715
38	1.304	1.686	2.024	2.429	2.712
39	1.304	1.685	2.023	2.426	2.708
40	1.303	1.684	2.021	2.423	2.704
41	1.303	1.683	2.020	2.421	2.701
42	1.302	1.682	2.018	2.418	2.698
43	1.302	1.681	2.017	2.416	2.695
44	1.301	1.680	2.015	2.414	2.692
45	1.301	1.679	2.014	2.412	2.690
46	1.300	1.679	2.013	2.410	2.687
47	1.300	1.678	2.012	2.408	2.685
48	1.299	1.677	2.011	2.407	2.682
49	1.299	1.677	2.010	2.405	2.680
50	1.299	1.676	2.009	2.403	2.678
51	1.298	1.675	2.008	2.402	2.676
52	1.298	1.675	2.007	2.400	2.674
53	1.298	1.674	2.006	2.399	2.672

α =	0.10	0.05	0.025	0.01	0.005
54	1.297	1.674	2.005	2.397	2.670
55	1.297	1.673	2.004	2.396	2.668
56	1.297	1.673	2.003	2.395	2.667
57	1.297	1.672	2.002	2.394	2.665
58	1.296	1.672	2.002	2.392	2.663
59	1.296	1.671	2.001	2.391	2.662
60	1.296	1.671	2.000	2.390	2.660
61	1.296	1.670	2.000	2.389	2.659
62	1.295	1.670	1.999	2.388	2.657
63	1.295	1.669	1.998	2.387	2.656
64	1.295	1.669	1.998	2.386	2.655
65	1.295	1.669	1.997	2.385	2.654
66	1.295	1.668	1.997	2.384	2.652
67	1.294	1.668	1.996	2.383	2.651
68	1.294	1.668	1.995	2.382	2.650
69	1.294	1.667	1.995	2.382	2.649
70	1.294	1.667	1.994	2.381	2.648
71	1.294	1.667	1.994	2.380	2.647
72	1.293	1.666	1.993	2.379	2.646
73	1.293	1.666	1.993	2.379	2.645
74	1.293	1.666	1.993	2.378	2.644
75	1.293	1.665	1.992	2.377	2.643
76	1.293	1.665	1.992	2.376	2.642
77	1.293	1.665	1.991	2.376	2.641
78	1.292	1.665	1.991	2.375	2.640
79	1.292	1.664	1.990	2.374	2.640
80	1.292	1.664	1.990	2.374	2.639
81	1.292	1.664	1.990	2.373	2.638
82	1.292	1.664	1.989	2.373	2.637
83	1.292	1.663	1.989	2.372	2.636
84	1.292	1.663	1.989	2.372	2.636
85	1.292	1.663	1.988	2.371	2.635
86	1.291	1.663	1.988	2.370	2.634
87	1.291	1.663	1.988	2.370	2.634
88	1.291	1.662	1.987	2.369	2.633
89	1.291	1.662	1.987	2.369	2.632
90	1.291	1.662	1.987	2.368	2.632
91	1.291	1.662	1.986	2.368	2.631
91	1.291	1.662	1.986	2.368	2.631
92	1.291	1.662	1.986	2.368	2.630

α =	0.10	0.05	0.025	0.01	0.005
93	1.291	1.661	1.986	2.367	2.630
94	1.291	1.661	1.986	2.367	2.629
95	1.291	1.661	1.985	2.366	2.629
96	1.290	1.661	1.985	2.366	2.628
97	1.290	1.661	1.985	2.365	2.627
98	1.290	1.661	1.984	2.365	2.627
99	1.290	1.660	1.984	2.365	2.626
100	1.290	1.660	1.984	2.364	2.626
120	1.289	1.658	1.980	2.358	2.617
∞	1.282	1.645	1.96	2.326	2.576

Source: The *t*-coefficients were generated in Excel.

F Tables

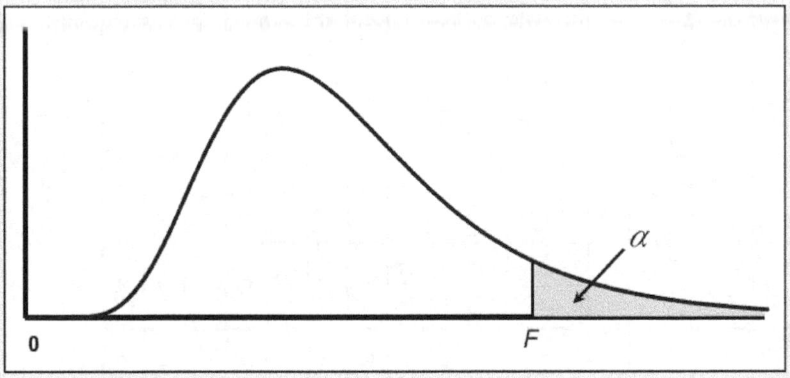

Each of the following *F*-Tables contains the value for the upper boundary of the *F*-distribution for a given numerator and denominator degree of freedom that marks off 0.10, 0.05, 0.025, and 0.01 of the area in the tail of the distribution.

F Table, $\alpha = 0.10$

denom df	num df 1	2	3	4	5	6	7	8	9	10	12	15	20	24	30	40	60	120	∞
1	39.86	49.50	53.59	55.83	57.24	58.20	58.91	59.44	59.86	60.19	60.71	61.22	61.74	62.00	62.26	62.53	62.79	63.06	63.33
2	8.53	9.00	9.16	9.24	9.29	9.33	9.35	9.37	9.38	9.39	9.41	9.42	9.44	9.45	9.46	9.47	9.47	9.48	9.49
3	5.54	5.46	5.39	5.34	5.31	5.28	5.27	5.25	5.24	5.23	5.22	5.20	5.18	5.18	5.17	5.16	5.15	5.14	5.13
4	4.54	4.32	4.19	4.11	4.05	4.01	3.98	3.95	3.94	3.92	3.90	3.87	3.84	3.83	3.82	3.80	3.79	3.78	3.76
5	4.06	3.78	3.62	3.52	3.45	3.40	3.37	3.34	3.32	3.30	3.27	3.24	3.21	3.19	3.17	3.16	3.14	3.12	3.10
6	3.78	3.46	3.29	3.18	3.11	3.05	3.01	2.98	2.96	2.94	2.90	2.87	2.84	2.82	2.80	2.78	2.76	2.74	2.72
7	3.59	3.26	3.07	2.96	2.88	2.83	2.78	2.75	2.72	2.70	2.67	2.63	2.59	2.58	2.56	2.54	2.51	2.49	2.47
8	3.46	3.11	2.92	2.81	2.73	2.67	2.62	2.59	2.56	2.54	2.50	2.46	2.42	2.40	2.38	2.36	2.34	2.32	2.29
9	3.36	3.01	2.81	2.69	2.61	2.55	2.51	2.47	2.44	2.42	2.38	2.34	2.30	2.28	2.25	2.23	2.21	2.18	2.16
10	3.29	2.92	2.73	2.61	2.52	2.46	2.41	2.38	2.35	2.32	2.28	2.24	2.20	2.18	2.16	2.13	2.11	2.08	2.06
12	3.18	2.81	2.61	2.48	2.39	2.33	2.28	2.24	2.21	2.19	2.15	2.10	2.06	2.04	2.01	1.99	1.96	1.93	1.90
15	3.07	2.70	2.49	2.36	2.27	2.21	2.16	2.12	2.09	2.06	2.02	1.97	1.92	1.90	1.87	1.85	1.82	1.79	1.76
20	2.97	2.59	2.38	2.25	2.16	2.09	2.04	2.00	1.96	1.94	1.89	1.84	1.79	1.77	1.74	1.71	1.68	1.64	1.61
24	2.93	2.54	2.33	2.19	2.10	2.04	1.98	1.94	1.91	1.88	1.83	1.78	1.73	1.70	1.67	1.64	1.61	1.57	1.53
30	2.88	2.49	2.28	2.14	2.05	1.98	1.93	1.88	1.85	1.82	1.77	1.72	1.67	1.64	1.61	1.57	1.54	1.50	1.46
40	2.84	2.44	2.23	2.09	2.00	1.93	1.87	1.83	1.79	1.76	1.71	1.66	1.61	1.57	1.54	1.51	1.47	1.42	1.38
60	2.79	2.39	2.18	2.04	1.95	1.87	1.82	1.77	1.74	1.71	1.66	1.60	1.54	1.51	1.48	1.44	1.40	1.35	1.29
120	2.75	2.35	2.13	1.99	1.90	1.82	1.77	1.72	1.68	1.65	1.60	1.55	1.48	1.45	1.41	1.37	1.32	1.26	1.19
∞	2.71	2.30	2.08	1.94	1.85	1.77	1.72	1.67	1.63	1.60	1.55	1.49	1.42	1.38	1.34	1.30	1.24	1.17	1.00

F Table, $\alpha = 0.05$

denom df	num df 1	2	3	4	5	6	7	8	9	10	12	15	20	24	30	40	60	120	∞
1	161.4	199.5	215.7	224.6	230.2	234.0	236.8	238.9	240.5	241.9	243.9	245.9	248.0	249.1	250.1	251.1	252.2	253.3	254.3
2	18.51	19.00	19.16	19.25	19.30	19.33	19.35	19.37	19.38	19.40	19.41	19.43	19.45	19.45	19.46	19.47	19.48	19.49	19.50
3	10.13	9.55	9.28	9.12	9.01	8.94	8.89	8.85	8.81	8.79	8.74	8.70	8.66	8.64	8.62	8.59	8.57	8.55	8.53
4	7.71	6.94	6.59	6.39	6.26	6.16	6.09	6.04	5.00	5.96	5.91	5.86	5.80	5.77	5.75	5.72	5.69	5.66	5.63
5	6.61	5.79	5.41	5.19	5.05	4.95	4.88	4.82	4.77	4.74	4.68	4.62	4.56	4.53	4.50	4.46	4.43	4.40	4.36
6	5.99	5.14	4.76	4.53	4.39	4.28	4.21	4.15	4.10	4.06	4.00	3.94	3.87	3.84	3.81	3.77	3.74	3.70	3.67
7	5.59	4.74	4.35	4.12	3.97	3.87	3.79	3.73	3.68	3.64	3.57	3.51	3.44	3.41	3.38	3.34	3.30	3.27	3.23
8	5.32	4.46	4.07	3.84	3.69	3.58	3.50	3.44	3.39	3.35	3.28	3.22	3.15	3.12	3.08	3.04	3.01	2.97	2.93
9	5.12	4.26	3.86	3.63	3.48	3.37	3.29	3.23	3.18	3.14	3.07	3.01	2.94	2.90	2.86	2.83	2.79	2.75	2.71
10	4.96	4.10	3.71	3.48	3.33	3.22	3.14	3.07	3.02	2.98	2.91	2.85	2.77	2.74	2.70	2.66	2.62	2.58	2.54
12	4.75	3.89	3.49	3.26	3.11	3.00	2.91	2.85	2.80	2.75	2.69	2.62	2.54	2.51	2.47	2.43	2.38	2.34	2.30
15	4.54	3.68	3.29	3.06	2.90	2.79	2.71	2.64	2.59	2.54	2.48	2.40	2.33	2.29	2.25	2.20	2.16	2.11	2.07
20	4.35	3.49	3.10	2.87	2.71	2.60	2.51	2.45	2.39	2.35	2.28	2.20	2.12	2.08	2.04	1.99	1.95	1.90	1.84
24	4.26	3.40	3.01	2.78	2.62	2.51	2.42	2.36	2.30	2.25	2.18	2.11	2.03	1.98	1.94	1.89	1.84	1.79	1.73
30	4.17	3.32	2.92	2.69	2.53	2.42	2.33	2.27	2.21	2.16	2.09	2.01	1.93	1.89	1.84	1.79	1.74	1.68	1.62
40	4.08	3.23	2.84	2.61	2.45	2.34	2.25	2.18	2.12	2.08	2.00	1.92	1.84	1.79	1.74	1.69	1.64	1.58	1.51
60	4.00	3.15	2.76	2.53	2.37	2.25	2.17	2.10	2.04	1.99	1.92	1.84	1.75	1.70	1.65	1.59	1.53	1.47	1.39
120	3.92	3.07	2.68	2.45	2.29	2.18	2.09	2.02	1.96	1.91	1.83	1.75	1.66	1.61	1.55	1.50	1.43	1.35	1.25
∞	3.84	3.00	2.60	2.37	2.21	2.10	2.01	1.94	1.88	1.83	1.75	1.67	1.57	1.52	1.46	1.39	1.32	1.22	1.00

F Table, $\alpha = 0.025$

denom df	num df 1	2	3	4	5	6	7	8	9	10	12	15	20	24	30	40	60	120	∞
1	647.8	799.5	864.2	899.6	921.8	937.1	948.2	956.7	963.3	968.6	976.7	984.9	993.1	997.2	1001	1006	1010	1014	1018
2	38.51	39.00	39.17	39.25	39.30	39.33	39.36	39.37	39.39	39.40	39.41	39.43	39.45	39.46	39.46	39.47	39.48	39.49	39.50
3	17.44	16.04	15.44	15.10	14.88	14.73	14.62	14.54	14.47	14.42	14.34	14.25	14.17	14.12	14.08	14.04	13.99	13.95	13.90
4	12.22	10.65	9.98	9.60	9.36	9.20	9.07	8.98	8.90	8.84	8.75	8.66	8.56	8.51	8.46	8.41	8.36	8.31	8.26
5	10.01	8.43	7.76	7.39	7.15	6.98	6.85	6.76	6.68	6.62	6.52	6.43	6.33	6.28	6.23	6.18	6.12	6.07	6.02
6	8.81	7.26	6.60	6.23	5.99	5.82	5.70	5.60	5.52	5.46	5.37	5.27	5.17	5.12	5.07	5.01	4.96	4.90	4.85
7	8.07	6.54	5.89	5.52	5.29	5.12	4.99	4.90	4.82	4.76	4.67	4.57	4.47	4.41	4.36	4.31	4.25	4.20	4.14
8	7.57	6.06	5.42	5.05	4.82	4.65	4.53	4.43	4.36	4.30	4.20	4.10	4.00	3.95	3.89	3.84	3.78	3.73	3.67
9	7.21	5.71	5.08	4.72	4.48	4.32	4.20	4.10	4.03	3.96	3.87	3.77	3.67	3.61	3.56	3.51	3.45	3.39	3.33
10	6.94	5.46	4.83	4.47	4.24	4.07	3.95	3.85	3.78	3.72	3.62	3.52	3.42	3.37	3.31	3.26	3.20	3.14	3.08
12	6.55	5.10	4.47	4.12	3.89	3.73	3.61	3.51	3.44	3.37	3.28	3.18	3.07	3.02	2.96	2.91	2.85	2.79	2.72
15	6.20	4.77	4.15	3.80	3.58	3.41	3.29	3.20	3.12	3.06	2.96	2.86	2.76	2.70	2.64	2.59	2.52	2.46	2.40
20	5.87	4.46	3.86	3.51	3.29	3.13	3.01	2.91	2.84	2.77	2.68	2.57	2.46	2.41	2.35	2.29	2.22	2.16	2.09
24	5.72	4.32	3.72	3.38	3.15	2.99	2.87	2.78	2.70	2.64	2.54	2.44	2.33	2.27	2.21	2.15	2.08	2.01	1.94
30	5.57	4.18	3.59	3.25	3.03	2.87	2.75	2.65	2.57	2.51	2.41	2.31	2.20	2.14	2.07	2.01	1.94	1.87	1.79
40	5.42	4.05	3.46	3.13	2.90	2.74	2.62	2.53	2.45	2.39	2.29	2.18	2.07	2.01	1.94	1.88	1.80	1.72	1.64
60	5.29	3.93	3.34	3.01	2.79	2.63	2.51	2.41	2.33	2.27	2.17	2.06	1.94	1.88	1.82	1.74	1.67	1.58	1.48
120	5.15	3.80	3.23	2.89	2.67	2.52	2.39	2.30	2.22	2.16	2.05	1.94	1.82	1.76	1.69	1.61	1.53	1.43	1.31
∞	5.02	3.69	3.12	2.79	2.57	2.41	2.29	2.19	2.11	2.05	1.94	1.83	1.71	1.64	1.57	1.48	1.39	1.27	1.00

F Table, $\alpha = 0.01$

denom df	num df																		
	1	2	3	4	5	6	7	8	9	10	12	15	20	24	30	40	60	120	∞
1	4052	5000	5403	5625	5764	5859	5928	5981	6022	6056	6106	6157	6209	6235	6261	6287	6313	6339	6366
2	98.50	99.00	99.17	99.25	99.30	99.33	99.36	99.37	99.39	99.40	99.42	99.43	99.45	99.46	99.47	99.47	99.48	99.49	99.50
3	34.12	30.82	29.46	28.71	28.24	27.91	27.67	27.49	27.35	27.23	27.05	26.87	26.69	26.60	26.50	26.41	26.32	26.22	26.13
4	21.20	18.00	16.69	15.98	15.52	15.21	14.98	14.80	14.66	14.55	14.37	14.20	14.02	13.93	13.84	13.75	13.65	13.56	13.46
5	16.26	13.27	12.06	11.39	10.97	10.67	10.46	10.29	10.16	10.05	9.89	9.72	9.55	9.47	9.38	9.29	9.20	9.11	9.02
6	13.75	10.92	9.78	9.15	8.75	8.47	8.26	8.10	7.98	7.87	7.72	7.56	7.40	7.31	7.23	7.14	7.06	6.97	6.88
7	12.25	9.55	8.45	7.85	7.46	7.19	6.99	6.84	6.72	6.62	6.47	6.31	6.16	6.07	5.99	5.91	5.82	5.74	5.65
8	11.26	8.65	7.59	7.01	6.63	6.37	6.18	6.03	5.91	5.81	5.67	5.52	5.36	5.28	5.20	5.12	5.03	4.95	4.86
9	10.56	8.02	6.99	6.42	6.06	5.80	5.61	5.47	5.35	5.26	5.11	4.96	4.81	4.73	4.65	4.57	4.48	4.40	4.31
10	10.04	7.56	6.55	5.99	5.64	5.39	5.20	5.06	4.94	4.85	4.71	4.56	4.41	4.33	4.25	4.17	4.08	4.00	3.91
12	9.33	6.93	5.95	5.41	5.06	4.82	4.64	4.50	4.39	4.30	4.16	4.01	3.86	3.78	3.70	3.62	3.54	3.45	3.36
15	8.68	6.36	5.42	4.89	4.56	4.32	4.14	4.00	3.89	3.80	3.67	3.52	3.37	3.29	3.21	3.13	3.05	2.96	2.87
20	8.10	5.85	4.94	4.43	4.10	3.87	3.70	3.56	3.46	3.37	3.23	3.09	2.94	2.86	2.78	2.69	2.61	2.52	2.42
24	7.82	5.61	4.72	4.22	3.90	3.67	3.50	3.36	3.26	3.17	3.03	2.89	2.74	2.66	2.58	2.49	2.40	2.31	2.21
30	7.56	5.39	4.51	4.02	3.70	3.47	3.30	3.17	3.07	2.98	2.84	2.70	2.55	2.47	2.39	2.30	2.21	2.11	2.01
40	7.31	5.18	4.31	3.83	3.51	3.29	3.12	2.99	2.89	2.80	2.66	2.52	2.37	2.29	2.20	2.11	2.02	1.92	1.80
60	7.08	4.98	4.13	3.65	3.34	3.12	2.95	2.82	2.72	2.63	2.50	2.35	2.20	2.12	2.03	1.94	1.84	1.73	1.60
120	6.85	4.79	3.95	3.48	3.17	2.96	2.79	2.66	2.56	2.47	2.34	2.19	2.03	1.95	1.86	1.76	1.66	1.53	1.38
∞	6.63	4.61	3.78	3.32	3.02	2.80	2.64	2.51	2.41	2.32	2.18	2.04	1.88	1.79	1.70	1.59	1.47	1.32	1.00

CHI-SQUARE TABLE

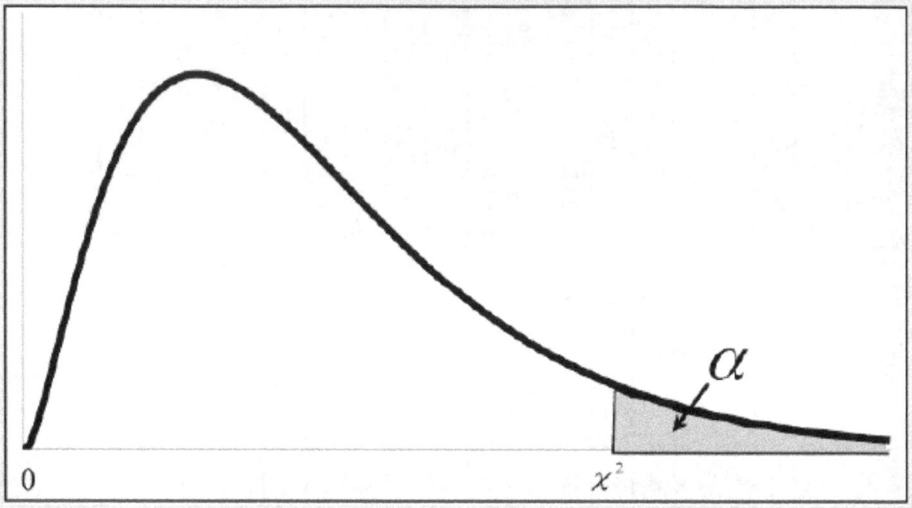

df	0.10	0.05	0.025	0.01	0.005
1	2.706	3.841	5.024	6.635	7.879
2	4.605	5.991	7.378	9.210	10.597
3	6.251	7.815	9.348	11.345	12.838
4	7.779	9.488	11.143	13.277	14.860
5	9.236	11.070	12.833	15.086	16.750
6	10.645	12.592	14.449	16.812	18.548
7	12.017	14.067	16.013	18.475	20.278
8	13.362	15.507	17.535	20.090	21.955
9	14.684	16.919	19.023	21.666	23.589
10	15.987	18.307	20.483	23.209	25.188
11	17.275	19.675	21.920	24.725	26.757
12	18.549	21.026	23.337	26.217	28.300
13	19.812	22.362	24.736	27.688	29.819
14	21.064	23.685	26.119	29.141	31.319
15	22.307	24.996	27.488	30.578	32.801
16	23.542	26.296	28.845	32.000	34.267
17	24.769	27.587	30.191	33.409	35.718
18	25.989	28.869	31.526	34.805	37.156
19	27.204	30.144	32.852	36.191	38.582
20	28.412	31.410	34.170	37.566	39.997

df	0.10	0.05	0.025	0.01	0.005
21	29.615	32.671	35.479	38.932	41.401
22	30.813	33.924	36.781	40.289	42.796
23	32.007	35.172	38.076	41.638	44.181
24	33.196	36.415	39.364	42.980	45.559
25	34.382	37.652	40.646	44.314	46.928
26	35.563	38.885	41.923	45.642	48.290
27	36.741	40.113	43.195	46.963	49.645
28	37.916	41.337	44.461	48.278	50.993
29	39.087	42.557	45.722	49.588	52.336
30	40.256	43.773	46.979	50.892	53.672
31	41.422	44.985	48.232	52.191	55.003
32	42.585	46.194	49.480	53.486	56.328
33	43.745	47.400	50.725	54.776	57.648
34	44.903	48.602	51.966	56.061	58.964
35	46.059	49.802	53.203	57.342	60.275
36	47.212	50.998	54.437	58.619	61.581
37	48.363	52.192	55.668	59.893	62.883
38	49.513	53.384	56.896	61.162	64.181
39	50.660	54.572	58.120	62.428	65.476
40	51.805	55.758	59.342	63.691	66.766
41	52.949	56.942	60.561	64.950	68.053
42	54.090	58.124	61.777	66.206	69.336
43	55.230	59.304	62.990	67.459	70.616
44	56.369	60.481	64.201	68.710	71.893
45	57.505	61.656	65.410	69.957	73.166
46	58.641	62.830	66.617	71.201	74.437
47	59.774	64.001	67.821	72.443	75.704
48	60.907	65.171	69.023	73.683	76.969
49	62.038	66.339	70.222	74.919	78.231
50	63.167	67.505	71.420	76.154	79.490
60	74.397	79.082	83.298	88.379	91.952
70	85.527	90.531	95.023	100.425	104.215
80	96.578	101.879	106.629	112.329	116.321
90	107.565	113.145	118.136	124.116	128.299
100	118.498	124.342	129.561	135.807	140.169